BAD TRIPS

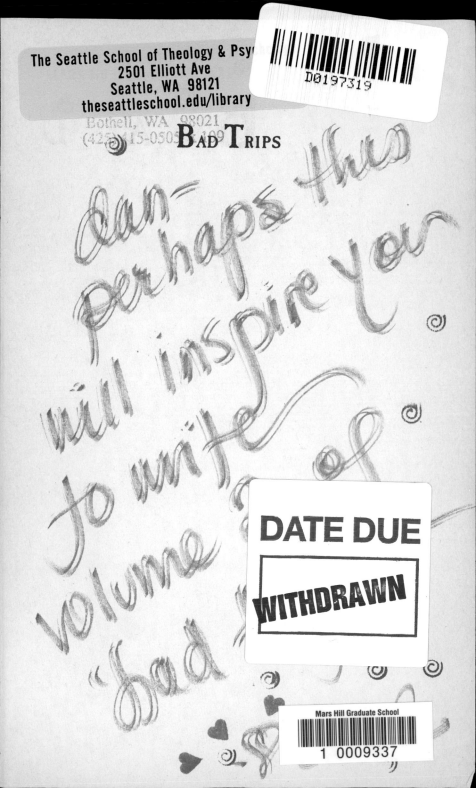

dan—
Perhaps this
will inspire you
to write
volume
"bad

B A D

TRIPS

Edited
and with an introduction by
Keath Fraser

Vintage Books   *A Division of Random House, Inc.*   *New York*

VINTAGE DEPARTURES

A VINTAGE DEPARTURES ORIGINAL

FIRST EDITION, APRIL 1991

Copyright © 1991 by Keath Fraser

Library of Congress Cataloging-in-Publication Data
Bad trips / edited and with an introduction by Keath Fraser.—1st ed.
p. cm.
ISBN 0-679-72908-9
1. Voyages and travels—1981– I. Fraser, Keath.
G465.B32 1991
910.4—dc20   90-50618
CIP

Book design by Jacek Przybyszewski

Manufactured in the United States of America
579B864

For George and Inge Woodcock,
Travelers and Founders

Exploring is delightful to look forward to and back upon,
but it is not comfortable at the time, unless it be of such
an easy nature as not to deserve the name.

—Samuel Butler, *Erewhon*

CONTENTS

CONTENTS

CONTENTS

INTRODUCTION

Here is one way to have a bad trip.

You are lying in your underwear on a bed in a Havana hotel room in the late sixties when travel to Cuba is still widely restricted, and a young man in the next bed refuses to discuss anything about money until you follow him into the bathroom. Only here will he let you continue counting aloud the Cuban pesos in your wallet. We're being watched he says.

You walk back into the bedroom and discover it's true. Tapestry palms hanging on either side of the large mirror aren't embroidered on a cloth so much as planted in a kind of webbing common to old-fashioned radio speakers set into the wall. You prod the coconuts, nestling in behind a design of iron filigree, and discover the adjoining mirror is also lodged into the wall. It doesn't take much imagination to figure it goes both ways.

Suppose you have been trading in black market currency with a Pakistani diplomat the evening before in his colonial suburban home. And now your conversation has been careless. It's a hot day in December, say. The ceiling fan cranks slowly.

Your journey is already a debacle, with an Ilyushin that had mechanical trouble reaching Cuba, forcing it to re-land in Mexico City and then take off again—bringing you into San Martí airport long after dark, on a Cubana flight that oddly enough felt hijacked (the sixties' new mode of arrival in Havana). But worse, in the days that follow, officials are loath to let you leave Cuba, where, while no visa was required to enter the country, an exit visa is now harder to come by than a peace medallion on a leather thong. They're toying with you.

Perhaps you've been eating too well in the dining room, spending too freely on boxes of Havana cigars.

You are an odd couple, you see now, you and this neurotic French Canadian, meeting by chance at the airport in Mexico City, flying in as celebration of the Revolution's tenth anniversary happens to be getting under way, a pair of gringo good-timers in an otherwise discreet pool of earnest Russian advisors. It's important for Cuban agents to harass you. It's their duty.

Even then, while trotting from pillar to post, you know that some day you will use your journey. You feel fortunate to be suffering. Perhaps a Catholic childhood prepared you for worse. On this, your first trip abroad, travel has become after reading and eating out the third great pleasure in life. It has also become, like repetition and indigestion, a curse. A demon to be exorcised in a little black diary. It's important to record this. It's your duty.

You are coming to learn that destination achieved is seldom what it promised when you first set off. "Ay," as Touchstone says, "now am I in Arden, the more fool I. When I was at home, I was in a better place, but travelers must be content." Not content, but rather, as the writers in this volume will show, interested in exploring the folly in forsaking more familiar surroundings.

Home in an absolute sense is where we come from. The thoughtful traveler willy-nilly is instructive about the moral differences between the relative and absolute meanings of that place. In the relative sense home is as likely to be a ledge with two sleeping bags on the side of a mountain in the Hindu Kush as it is a bugged hotel room in weather-beaten Havana. The relative meaning, we suspect, is but a convenience on some exotic way to the other meaning, however idealized real home may become in the struggle to survive the perils of the road.

Whoever claimed that travel is merely home in motion was traveling in an armchair—or else engaged in travel (as Samuel Butler once put it) too easy to deserve the name. Travel still suggests "travail" to those who know that by leaving home they risk wire-walking without a net.

Among living writers, Redmond O'Hanlon goes further than many in mining the gap between home and wherever it is he finds himself—usually up a jungle river full of tropical dread and having the worst journey of his life. His book *In Trouble Again* has the ideal title, coming as it does from a writer determined to be funny about trouble. So has *Arabian Sands*, from another writer determined to traverse the waterless desert of Arabia's Empty Quarter. Assuming "the worst" to be over, after crossing what he has taken to be the grueling dunes of the Uraq al Shaiba, Wilfred Thesiger is told it isn't and they weren't. "For a moment, I thought he was joking, and then I realized that he was serious, that the worst of the journey which I had thought was behind us was still ahead."

In recalling Apsley Cherry-Garrard's account of Scott's Antarctic expedition in *The Worst Journey in the World*, George Woodcock may be right when he observes that a worst journey, in an absolute sense, is one that ends in death. Anything this side must presumably be governed by what Martha Gellhorn considers the subjective nature of all the other "horror journeys." Thus in Saigon, we learn that when James Fenton narrates a grotesque encounter with an apparently dying baby, "There was not the slightest element of drama. Indeed, I began to see that I was now the only person who was panicking." Indeed, not even the ghastliest cities nor vilest bureaucracies have managed to dissuade the peripatetic Jan Morris that she has *had* a bad journey. She won't stop smiling. "*What a lovely journey this is!*" Invited to tell of her worst journey she is thus forced to make one up—we presume with the same zest used to cook up her favorite and apocryphal city of Hav, also situated in the Levant.

No entire journey, nor even the greatest portion of it, is likely to be bad. Edward Hoagland considers himself a rhapsodist and essentially a Good Trip man who discerns no value in making an "ado" about bad journeys. But he concedes, "In Mexico and the southern Sudan I've seen whimpering hunger. In Casablanca and Chicago I've seen people viciously clubbed. I know that life is an abyss, among other things, and like other travel writers, I enjoy wire-walking a bit, courting, in a sense, a catastrophe." Why?

"The only aspect of our travels that is guaranteed to hold an audience is disaster," Martha Gellhorn tells us in her preface to *Travels with Myself and Another*. "That's what [people] like. They can hardly wait for us to finish before they launch into stories of their own suffering in foreign lands. . . ." The skeptic is likely to point out that such cherishing really begins with the retrospective arrangement of these disasters (the shaping of what once seemed shapeless) in reclaiming control of a temporarily disarranged self. In ascribing significance to what looked like hopeless boredom at the time, a good writer will discern humor where it never before revealed itself. She will no doubt tinker till a bad journey is, at least for her, a resolution of anxiety, indifference, fear. Gellhorn would agree: "As a student of disaster, I note that we react alike to our tribulations: frayed and bitter at the time, proud afterwards. Nothing is better for self-esteem than survival."

It is no wonder survival is central to the journeys writers record. It makes them feel good. "Look, we have come through!" wrote Lawrence of his and Frieda's rocky journey of elopement. "They may have come through," replied Bertrand Russell, "but I see no reason to look." Armchair travelers have no such scruples. We are voyeurs, carefully set up by the writer.

Martin Amis sets us up, with his confessed fear of flying and the emergency landing that follows, before he undresses even more: "Now, all writers secretly maintain a vampiric attitude to disaster; and, having survived it, I was unreservedly grateful for the experience." To no one's surprise Paul Theroux has gone so far as to conclude, in confessing his own bent as a professional travel writer, that "the worst trips make the best reading." Bad journeys, it seems, lead straight to the confession box. And as readers we take as much pleasure in listening to the blunders as writers do in confessing them. Invited to contribute to this collection, Anita Desai writes from Delhi: "Then, then at last I knew I had been had," aboard a small steamer in the dead of an Arctic winter night, having responded to a UN invitation to visit Norway to help celebrate the Decade of Women. Another contributor, William Trevor, responds by forgoing any account of a conventional trip in favor of a simple bus journey back to boarding school at the age of twelve. "What possessed me was dread," he confesses, "and the misery of anticipating the unavoidable." Such were the joys, all these travelers would agree, of recollections in misfortune.

....

Travel writing is a genre, but the literature of travel isn't, with ante-
cedents as much in imaginary literature as in explorers' logbooks. Before Eric Newby's *A Short Walk in the Hindu Kush*, Norman Lewis's
Golden Earth, Graham Greene's *Journey Without Maps*, all classics of
twentieth-century travel—and earlier, before Robert Louis Stevenson's
The Amateur Emigrant, Melville's *Typee*, and Alexander Kinglake's
Eothen—easily lay the fictions of *Gulliver's Travels*, *Robinson Crusoe*,
and *The Unfortunate Traveller*. If writing impelled by travel is circum-
scribed by an ever unruly exotic (the case in all these books, and in
The Odyssey, come to think of it), then it will probably follow that
survival flirts with us from the center of such travel, because the storyteller has understood as much if not more about human nature than
the sociologist and historian. Lévi-Strauss has suggested, "The first thing
we see as we travel round the world is our own garbage, flung into the
face of mankind." Escape this, presumably, and we escape ennui,
though the journey to that point may be difficult. To escape the self,
to remake Caliban's face in the mirror, the writer as traveler uses his
journey to see home even while distancing himself from it.

In John Updike's "Venezuela for Visitors" we are offered a mock
anthropological report on a third-person journey into discomfort by
contrast, which distances the traveler from poor Indians on one side—
their lives "not paradise but full of anxiety"—and the rich who exploit
them. We are not so far from home as we imagine, for introduced slyly
is flirting, a cultural habit indigenous to the locally insignificant middle-
class. Elsewhere, Updike has admitted that the helicopter crash on a
mountaintop in Venezuela nearly killed him. He is strangely casual
about it here, and possibly for a reason. This original piece of travel
writing first appeared in pages of *The New Yorker* normally reserved for
fiction; something stranger than fiction might have ruined its welcome.

Our itinerant wanders unbounded, much taken by what travel
can tell us of the self and of the world it would escape to and be
transformed by. A bad journey mirrors its exotic circumference, throwing back an image of the writer in extremis, who is willing to be tested,
mocked, and remain remarkably undaunted when it begins to rain on

his parade . . . when the rim of the troddened world degenerates into a *via dolorosa*.

Incidentally, it is doubtful whether my favorite title from nineteenth-century travel literature, *On Sledge and Horseback to Outcast Siberian Lepers*, by one intrepid lady traveler, misled many novel readers. But neither, for that matter, would Eric Hansen's recent title *Stranger in the Forest: On Foot Across Borneo*, though its dual declaration reminds us, with a novel's hint of mystery to the left of the centering colon, how far the travel book has come back (if that is the term) to mirroring the survival interests of fiction. "It was clear to me that at any moment I might be ambushed and killed." Hansen sounds a little like Crusoe, minus Defoe's cultural blinders.

The Australian novelist Murray Bail, whose novel *Homesickness* uncovers the kind of tourist ethnocentrism the real traveler reviles, raises the moral question of voyeurism and intervention on safari in Central Park, when a group of Australians visiting New York City finds itself in a tree house watching human predators attracted by darkness and a human prey. Obsessed with the way we see the world, the novel subverts travel in brilliant ways, not the least of them on this terrible journey into Central Park.

Tension and resolution, but also character and insight: these characteristics of the novel have been absorbed by many contemporary travel writers who may or may not be novelists. Graham Greene, Norman Lewis, Colin Thubron, Edward Hoagland, Paul Theroux, Peter Matthiessen, Jonathan Raban, Mary Morris—novelists know how central drama is to the stories they tell us in their travel books. We read these writers for the plots of their frequently self-inflicted predicaments. ("What do people *do* in Morgan City?" asks Jonathan Raban, finding himself in the "worst" motel room he has ever seen, having just motored two thousand miles down the Mississippi in a sixteen-foot boat. He finds out. "Fight. Get drunk. Pick up women.")

The novelist Timothy Findley, flying to Moscow in 1955 as a young actor in Peter Brook's production of *Hamlet*, describes how "increasingly, as the flight wore on, it became apparent that we really were in trouble. It became very cold in the plane. Everyone put on an overcoat. Blankets were offered. The pilot was attempting to climb above the storm, but he was failing to achieve his goal. The snow, apparently, went all the way to heaven." On an earlier leg of this flight, Findley has looked around the cabin to discover with some solace a furtive Graham Greene on the same journey to Moscow. "His knuckles, just like mine, were bone white and rigid." Findley's fear of flying scrambles for any metaphysical comfort he can find in his hope that perhaps God takes "special care of special people." So the fear of flight creates its own drama in a story.

So do the fears of fellow tourists, dark and squalid conditions of the road, mutterings of war, and possible death by rain forest Indians, thirst, or hypothermia. Survival is all. In the finest travel writing the storyteller resolves his fears through the catharsis of narrative. Without fear, travel has no meaning; the writer is without a secret. He goes on to create epiphanies where the scholar would be tempted merely to recycle the past. If the scholar is right, that we learn from history, even more may we learn from what fictional narrative teaches us about journeying in time.

Think of Sartre's autodidact. He is looking for "adventures" only because he thinks travel, which he has never done, is the best "school." (". . . Getting on the wrong train. Stopping in an unknown town. Losing your wallet, being arrested by mistake, spending the night in prison. Monsieur, it seems to me that you could define adventure as an event which is out of the ordinary without being necessarily extraordinary.") Yet even while longing for adventure, the autodidact fears the upheaval of travel, and moreover is unable to look at photographs and see journeys abroad as anything except confirmation of what he already knows. He knows history, but cannot tell a story. He lacks the imagination for metaphor.

(Not novelist Umberto Eco, who is able to use history in a bold and indivisible way. Listen to his mock horror on a culture crawl down the California coast in *Travels in Hyperreality*: "The poor words with which natural speech is provided cannot suffice to describe the Madonna Inn. . . . Let's say that Albert Speer, while leafing through a book on Gaudi, swallowed an overgenerous dose of LSD and began to build a nuptial catacomb for Liza Minnelli. But that doesn't give you an idea. Let's say Arcimboldi builds the Sagrada Familia for Dolly Parton.

Or . . ." etc. He can barely contain his imagination, set free by its recollected arrival amidst the *horror vacui* of pop vulgarity.)

In one obvious sense, then, a writer's worst journey is also his best. It contains the seed of a vivid story in which he is the welcome survivor. The worse the journey the more fortunate the writer. Long before Defoe, Thomas Nashe saw that a bad journey could be very useful in his imaginary story of Jack Wilton. *The Unfortunate Traveller* is suitably mistitled—as is James Fenton's recent *All the Wrong Places*, which of course points to all the *right* places for a writer to be in when trouble breaks out. Jack Wilton fortunately survives, as if the advice he is given on the requisite anatomy of a traveler—from a banished English earl who, in despising life abroad, believes that what the wandering Israelites consider to be an enslaving curse, masochistic Englishmen count as their chief boon—has somehow made the difference: "He that is a traveller must have the back of an ass to bear all, a tongue like the tail of a dog to flatter all, the mouth of a hog to eat what is set before him, the ear of a merchant to hear all and say nothing." Scoundrels, murderers, liars—why, wonders the earl, is Jack interested in trucking with foreigners abroad? Better learn of their treachery from books at home.

Well, we hasten to agree, home is a place of fortune that allows writers sufficient funds to leave it at their leisure. Writers who tell of bad trips through peaceful or even plentiful lands, not to mention war-torn and impoverished lands, recognize instinctively how fortunate they are to have their particular homes (those gauges of fortune) to return to. Compared with the struggling and even starving strangers they will certainly meet along the road, these travelers will indeed feel fortunate and perhaps morally sensitized.

Over the traveler's head hang evils Joseph Brodsky offers advice about avoiding, instructing us winningly on how to *prevent* a worst journey, in his imagined Asian landscape ("Advice to a Traveller"). Yet a traveler will find some way to thwart the evils of the road by turning misery to his advantage. Reflecting upon a lifetime of travel, little of it easy, the splendid English traveler Norman Lewis once observed that "insurgents and bandits, malaria, curtains of various kinds, whether lowered by politicians or by the priest-kings of their day . . . I am reminded that those parts of the world where I have travelled most happily . . . always seemed to suffer from these disadvantages. . . ." Lewis has always felt happiest traveling when the going was manifestly *not* good. As Edward Hoagland correctly grasps, T. E. Lawrence was not necessarily happier than V. S. Naipaul for having had trips that sounded more agreeable.

Happiness for the writer who travels certainly seems earned in proportion to exhaustion brooked. Note Graham Greene on his arduous journey to Palenque in the thirties: "I lay wet through with sweat for four hours—it was very nearly like happiness. In the street outside nobody passed: it was too hot for life to go on." Paul Theroux is also happiest when unhappy. The success of his own travel books owes something to the persona he creates for himself in the tradition of Evelyn Waugh and Greene himself. He's the antidote to Jan Morris. One might even wonder if, like her, he is here making *up* his worst journey, at home in his study once the hard traveling is past, and Limón has become a minor inconvenience with confessional potential. However contrived his drama, in his engaging little story of survival (no more or less contrived than other writers' stories), his unflattering portrait is recognizable to anyone who has visited the Caribbean coast of Costa Rica.

The fifty living writers collected here have engaged me in different ways and with varying degrees of drama. All these writers—whether as tourists, professional travel writers, war correspondents, poets, rugged explorers, memoirists, or imaginary travelers in the personae of novelists like Russell Banks or J. M. Coetzee with journeys of grim irony and moral dilemma—all transport me in directions I like my armchair to go. Writers remaking themselves remake us. By their surviving so do we, in mini catharses, in armchair journeys of descent and resurrection, feel life renewed.

The fruit of bad journeys should be redemptive. The writer escapes, feels wiser perhaps, survives to bring back tales of ennui and strangely focused mirrors. (Kicked out of Cuba, with a visa at last, you are refused a visa back into Mexico.) Peter Matthiessen in *The Snow Leopard* notes: "Tibetans say that obstacles in a hard journey, such as hailstones, wind, and unrelenting rains, are the work of demons, anxious to test the sincerity of the pilgrims and eliminate the fainthearted among them." In a beguiling sense the pilgrims today have become Matthiessen's readers. We as readers can be grateful to such fortunate travelers for bringing back reports of the demonic. Of the amusingly corrupt. Of bugs and hot hikes: "No," writes Wilfred Thesiger in *Arabian Sands*, "it is not the goal but the way there that matters, and the harder the way the more worthwhile the journey." These survivors, fortunate all, save us from faintheartedness.

··············

Not every writer, of course, who travels is a traveler—no more than is every traveler who writes a writer. Writers from a number of countries were invited to tell of their (mis)fortunes on the road. I would especially like to thank those who took time to contribute essays on their worst journeys, along with the rest and their publishers who were asked for excerpts from previously published works.

I suppose many landscapes described here in passing aren't really different in degree from the harsh ones of India—to which this collection of journeys happens to be devoted, and its people assisted by the generosity of these writers, who have agreed to donate all their royalties to Canada India Village Aid. CIVA is a registered, nonsalaried charity dedicated to building medical and agricultural facilities in some of the poorest areas of rural India.

In addition, I would like to extend my gratitude to Ed Carson, Louise Dennys, Cynthia Good, Ellen Levine, Michael Ondaatje, John O'Brien, and George Woodcock for their support and interest in this project in variously crucial ways; and to Trevor Carolan.

No thanks, of course, is ever really adequate to express the deep appreciation I feel for the continuous support of my wife, Lorraine.

Keath Fraser
Vancouver, 1990

BAD TRIPS

PART ONE

THE VERY IDEA OF A BAD TRIP

You define your own horror journey, according to your taste. My definition of what makes a journey wholly or partially horrible is boredom. Add discomfort, fatigue, strain in large amounts to get the purest-quality horror, but the kernel is boredom. I offer that as a universal test of travel; boredom, called by any other name, is why you yearn for the first available transport out. But what bores whom?

—Martha Gellhorn

JOSEPH BRODSKY

Born in Leningrad in 1940, Joseph Brodsky grew up in Russia and came to the United States in 1972, a reluctant exile. In the years since, he has published several volumes of poetry, including Elegy for John Donne and Other Poems, A Part of Speech, *and* To Urania, *and a collection of essays,* Less Than One. *He is Andrew Mellon Professor of Literature at Mt. Holyoke College, and lives in South Hadley, Massachusetts, and New York City. He won the Nobel Prize for Literature in 1987.*

•

··

ADVICE TO A TRAVELLER

I
Trekking in Asia, spending nights in odd dwellings, in
granaries, cabins, shacks—timber abodes whose thin
squinted windowpanes harness the world—sleep dressed,
wrapped in your sheepskin, and do your best
always to tuck your head into the corner, as
in the corner it's harder—and in darkness at that—to swing an axe
over your heavy, booze-laden gourd
and to chop it off nicely. Square the circle, in short.

II
Fear broad cheekbones (including the moon's), pock-marked
skin, and prefer blue eyes to brown eyes. Search hard
for the blue ones especially when the road takes you into the wood,
into its heart. On the whole, as for eyes, one should
watch for their cut. For at your last instant it's

better to stare at that which, though cold, permits
seeing through: ice may crack, yet wallowing in an ice-
hole is far better than in honey-like, viscous lies.

III
Always pick a house with baby-clothes hanging out
in the yard. Deal only with the over-fifty crowd:
a hick at that age knows too much about fate to gain
anything by attempting to bust your brain;
same thing, a squaw. Hide the money in your fur-coat's
collar, or if you are travelling light, in your brown culottes
under the knee—but not in your boots, since they'll find the dough
easily there. In Asia, boots are the first to go.

IV
In the mountains, move slowly. If you must creep, then creep.
Magnificent in the distance, meaningless closer up,
mountains are but a surface standing on end. The snail-
like and, it seems, horizontal meandering trail
is, in fact, vertical. Lying flat in the mountains, you
stand. Standing up, you lie flat. Which suggests your true
freedom's in falling down. That's the way, it appears,
to conquer, once in the mountains, vertigo, raptures, fears.

V
If somebody yells "Hey, stranger!" don't answer. Play deaf and dumb.
Even though you may know it, don't speak the tongue.
Try not to stand out—either in profile or
full face; simply don't wash your face at times. What's more,
when they rip a cur's throat with a saw, don't cringe.
Smoking, douse your butts with spittle. And, besides, arrange
to wear grey—the hue of the earth—especially underclothes,
to reduce the temptation to blend your flesh with earth.

VI
When you halt in the desert make an arrow from pebbles, so,
if suddenly woken up, you'll grasp which way to go

in the darkness. At nights, demons in deserts try
travellers' hearts. One who heeds their cry
is easily disoriented: one step sideways and—well, *c'est tout*.
Ghosts, spectres, demons are at home in the desert. You
too will discover that's true when, sand creaking under your sole,
all that remains of you is your soul.

VII

Nobody ever knows anything for a fact.
Gazing ahead at your stooping guide's sturdy back
think that you gaze at the future and keep your distance (if
that is possible) from him. Since, in principle, life
also means but a distance between here and there, and
quickening the pace pays only when you discern the sound
behind, of those running after you down the path
with lowered heads—be they murderers, thieves, the past.

VIII

In the sour whiff of rugs, in the burnt dung's fume,
prize the indifference of things to being regarded from
afar, and in turn lose your own silhouette, turning thus
unattainable for binoculars, gendarmes, mass.
Coughing in a cloud of dust, wading through mud, muck, map,
what difference does it make how you would look close up?
It's even better if some character with a blade
figures out you are a stranger a bit too late.

IX

Rivers in Asia are longer than elsewhere, more rich
in alluvium—that is, murkier. As you reach
for a mouthful, your cupped fingers ladle silt,
and one who has drunk this water would prefer it spilt.
Never trust its reflection. Crossing it, cross it on
a raft built with no other hands but the pair you own.
Know that the gleam of a campfire, your nightly bliss,
will, by sliding downstream, betray you to enemies.

X

In your letters from these parts don't divulge whom and
what you've seen on your way. If anything should be penned,
use your various feelings, musings, regrets, et al.:
a letter can be intercepted. And after all,
the movement of a pen across paper is,
in itself, the worsening of the break between you and those
with whom you won't any longer sit or lie down—with whom,
unlike the letter, you won't share—who cares why—a home.

XI

When you stand on an empty stony plateau alone
under the fathomless dome of Asia in whose blueness an aeroplane
or an angel sometimes whips up its starch or star—
when you shudder at how infinitesimally small you are,
remember: space that appears to need nothing, does
crave, as a matter of fact, an outside gaze,
a criterion of emptiness—of its depth and scope.
And it's only you who can do the job.

Translated from the Russian by the author and George L. Kline

JAN MORRIS

*It was as James Morris that Jan Morris established her rep-
utation as a stylish writer on travel to many corners of the
world, and even to its summit, where she accompanied Ed-
mond Hillary on the first successful Everest expedition and
wrote about it for* The Times. *Her many books include*
Conundrum, *an autobiographical account of changing her
sex, the* Pax Britannica *trilogy, and six volumes of collected
travel essays such as* Places *and* Among the Cities. *As well
as book-length accounts of Spain, Venice, Oxford, Man-
hattan, and Hong Kong, she has published a novel about
a fictional Mediterranean city,* Last Letters from Hav, *which
was nominated for the Booker Prize. Morris lives in Wales
and continues to wander everywhere, claiming to have visited
every chief city on earth over the last thirty-five years. She
left the 9th Queen's Royal Lancers in 1946.*

MY WORST JOURNEY

Two principles I resolved at the end of the Second World War: I would
have a glass of wine every day for the rest of my life, if there was wine
to be had; and after a youth that seemed to have been spent very largely
in the jammed and blacked-out corridors of troop trains, bouncing about
in the backs of 15-cwt trucks or being hurled around the interiors of
Sherman tanks—after a distinctly uncomfortable introduction to the
practice of travel, if I could possibly help it, I would never travel dis-
agreeably again.

On both counts, I am proud to say, I have stuck to my guns.

7

Rare indeed have been my days without wine, and rarer still the journeys I have not by hook or by crook obliged myself to enjoy. For forty years and more I have made a professional speciality of the happy journey. When things have gone wrong, I have resolutely forgotten them. When people have been unpleasant, I have shrugged them off. The most ghastly cities have unavailingly tried to depress me, the vilest bureaucracy has not been able to expunge the ingratiating leer from my face. I can outsmile them all. Join me in a glass of chardonnay, I cry! *What a lovely journey this is!*

So invited as I am now to recall the grimmest experience of a travelling life, all I can do is suggest a hypothetical conflation of separate small mishaps that have befallen me despite myself since 1945, and to imagine the position I might have been in if they had all happened at once: namely, to have been robbed of my passport and plane ticket, my luggage having already been lost in flight, while suffering from extreme diarrhea during a high summer heat wave and a severe water shortage, at a moment when the local electricity supply and telephone service have been cut off because of political disturbances, with nothing to read but a Robert Ludlum thriller, expecting a visit from the security police in a hotel room without a washbasin overlooking a railway freight yard on a national holiday in the Egyptian town of Zagazig.

But if I had ever found myself in such a combination of predicaments, would I have allowed myself a moment of self-pity? Certainly not. Why, I would have said to myself, how lucky I am that it isn't raining, and what a rare opportunity I have been given to watch the steam engines shunting their wagons back and forth immediately beneath my window! And if, Zagazig being the place it is, I were unable to have a glass of wine with my bean stew dinner that evening (if indeed I were able to face dinner at all, in the current state of my stomach), well, it would only go to show that principles of travel, like any other rules, can only be proved by exception. Never let it, I would tell myself firmly, on any account happen again.

GEORGE WOODCOCK

*One of Canada's most prolific men of letters, George Wood-
cock is the author of over fifty books of poetry, political
history, literary criticism, and biography. A wide and curious
traveler, Woodcock is also author of over half a dozen travel
books, including* Incas and Other Men, Faces of India, *and*
Asia, Gods and Cities. *Woodcock left Canada as an infant
and grew up in England, where such writers as George Orwell and Herbert Read later befriended him. A philosophical
anarchist, Woodcock returned to Canada in 1949, doing
much ever since to shape the way Canadians think about
their literature, culture, and politics. He helped to found
Canada India Village Aid in 1981 and lives in Vancouver.*

....

MY WORST JOURNEYS

My idea of a worst journey is conditioned by the fact that long ago, in
my boyhood, I read a book on Scott's Antarctic expedition, which came
to a tragic end only a few days before I was born in 1912. The book
was called *The Worst Journey in the World*, and even now, when I
think of bad journeys, that title by Apsley Cherry-Garrard echoes in
my mind. In an absolute sense, a worst journey is one that ends, like
Scott's or Bering's, in death. We admire the fortitude with which such
men endured their cumulative discomforts, and the kind of grim resignation projected in the last sentences of Scott's diary: "We shall stick
it out to the end, but we are getting weaker, of course, and the end
cannot be far. It seems a pity but I do not think I can write more."
This was after Scott and his companions had learned that their efforts

had been in vain, that Amundsen had reached the Pole before them. Adding to their sense of failure was the growing certainty that exhaustion, starvation, and the bitter weather were making it impossible for them to survive long enough to return to their base camp. Behind the stiffest of upper lips, fear must have been there, and a growing sense of the futility of heroism.

Physically and mentally, in its progress and its results, Scott's was in an absolute sense a "worst" journey. For those of us who have survived our travels, there are only worse journeys, since our experiences, on this side of dying along the way, are relative, not absolute. But that at least allows a degree of comparison.

In deciding which is the worst of worse journeys, there are many criteria to be considered, and when I think of them, each draws out of my memory different incidents. Am I thinking of extreme physical discomfort? I remember a bone-racking bus journey in the Mexican highlands, with a maimed driver who controlled the wheel with the stump of his left arm at bad corners while he crossed himself with the fingers of his right hand. And there were painful shoreward walks over sharp coral and tin cans—always watchful for deadly stonefish—when a copra boat dropped one thigh-deep in the South Sea lagoons. But I especially remember one night in the early 1950s, at a place called Monterrey at the centre of the Callejón de Huaylas in the Peruvian Andes.

Monterrey had been a parody of a European spa until the publicity for its "radioactive" springs suddenly began to scare away the valetudinarians who would come up from Lima to stay for a week or so of sparkling waters. The neglected baths were now green with weed. The hotel was dingy. The food was heavy in the Peruvian way, many dirty courses served about ten at night.

I was already suffering from the mountain sickness locally called *soroche*, a bit incoherent, fainting in the dining room. And then, in the middle of the night, Inge and I were both seized by violent attacks of dysentery. At the same time the electricity and water supply failed simultaneously, and no servants answered our plaintive calls for candles when we ventured into the dark corridors. So, attacked by recurrent spasms, we would make our stumbling ways to the bathroom, to shit and vomit, nauseated once again by the rising stench, until we would fall back exhausted on the bed. But even then, weary as we were, we could not sleep even fitfully, for it was the night of an Indian festival, which was probably where all the servants had gone. From farmsteads near the hotel came the beat of drums and harps, the shrilling of *quenas*, the high-pitched chant of women singing Quechua songs. We looked out from our wretched darkness and saw the people dancing round their fires in what at that moment seemed to us an obscene and mocking sabbath.

The night passed. In the morning the water came on again and we staggered down exhausted to get on a bus for the next stage of our mountain journey. I was too comatose to be alarmed when the bus was stopped along the road by a squad of the jackbooted and spurred *guardia civil* who were then the terror of the *antiplano*. They pushed the Indians off the bus, poking at their bundles and roughing them up with a cruel impersonality that did not arouse a yelp of protest from the opaque-eyed victims.

They ordered me into their office, a grim granite guardhouse by the roadside. "Do not let him go alone, señora," a man behind us whispered, and so Inge and I went together. Perhaps the indifference of tiredness disarmed the epauletted figures who sat behind a large desk as we entered, with vast leather-bound books before them, for all at once they became officers and gentlemen instead of the tyrants of the countryside, offering us seats, plying us with coffee, and accepting cigarettes, as they laboriously entered the particulars of our passports and the intent of our journey into their great registers. My appearance of dignity, due entirely to weariness, was spoilt when I had to ask the sergeant in attendance to show me the smeared and stinking latrine at the back of the post. He was a ferocious-looking giant with Hohenzollern mustaches and a sword whose loosely slung scabbard clinked over the stones as he walked slightly behind me. In less urgent need I might have been scared of him.

We were let go in the end, got back on the bus with the maltreated Indians, and dozed almost the whole time until we reached the town where we meant to stay the next night. The sun was just setting, and as we walked up to the hotel door I saw a *guardia civil*, also heavily mustached, stepping out from under the shadow of a great eucalyptus to take a good look at us. Our movements had obviously been telephoned ahead. But by now whatever one took in those days to slow down one's bowels was beginning to work, the altitude was lower, and we could laugh at our adventure. A bad bit of journeying, but not the worst.

....

There is a special ambivalence to journeys in which one's own discomfort seems mitigated by an awareness of the much greater misery of the people around one—though that mitigation adds another dimension of discomfort, the mental spasm of guilt.

I first experienced this on a journey I had made in the very early 1930s, when I was about twenty. It was the height of the depression, and I was—relatively speaking—one of the fortunate ones, cliff-hanging to a wretchedly paid job in London which I hated. But I was earning enough money to do a little more than merely survive: I could spare some to buy the occasional sixpenny Penguin, to see Charles Laughton in *Cherry Orchard* at the Old Vic for fivepence in the gallery, and occasionally treat a girl to ravioli at Poggiolis in Charlotte Street at ninepence a time. I did not have to undergo the humiliation of those who for years had been living on a near starvation dole, subject to the weekly insolence of the petty bureaucrats who administered such grudging largess. I had a Welsh aunt in a small Glamorgan town who provided free holidays. One day, when I was visiting her, I decided to take a bus and visit the Rhondda area, the heart of the South Wales mining district. Rhondda has a special place in the thoughts of those with Welsh connections, for one of the finest of all Welsh songs—stunning when the *daios* from the valley sing it at a rugby match—is called "Cwm Rhondda," the hill of Rhondda. There are actually two valleys— Rhondda Mawr, Great Rhondda or the main valley, and Rhondda Fach, the lesser valley of little Rhondda that branches off from it. I intended to go up Rhondda Mawr, cross over the intervening hills, and come down into Rhondda Fach, which I would descend and then make my way back to Bridgend, where I was staying.

It was the worst of times in Rhondda, though it probably looked just a little better than the best of times, since most of the mines were not working, and the smoke that would normally have given a dark, satanic aspect to the landscape was less evident than in more prosperous days. Still, it was dismal enough: a long ribbon of a main road with no real gap in the houses, so that it seemed like a single serpentine town, thickening out at each village centre like knots on a string. The houses were mostly built of gray stone long turned black from soot. In the middle distance reared up the gaunt towers and immense wheels of the pitheads and the truncated pyramids of the slag heaps. There were a few sickly trees among the houses, but the hills on each side were bare and greenish brown; spring had hardly begun.

It had the feeling of occupied territory. Many of the shops had gone out of business, the mines had slowed down years ago, and the General Strike of 1926—disastrous for the workers—had delivered the coup de grace to the local economy. The people were shabby and resentful. Groups of ragged men squatted on their haunches, as miners do, and played pitch-and-toss with buttons; they had no halfpennies to venture. A man came strolling down the street, dejectedly whistling "The Red Flag" in slow time as if it were a dirge.

The people of Rhondda had double reason for resentment. In those days before Welsh nationalism became fashionable, they clung to their language as the last vestige of their identity as a people, sang it splendidly, and despised the anglicized Welsh of the towns, who mocked them in turn. And they believed, rightly, that they had been made to pay more heavily than anyone else for the difficulties of the coal industry at that period; the fact that English interests controlled the mines reinforced their ethnic resentments. Significantly, the two areas in Britain where the Communists, entirely in their role of extreme radical rebels, always gained large votes were Rhondda, where Welsh feeling was combined with exceptional poverty, and Clydebank, where exceptional poverty was combined with ancient Scottish grievances against the English. So it was not surprising that though there was not a policeman or a soldier in sight, I had this uneasy feeling, without being menaced in any physical way, that I was in occupied territory as I walked up the long street of Rhondda Mawr.

I came to the blunt end of the valley, went into a cut price shop to buy a bag of broken chocolate as cheap insurance against hunger, and took a lane that led towards the hills. It soon became a path up a gulch with a few dejected alders. Then I was on the bare pathless hillside, and as I climbed higher, with a few small inquisitive mountain sheep my only companions, I walked over a moorland where the peat had accumulated for millennia—it was as soft and springy and easy to walk on as the tundra of the Canadian Arctic. Streams had cut deep trenches down to the gravel, and to cross them I would scramble down and up the eight-foot banks of what looked like chocolate sponge cake. But these gullies offered no shelter when a storm suddenly burst over the mountain, a driving downpour that drenched me in a minute, for I had no raincoat. There was nothing for me to do but stumble on, finding the gullies more difficult to cross as the water began to rush down them in brown spates into which I slipped several times up to my knees. At last I came to the slope leading down into Rhondda Fach, and the rain ceased.

I was a sad, sodden object, my clothes heavy with water, and the chill of the mountainside hitting through the wet tweeds as I came down into the valley beside a slag heap where fifty or so men and women were industriously picking over the ground. I caught up with a man walking along the overgrown road from the mine into the village, whose damp slate roofs I could see glistening about half a mile away. He was pushing a rusty old bicycle that had no saddle and no tires, but it served to transport the dirty gunnysack he had tied onto the handle bars. He had been picking coal from the lagheap. "No bigger nor walnuts, man," he explained. The big coal had been taken years ago, so long ago it was since work had been seen in the village. I asked him how long he had been unemployed. "Ach y fi, man, it's nine years I've been wasting and wasted." Yet he was friendly, perhaps because I looked such a wretched object that he saw me as an equal in misery. He apologetically remarked that these days nobody had a fire in the village except to cook the mid-day dinner, if there was anything to cook, so I'd find it difficult to dry my clothes. Then he suddenly brightened. "Try the Brachi Shop, man. They'll have a fire, sure to goodness. And it's glad they'll be for a couple of pence to dry your clothes."

Long ago an Italian named Brachi had found his way into one of the Welsh mining valleys and had established a modest cafe. Others had followed him, but his name had clung, and Italian cafes in the Rhondda were generically called Brachi Shops. The Brachi Shop in Rhondda Fach was a melancholy place, its front in need of paint, a sheet of old cardboard filling the broken part of the window in which stood a few dummy packets of tea and biscuits. A dejected girl came from the back. Her black hair and olive complexion were Mediterranean, but her voice had the lilt of Wales. She looked at me hostilely when I talked about a fire, and I think it was because I was humiliating her into admitting that they, too, lit the fire only at their mealtimes. Nobody came for meals anymore. So I spent my tuppence on a cup of tea, which she languidly made on a primus stove. She thawed a little as the kettle warmed up, and talked of longing to go to London. I hope she got there.

My clothes dried stiffly on me as I travelled back on various buses. I had a shilling left, and at a town where I changed lines I went into a pub and spent it on grog to warm me up, and took no harm from my drenching. It was a bad journey and a sad one, and whenever people talk of the depression the image of Rhondda Fach and the workless men and the Italian girl with a Welsh accent come into my mind. But it was not the worst of my worse journeys; after all I could have slipped and drowned in one of the flooding streams on the mountain; I could have caught pneumonia, which in those days was still a killing sickness.

················

Such journeys, combining one's own physical discomfort with a close view of the misery of others, haunt the memory and come back often. There was another, even more harrowing, in Bangladesh, which was then East Pakistan. Inge and I ended up in Chittagong, the dirtiest, ugliest, most wretched and hopeless town I had ever seen—"rectum mundi," as I then described it. In the "best" and only possible hotel, where the officers from the freighters stayed and drank themselves sodden from boredom, the "luxury suite" had a "bathroom" that was really a section of balcony where one squatted to shit into a hole and showered under a pipe jutting from the wall, with only a four-foot screen to give a scanty privacy. The nets over the beds were full of holes, through which mosquitoes flew at will. The palms were dying in the gardens and the fountain in the courtyard was dry and filled with rubbish. Around it the beggars clustered, not in ones and twos, but in families and tribes, many of them with limbs deformed and faces partly eaten away by leprosy and other sicknesses. Occasionally the hotel manager— a Eurasian who talked pathetically of England as "home" though he had never been there—would dart out and urge his porters to drive them away. "A scandal! In the front of a first-class hotel!" he would shout, and rush in to telephone the police. The police never came and the beggars always drifted back, stumbling in one's way, plucking one's clothes, speaking in a professional whine. They were everywhere in Chittagong; one was free of them only when driving in a taxi through the lanes of mud-stained hovels. They were dejected beggars, hopeless beggars, without the energy to be aggressive; in any case, that would have been pointless, for there were far too many of them for the supply of visitors, and I wondered how they clung to the edge of survival.

Of course our own wretched hotel life, kept awake by the mosquitoes, eating tasteless and suspect food, hating everything we saw and heard and smelt, was in local terms the height of privileged comfort, even though it resembled in no way what we had expected from the posters put up in Dacca to show the palm-fringed beaches of Chittagong. "Beaches? What is this about beaches?" the hotel manager had asked; the nearest thing we saw to them were the sand banks that the muddy river deposited as it flowed out to the Bay of Bengal. We flew out eventually via Calcutta to Bangkok, where the modest standards of the Thais looked, in comparison, like those of rich men.

Chittagong is high among my bad journeys, but since I survived and came nowhere near death, and ended up with the bonus of that curious moral satisfaction that comes when one's own discomfort makes one see more clearly into the misery of others, it was not the worst of worse journeys. The element missing, I think, was fear. Well-founded fear, which takes one through the valley of the shadow of death without abandoning one there, is what makes the worst of worse journeys; the situation is made all the more intense when the fear is somehow mingled with delight.

So in the hierarchy of my worse journeys I would place at the summit a trip we made in 1972 to Apolima, the smallest of the islands of Western Samoa. It was an historic island, a kind of natural fortress formed from the peak of an ancient volcano, broken down on one side to allow a little harbour to form in the crater. At one period, a high Samoan chief had held out here for a decade when the rest of the chain was occupied by invading Tongans, and had eventually sailed out to defeat them. The name of Apolima meant "Held in the palm of one's hand," and indeed it did look like a hand held with the palm flat and the fingers raised. Since Apolima is a very traditional island, we had to go there accompanied by a man of high chiefly lineage, a school inspector named Afamasaga. We travelled in a beat-up old whale boat with an outboard motor, chugging across the lagoon of the main island of Upolu and through the reef into the open sea, which in the morning had a steady manageable swell. The cone of Apolima came into sight, and we circled until we were facing the great natural amphitheatre of the standing walls of the crater, their gray crags and combs half sub-merged under the surging tropical vegetation.

Another kind of surge soon preoccupied us, for the reef at Apolima was an unusual and very dangerous one. It was not a coral reef, but the actual broken-down and sea-worn lava wall of the crater; and it was entered through a narrow L-shaped passage between the great rock slabs where, only a week before, Afamasaga told us, the boat carrying the island's new teacher had been swamped, and, though he was saved with difficulty, his books had been lost. By now the swell had grown higher, and it was sweeping in tall, green waves over the gray rock and returning in a seething white race. At first we could distinguish no break at all in the reef, until Afamasaga pointed to an area where the flow, though no less powerful, seemed at least less white and broken.

The boat moved into position. "They always wait for the seventh wave," Afamasaga said, as the boat tossed and the crews shifted into their posts. One crewman clambered into the bows and stood poised with a pole in his hand. Another climbed onto the awning and sat watching the water, with his hands dangling on each side so that the steersman in the stern could see them. The man in the bows made a gesture, the engines sprang into life, and suddenly we were moving full speed with the blue-green wave towards the gap, and in a few seconds were between the dark rock masses that loomed in the tumbling water.

17

The passage ahead seemed hardly wider than the boat. The man on the awning gestured frantically, left hand and then right hand. We wavered slightly, and then we were in the passage, forging ahead and curving as we went, with the poleman fending off the rock on the port side as we swung round through the L-shaped kink and out with the last rush of the wave into the bay, the calm water, and the sudden release of quick fear.

I looked at Afamasaga. He laughed softly. "Only men from Apolima can do that. Now you see why it's a great fortress. No Tongan boat ever sailed into this harbour."

Once we were in calm waters, an idyll of charm and calculation was enacted. A tall, powerfully built Polynesian stood on the beach to welcome us, in a tartan shirt and a flowered lavalava. He was the second chief on the island, the *tulefale* or orator. He made a great pretence that our visit was unexpected, and led us to the open-sided, palm-thatched meeting house that stood on a greensward looking over the little harbour. Almost immediately two other men appeared, looking like a South Sea version of Don Quixote and Sancho Panza. The gaunt Don was the *ali'i* or hereditary high chief of the island; fat Sancho was the local pastor.

We were welcomed with green coconuts and introduced by Afamasaga with titles of nobility made up on the spot. Then the two chiefs slipped away and returned with twisted gray roots of the kava plant, which they offered us as tokens of peace between us. There followed the traditional ceremony of preparation and partaking of kava as a sacred and mildly narcotic drink; and a round of bombastic oratory in which I was posthumously helped by the example of the Welsh preacher uncles of my childhood; and finally a traditional island feast, borne in by a long file of youths and maidens carrying all the Polynesian delicacies of sea and land. After that we settled down to a session of obliquely self-interested conversation.

I was anxious to find out how the most traditional community I had yet encountered in the Polynesian world actually worked, how the apparently complete acceptance of a rather evangelical kind of Christianity was reconciled with an equally strong adherence to *fa'a Samoa*, the perpetuation in the modern world of the Samoan way of life.

The chiefs and the pastor were equally intent on finding what

18

advantage might be reaped from this windfall visit of a *palangi* (the customary local term for a white man which literally means "heaven-breaker") whose power, thanks to Afamasaga's flowery introduction, they imagined to be great and far-reaching.

The chiefs suggested it might be appropriate to confer on me the honorary title of *Matai*, or clan chief. I had already been forewarned by a Samoan writer in Apia that I might receive such an offer, and that acquiescence would mean I would be responsible for providing benefits for my adopted community that I might not be able to afford. Afamasaga merely told me that I must be decisive one way or another; hesitation would be taken as acceptance. So I elaborately proclaimed my unworthiness, even though I already bore the respected Stevensonian title of *tusitala* (story-teller), to become a chief on such a celebrated island as Apolima.

My decision—and my gift of good Australian silver dollars and a large tin of *pisupo* (corned beef)—were accepted with sangfroid. This was still my island and my village, the *tulefale* assured me; I would always be welcome back—and if I could get them a new power boat and a short-wave radio, it would be appreciated.

While all this had been going on, there had been a great shouting of children from the beach. We all rose and went to look in the harbour, where a high wave had come sweeping in over the reef, lifting our boat so that it lay broadside and tilting. It was soon righted, but the leading boatman came to tell us that we should not be too late in leaving, for the wind was beating up the channel between Apolima and Upolu.

But the orations and the tea drinking, the smoking and gift giving, could not be interrupted. And Afamasaga had to do at least a routine school inspection to justify his visit officially. The boatman came back to say that we really must leave; further delay would be dangerous. But more green coconuts had to be drunk, the final speeches made, the last gifts pressed to the brow, before we went down to the beach, where baskets of breadfruit and coconuts were put on board and the *tulefale* and the young men of the village waded into the harbour to bid us farewell. The pastor had decided to accompany us to the main island, and a couple of women came as well with baskets of gifts for their relatives.

We shot the reef in great style, but the boatmen had been correct in their warnings. The risk was great, and the fear slow and cumulative. The swell rose high, and the old and open boat was rolled like a shell on a beach—sometimes shuddering, through all its fragile timbers, under the impact of a wave; sometimes rising before a crest like the boat in Hokusai's famous print, and scudding down sickeningly into the trough. Many times we shipped water, and the boatman bailed steadily most of the way. I felt that any moment we would be swamped or capsized or that the boat would merely break apart in the heavy waters, and so did Inge. We did not mention our fears until we reached dry land, though silently and almost like automatons, we exchanged things, Inge giving me my passport, which she was carrying, I passing money to her, so that if one survived she or he would not be stranded.

Even Afamasaga looked grave, which perturbed me in a man who knew these waters. The pastor closed his eyes and began to mutter prayers, and the women followed his example. One of them whimpered. But I did not begin to feel fear rising to panic until I looked at the hand with which Afamasaga was holding one of the upright struts of the awning, and saw it was so tightly clenched that it was turning white.

But we did not drown, and eventually slipped into the great Lagoon of Upolu, where the waters were calm. Yet I felt nearer to death on that journey than on any other, perhaps because fear was prolonged, and therefore, despite the delights that accompanied the terror, I now regard it as the worst of my worse journeys. But not the worst journey. That is yet to come.

DAVID MAMET

Born in Chicago in 1947, David Mamet has written many plays, including Sexual Perversity in Chicago, American Buffalo, *and* A Life in Theater. *He is the author of several screenplays and two collections of essays, the more recent of which is* Some Freaks. *He won the Pulitzer Prize and the New York Drama Critics Circle Award for* Glengarry Glen Ross. *He lives in Massachusetts and Vermont. The following essay is taken from* Writing in Restaurants (*1986*). *In it Mamet's expectations about a trip with his family to the Caribbean are subverted.*

A FAMILY VACATION

My people have always been anxious about traveling. I think this dates back to the Babylonian Exile. In any case, when I was growing up, the smallest move was attended by fear, puttering, and various manifestations of nerves. My father and mother would fight, we would invariably get lost, we would miss meals, bedtimes, and destinations entirely.

My parents' fears took many convenient forms: fear of polio, of contamination from drinking fountains, of drowning from swimming too close on the heels of eating . . . all of these were just handy guises for the severest xenophobia, which I saw all around me as a child, in my home and my friends' homes.

Looking back, the fear of the strange that I saw around me is understandable, and I am only half kidding in referring to it as a cultural trait. My parents and the parents of my friends were one short generation removed from The Pale of Settlement in Russo-Poland; and to *their* parents the shortest trip away from home offered real possibilities of real trouble: difficulty of obtaining food acceptable to their religious laws, of confusion as to the local customs, of persecution and murder itself.

So this was the jolly burden which my parents inherited from their parents and passed down to me; and seventy years removed from the Cossacks I was still unable to take a vacation.

On our honeymoon, my wife and I went to Paris and I spent two days curled up on the bed. Yes, you will say, correctly, that probably had something to do with getting married—but isn't that a journey of a sort as well?

The above specious observation to the contrary notwithstanding, in eight years of marriage, and based on our informative experiences on the honeymoon, we have not really had a vacation.

But this year it occurred to both of us that we were not going to live forever, that our daughter was not forever going to stay a fascinating, loving, three-year-old, and that on our respective deathbeds we were going to be unlikely to say, "I'm glad I advanced my career in 1986."

So my wife, speaking not for herself, but for the Group, signed us up to take a vacation. A model husband, I, of course, agreed and congratulated her on her decision, knowing that as the time came to leave, I could find some pull of work that kept me at home, or at the very best, feign sickness, and failing that, I could actually *become* sick.

The last being a tactic I'd employed before and to advantage: "*You* girls go away, don't worry about me, go and refresh yourselves," and then they'd go, and I could stretch out over the whole bed and smoke cigars in the living room.

But this time it was not to be. And, as the day set for departure drew near, I told my wife that I was heartbroken, but I could not accompany them; to which she replied that she had checked my date-book, and I had nothing scheduled for the week in question save a haircut appointment, which she had canceled for me; and that she had already told the kid how Daddy was going to come down for a week and "not work."

Well, I fought a holding action on the rectitude of her having unilaterally canceled my haircut appointment, and on the collateral issue of my well-known inability to enjoy myself when my hair is too long. To which arguments my wife responded, "Tough," and off we went to fun and frolic in the Caribbean surf.

On the way to the airport, the cabbie asked us why we were going to vacation on an island which was currently being decimated by a hurricane. I thought, Aha! The cavalry arrives. But my wife said, "We're going down there to find out, and if it has not passed we'll just come home, and that's what we're going to do." We prepared to get on the plane.

I explained to my wife that on the plane going down I was going to have to do research, and she said, "Fine." My research consisted of reading the galleys of a detective novel someone wanted to make into a movie, and my enjoyment of it would have been increased if she had resisted, but she did not. So I struggled through the book. My daughter watched *Romancing the Stone*, and my wife colored in the kid's coloring book for three and a half hours.

At the island we found that the hurricane had indeed passed, so I scowled and we went off to our hotel. We got to the hotel, and I braced for what the Semitic Traveler will of course recognize as the interlude of: I am here, I am paying good money, everything is wrong. Change everything immediately and make it different or I am going to die.

The bellman put the bags in the room, I opened the doors to the patio beyond which was the sand beach and the Caribbean, and a football landed with a huge "plop" in the water outside.

Fine, I thought, here I'm paying good money for some peace and quiet, and some overly American jock who can't leave home without his props is going to ruin my vacation.

Then as I watched, the football opened its wings and revealed itself to be a pelican which had just dived for a fish.

Okay, I thought, I'll try. And I did try. I changed into my suit and sat on the beach. I thought about Somerset Maugham and his sea stories. I thought about Joseph Conrad. I picked up a seashell and thought how very Victorian it looked, and wondered at the Multiplicity of Nature.

The sun went down, we put the baby to bed, and my wife and I went to dinner. We sat in a beautiful restaurant, hanging out on a cliff over the beach. There was a "popping" sound below, like far-off fire-works. I looked and saw the sound was made by the undertow, dragging the stones behind it. I said, "The stones on the beach being dragged sound like far-off fireworks." My wife said nothing. I said, "It occurs to me that the teaching of literature is completely *wrong*. Now: here we have a lovely simile—but the point is not the *simile* . . . the point is not the writer's knack at making a *comparison*—the point is the *stone*!"

My wife said, "Why don't you take a vacation?"

Well, I had another drink, then I had *another* drink, then we went back to our room and we fell asleep, and I slept for eighteen hours on each of the next two days, and on the third day I wasn't thinking about Joseph Conrad anymore.

My daughter asked me to come out and make "flour," and rather than responding "Just a minute" I went out and made flour. Making flour consisted of pouring sand into a palm leaf, and I was surprised to find it just as enjoyable as (and certainly more productive than) a business lunch at the Russian Tea Room.

The punch line was that we had a grand old time. We swam and went waterskiing, we had breakfast on the patio. The baby went naked on the beach for a week with a strand of beads around her neck, and her hair got bleached and streaked.

Some good friends were vacationing on a neighboring island, and they came over for a day and we all got drunk and went skinny-dipping in the moonlight; my daughter and I bounded on a trampoline a couple of hours every day; and all in all, it was the trip of a lifetime.

I thought: we are Urban people, and the Urban solution to most any problem is to do more: to find something new to eat in order to lose weight; to add a sound in order to relax; to upgrade your living arrangements in order to be comfortable; to buy more, to eat more, to do more business. Here, on the island, we had nothing to do. Everything had been taken away but the purely natural.

We got tired as the sun went down, and active when it rose; we were treated to the rhythm of the surf all day; the heat and the salt renewed our bodies.

We found that rather than achieving peace by the addition of a *new idea* (quality time, marital togetherness, responsibility), we naturally removed the noise and distractions of a too-busy life, and so had *no need* of a new idea. We found that a more basic idea sufficed: the unity of the family.

I did leave the island two days earlier than they, as I had to be in Los Angeles on business. As I got on the plane, I harbored a small secret joy at my forthcoming return to the addiction of busy life: I would have meetings and talk on the phone and lounge across the bed and smoke cigars in the hotel room.

I waved from the plane window and put my writer hat back on, and several thoughts occurred to me. The first was of Thorstein Veblen, who said that nobody traveling on a business trip would ever have been missed if he did not arrive. And I said to myself, you know, that's true.

And I thought of Hippocrates, and his hospital on the island of Cos, where the sick were treated to a peaceful view, and warm winds, and the regenerative rhythm of the surf—to a place where man could be healed because the natural order was allowed to reassert itself; and I missed my family, and was very grateful for the week that we spent with each other on the beach.

WILLIAM TREVOR

William Trevor was born in Mitchelson, County Cork, in 1928 and spent his childhood in provincial Ireland. He attended a number of Irish schools, one of them portrayed in the following essay, and later Trinity College, Dublin. A prolific story and novel writer he is also a dramatist, a member of the Irish Academy of Letters, and the recipient of an honorary C.B.E. Among his recent books are The Silence in the Garden, The News from Ireland, Beyond the Pale, *and* The Oxford Book of Irish Short Stories, *which he edited in 1989. He lives in Devon with his wife and travels regularly to the continent for extended periods.*

THE SECOND JOURNEY

There have been terrible, ugly journeys that are remembered by me now for different aspects of distress. Races against time have been lost. Delays at airports have triumphantly ruined weekends. Night has come down too soon when walking in the Alps. Theft has brought travel to a halt, toothache made a nightmare of it. Once a ferry mistakenly took off before its passengers had arrived on the quayside. Once the wheels of an aircraft did not come down. "Kaput!" a German garage mechanic declared of an old A.30 on an autobahn, and that was that.

But the worst journey of my life involved neither hardship, pain, nor danger. It was not particularly uncomfortable. I suffered neither undue hunger nor thirst, extremes of neither heat nor cold.

What possessed me was dread, and the misery of anticipating the unavoidable. I was twelve years old on the morning of April 28th, 1941.

I was returning to boarding school and I knew what awaited me. The journey took place by bus, from the town of Enniscorthy, in the southeast corner of Ireland, to Dublin. Some time in January I had made this journey for the first time. I had waited with my brother outside the paper shop where the bus drew in at the bottom of Slaney Hill. Our two trunks and our bicycles were on the pavement; other members of the family had come to wave good-bye. Too excited to say anything, we had watched the red-and-cream-coloured bus approaching on the other side of the river, crossing the bridge, then slowing down. We had egg sandwiches and Toblerone. Our spirits were high.

On this second occasion I was alone because my brother was ill. Otherwise everything was apparently the same. People had come to wave good-bye, bicycle and trunk were hoisted onto the roof of the bus and secured beneath a tarpaulin. A washbag and anything else necessary for the night was packed into a small suitcase known at the school as a pyjama suitcase. But everything was different also, dogged by a bleak melancholy that the thirteen weeks following that first occasion had inspired. Journey to hell, I said to myself as the conductor handed me my ticket and my change. "How're you doing?" he enquired, red-faced and cheery.

By the time we reached Bunclody the odour of long-boiled cabbage that hung about the school's kitchen and dining room was beginning to mingle with the bus's exhaust fumes. By Kildavin, the noise of the play yard echoed; by Tullow, Monsieur Bertain was striking the blackboard in a fury. "Tell us why, if you would," the sarcastic science master invited in Rathvilly. "Tell us why you lack intelligence."

An old man had halted the bus at Ballycarney crossroads and now sat beside me, shredding a plug of tobacco. He wore a cap and a rough grey suit, neither collar nor tie. He had entered the bus with a brown paper parcel under his arm, greeting everyone as he made his way along the aisle. He was travelling to Dublin to see his daughter who'd just been taken into hospital. He whispered hoarsely, telling me this. The parcel contained a nightdress he'd borrowed from a neighbour. "She sent me a wire to bring a nightdress," he said.

When my brother and I made the first journey to school our delight had increased with every mile. There would be dormitories, we had been told; games we'd only heard about would be played. A shop-man in Enniscorthy who had been at this school assured us that we'd love it, since he had loved it himself. We imagined the playing fields, and the day boys arriving on their bicycles every morning, the boarders going for walks at the weekends. Going for walks, and visits to the museum and the zoo, were mentioned in the prospectus. So was the excellence of the food, attention paid to health and well-being, the home-from-home atmosphere. The motherliness of the housekeeper was not mentioned, but we'd heard about it from the shopman. He said the headmaster had played cricket for the Gentlemen of Ireland, a man you could look up to, ex–Grenadier Guards.

"You're off for the two days?" The old man had coaxed his pipe to smoulder to his satisfaction and was emitting billows of acrid smoke. He didn't listen when I told him I was going back to school, but continued about his daughter being admitted to hospital. A worse mis-fortune had occurred in the past, when she'd married a Dublin man.

"He has her short of garment money," the old man said. "That's why she sent the wire."

His daughter had two broken legs. She'd been on the roof of a hen shed when it gave way. He crossed himself. She was lucky she hadn't been killed. It was a sunny day. The side of my face next to the window was warm. Cows rested in the fields we passed, not even chew-ing their cuds. A few stood on a riverbank, drooping over it, too lazy to drink. Primroses were in bloom.

"Plenty more for anyone!" The stern voice of the motherly house-keeper echoed, as the other voices had. In the middle of each morning the entire school congregated in the kitchen passage and received a Bakelite tumblerful of soup. It was a yellowish colour, with globules of grease floating on the surface. Chunks of potato and turnip sank to the bottom, and an excess of barley made the mixture difficult to consume: you had to open your mouth as wide as you could and tip the tumbler into it, feeling sick while you did so.

"A right gurrier," the old man said. His daughter's husband had ordered her up on the roof to repair it. "Roasting himself at the range while she's risking her limbs on old corrugated iron. A lead-swinger from Tallagh. Useless."

We'd have giggled, my brother and I. We'd have listened to all

28

that with pleasure if we'd heard it on our first journey to school. We'd have egged the old man on.

"Dooley's coming up!" the conductor called out. "Anyone for Dooley's?"

The early morning, when you first woke up, was the worst. You lay there listening to the noises coming from the three other beds—someone muttering in his sleep, someone softly snoring, the bedsprings creaking when there was a sudden movement. There were no curtains on the windows. The light of dawn brought silhouettes first and then the reality of the room: the blue top blankets, the boarded-up fireplace. You didn't want to go back to sleep because if you did you'd have to wake up again. "Get out of that bed," the Senior Boarder ordered when the bell went. If the bell hadn't roused him it was Rausmann, the German, who did the shouting. "Out at the double, pull the bedclothes back. Quick now!" They didn't get out themselves. Rausmann glared from the sheets, his acned features ugly on the pillow. The Senior Boarder, destined for the Church, was said to pray before he rose.

"Isn't that a grand day?" a woman shouted into the bus when it drew in at Dooley's, a wayside public house. She pushed a parcel in and the conductor ambled down to collect it. A grand day, he agreed. When the bus moved on the woman stood there, waving after it, smiling in the sunlight. GUINNESS IS GOOD FOR YOU the sign in the public house window said. A sweeping brush stood in the open doorway, propped against the door frame. Tulips grew in a tin bath that had been painted green.

Harrison 2 used to pretend he was going to brand you. He'd put a poker in the open fire in the Fourth Form and two of his buddies would hold your arms and leg, a third guarding the door. When the poker was red hot it would be held close to your cheek and you could feel the heat. "Don't blub," the one with the poker warned. "You'll get it if you blub." Old Boots, as the motherly housekeeper was known, was renowned for her toughness. The Bull was what we called the headmaster you could look up to because he roared like one when bad temper got the better of him.

"Two broken legs." The old man had twisted himself round to address the woman in the seat behind.

"God help her," the woman sympathised.

In the dormitory Corrigan, from Mullingar, would tell us about his adventures with the maid. After lights out his voice would drone on, no one believing a word he said. Little Meadows would snuffle into the bedclothes. "Shut up that bloody filth, Corrigan!" Rausmann would finally shout, his raised voice causing Old Boots to knock with the window-pole on the ceiling of the room below. Rausmann had huge blackheads all over his back which he'd try to make you squeeze out for him.

On the bus I closed my eyes. It might crash, and I might be taken to a hospital like the old man's daughter instead of having to continue the journey on my bicycle, out to the suburb where the school was. "Don't be a child," the Senior Boarder had a way of saying if you said you couldn't eat something, or if you didn't want to play the boarders' game of catching a tennis ball when it rolled off the roof of the big schoolroom, wet and dirty from the gutter water.

"I never heard the like," the woman behind me indignantly exclaimed. "She could've been lying there dead."

If the bus crashed there might be an instant blackness and you'd be lying there dead yourself. You wouldn't know a thing about it. You'd be buried in the graveyard by the church and everyone would be sorry that you'd been made to go on this fateful journey. Little Meadows would snuffle all night when he heard the news. "Don't be a child," the Senior Boarder would snap at him.

The bus stopped in Baltinglass and I thought I'd maybe get out. I imagined slipping away and nobody noticing, my bicycle and trunk still under the tarpaulin, carried on to Dublin. I imagined walking through the fields, warmed by the sun, not caring what happened next. At breakfast there were doorsteps of fried bread, one for each boarder, not crispy like fried bread was at home but sodden and floppy with fat. The Senior Boarder poured out tea that tasted of metal. Rausmann was the Second Boarder, the Second in Command, the Bull called him. "What's this?" Old Boots sniffily demanded, examining your darned pullover. She'd never seen worse darning, she declared, and you remembered your mother threading wool through a needle and then carefully beginning the small repair.

The bus arrived at the first straggle of Dublin's outskirts, then pressed relentlessly on through Templeogue and Terenure and into the city proper. When it finally drew up on Aston Quay it felt for the first time like a friend, its smoky, hot interior a refuge I had never valued. "Are you right there, son?" The cheery conductor wagged his head at me.

On the street I strapped the pyjama suitcase onto the carrier of my bicycle. I dawdled over that; I watched the old man who'd sat beside me crossing the street, the brown paper parcel containing his daughter's nightdress under his arm. Other passengers from the bus were moving away also. I mounted my bicycle, a Golden Eagle, and rode into the traffic of Westmoreland Street. The trunk would be delivered to the school later, with all the other trunks.

Arrival is an end; the journey is over, at last a destination is reached. That is usually so, but on this occasion journey and destination were one; this time there was no sigh of gratitude from the weary traveller, no long-earned moment of relief. My Golden Eagle carried me only to a realm in which the highways and byways were sealed against escape, a part of hell in which everyone was someone else's victim.

Irrelevantly, trams clanked by. Crowds bustled on the pavements. "Tell us why, if you would," the science master requested, and the Senior Boarder drove his elbow into a passing stomach, which was a habit he had. Corrigan from Mullingar retold his adventures with the maid; Rausmann showed off his blackheads. Mechanically, as though I had no will, my feet worked the pedals. When a red light demanded it, I applied the brakes, obedient in all things. "Spell fuchsia," the Bull commanded, coming across you somewhere. I could taste the yellow soup.

I turned out of Harcourt Street into Charlemont Street and later crossed the Grand Canal. My egg sandwiches and Toblerone remained uneaten. The chocolate would have melted into my pyjamas and wash-bag: dully, it passed through my mind that Old Boots would have an excuse to say something harsh almost as soon as she saw me. In Ranelagh I turned into the short avenue that led to the school. I rode past the carpentry hut and pushed the Golden Eagle into its numbered place in the bicycle shed. I walked through the play yard, continuing that endless journey.

MARTHA GELLHORN

Born in St. Louis, Missouri, in 1908, Martha Gellhorn set out in 1937 to cover the war in Spain. Over the following nine years she covered five wars around the world and nourished a career as a novelist and short story writer. She has published five novels, two collections of stories, and four collections of novellas. Her nonfiction books include The View from the Ground *and the volume from which the following essay is taken,* Travels with Myself and Another *(1978)—which she describes as "not a proper travel book" but rather "an account of my best horror journeys, chosen from a wide range, recollected with tenderness now that they are past." Hers is the bravado of a peripatetic ambition. She was once married to Ernest Hemingway.*

....

WHAT BORES WHOM?

In 1971, I made my fifth journey through Israel; purpose of journey, a book that never jelled. Tired of being serious and taking notes, I went to Eilath to swim. Outside Eilath, on the bare hills and wadis by the Red Sea, the travelling young of the world congregated, the new-style travellers, the hippies, the young who roam as a way of life, a vocation. I was very interested, hoping for "insights" into travel, and spent much time in a discarded water tank which housed seven of them, and in shacks made of cardboard and tin scraps, and beside camp fires, listening.

I was convinced that they smoked hash, a commodity traded by Bedouins, because they were bored nearly to death, and didn't know it. Hash soothed the gnawing ennui and induced giggling or dreaminess. They talked of little else. Like their bourgeois elders, who swap names of restaurants, they told each other where the hash was good. It is impossible to escape a painful amount of dull conversation in this life but for sheer one-track dullness those kids took the cookie.

They had been everywhere. Their Mecca was India and ashrams and the pure soul-state of the spiritual East. Some had actually made the journey, a tough one without money through Iran and Afghanistan; they deserved respect for guts and grit. I do not intend to go that road (God willing) and asked about the terrain; the name, Khyber Pass, singing its predictable siren song to me. Great, gee it's great, they murmured. Three words sufficed for the experience of travel: great, beautiful, heavy.

Why, why, I kept asking, bribing them to talk with groceries and Mount Carmel wine. Why did they travel? I wasn't prying, I only wanted to understand. Yes, I can see why you ran away from Long Island and lovely Copenhagen and Tokyo—who wouldn't run from Tokyo?—if your parents were heavy. But after you have fled your homes, what do you find? *What is it?* As their basic rule is live and let live, they were patient with me and my questions.

Only two young Israelis lived in this settlement, taking a holiday from life. And I met only two foreign Jews, Americans. It was a Gentile drop-out transient camp including the Japanese. The Japanese kept to themselves, kept their hillside startlingly neat, kept fit by fierce exercises. They grew their hair long, smoked hash with bright-eyed wonder—the joy of crime—and were in a state of beaming happiness like kids let out of reform school. Which is what they were, all scheduled to cut their hair sadly and return to careers in the Tokyo rat race.

Books were either non-existent or a hidden vice. No one expressed any interest in man-made beauty; art and architecture were for old squares. They littered the landscape (superb landscape) while condemning Israelis for doing the same. People who foul landscapes do not take their sustenance from the natural world. I decided that what they found were companions of the road but their code forbade them much conversation apart from long-winded stories about how stoned somebody was. Either they despised words or hadn't yet dominated their

33

use. Did they communicate like birds who manage all right with a limited range of notes?

Alone with me on the beach or sitting in a wadi, they were less chary of speech. In their view, they were travelling to find themselves, rather as if oneself were a missing cufflink or earring that had rolled under the bed. They admired those among them who meditated in the lotus position for a fixed period of time each day. Like I mean he's really into meditation. The meditators were closer to finding themselves. I couldn't imagine any of them ten years hence, having never known such shapeless people.

I asked about their parents; nobody came here from stately homes and filthy riches. A few disliked their parents but most pitied the poor slobs who spent their lives working to make money, for what? Well, to rear these children and give them all the little luxuries like food, clothing, shelter and as much education as they would take. Money orders from home were welcome but accepted as due; the old man worked, he could afford the cash. Work was a four-letter word meaning slavery. They were not going to be slaves of the system.

I can now hear young voices telling me to knock it off, the kids were putting me on. (Did Margaret Mead ever suspect that the Samoans were putting her on?) True, someone who smokes nicotine not hash in such company is like a teetotaller in a saloon. I explained that I had tried pot once, before they were born or anyway lapping up baby food, and once was enough. For twelve hours I lay like a stone statue on a tomb, unable to move or sleep, while a few flies circled around, as loud large and terrifying as bombers. They said probably the vibes were bad. I said the vibes were first-rate, the trouble was me, I was allergic to pot and besides Mount Carmel wine did for me what joints did for them.

They thought I was crazy to smoke cigarettes, didn't I know cigarettes gave you lung cancer? I said I was living dangerously, like them. In fact, apart from their hash and sex intake, they were living like a Boy Scout's dream of camping, but much rougher than Boy Scouts' well-equipped excursions. I think they hardly noticed me, being half-sloshed most of the time. In the water tank, daylight filtered through a small square hole in the roof; I was also hardly seen. When a hump of blankets started to hump energetically, I wondered whether the blankets were due to my presence but, after further study, decided that this was daytime style for copulation.

They had no cliques or sets. Even if they thought someone heavy or otherwise a nuisance, they never shut anyone out. Children learn and adults perfect the social tricks for making a fellow being feel unwelcome. They did not practise this sort of unkindness. They were generous; whoever had anything spread it around. These are the good manners of the heart and altogether praiseworthy. I couldn't tell whether a diet of hash explained a general lack of intelligence.

The girls surprised and amused me by confirming that the secret of success with boys is the same for hippy chicks as for debutantes, has always been the same for all girls: appreciative listening, tender care of male vanity, keeping your place in the background. How to be popular in a water tank. Poor little girls. Physically less resistant than the boys, they were often wrapped in a lonely blanket, coughing their heads off, shivering with fever, weak from diarrhoea. If attached to one man, they seemed like Arab women, permanently bringing up the rear. If unattached, they still did the cooking and washed the pots and plates under a distant spigot.

Like birds, they had all winged their way south to the slum they created at the tip of Israel, remarking that it was a pretty good place in the winter, as warm as you'd find. They knew nothing about Israel and didn't approve of it; the fuzz was heavy. At least they knew something of the cops wherever they'd been, which is one way to learn about a country. At the end of a week, they began to make me nervous; I was afraid I might grow up to be like them.

Thinking of those kids at Eilath has given me a new slant on horror journeys. They are entirely subjective. Well of course. If I had spent any time analysing travel, instead of just moving about the world with the vigour of a Mexican jumping bean, I'd have seen that long ago. You define your own horror journey, according to your taste. My definition of what makes a journey wholly or partially horrible is boredom. Add discomfort, fatigue, strain in large amounts to get the purest-quality horror, but the kernel is boredom. I offer that as a universal test of travel; boredom, called by any other name, is why you yearn for the first available transport out. But what bores whom?

The young hippies had not been condemned to an indefinite

sentence of aimless hardship travel. They believed they were living; the rest of us were merely existing. At their age, I travelled around Europe with a knapsack too but would have thought their doped and dirty communal drifting a horror journey then, as I did now. At the opposite extreme, people enjoy grand culture tours with an attendant charming scholar lecturer to inform and instruct. They are guided round the antiquities of Greece, the Coptic churches of Ethiopia, the mosques of Persia, and other splendours. The companions of the road are civilized and couriers spare them the trying aspects of travel. I would die of it.

As also I would die of a cruise which is a super delight to vast numbers of travellers. It bores me even to think of such a trip, not that I mind luxury and lashings of delicious food and starting to drink at 11 a.m. with a glass of champagne to steady the stomach. But how about the organized jollity, the awful intimacy of tablemates, the endless walking round and round because you can't walk anywhere else, the claustrophobia? One of the highly extolled features of a cruise is restfulness. If you really want the top in rest cures, take a three months' cruise on the Q E 2, the penthouse staterooms at £100,000 would be best but you can relax in some sort of hutch for a mere £5,000.

The longest time I ever passed upon the waves was eighteen days in 1944, crossing the Atlantic on a dynamite ship. The ship was manned by Norwegians, forty-five of them, the Captain and the First Mate had a working command of English, talk was basic. The deck cargo was small amphibious personnel carriers, which left hardly any space to stretch the legs. The hold was filled with high explosives. There were no lifeboats. I was the only passenger. Smoking was forbidden though by special permission of the Captain I could smoke in my cabin with a big bowlful of water as ashtray. The food was terrible and we had nothing to drink.

Though we didn't know it, this enormous convoy was part of the enormous final build-up for D-Day, eleven days after we reached Liverpool. It was freezing cold and the diversions were icebergs, a morning of splendidly snafu manoeuvres, evasive action against submarines, the air rent by curses, and gunnery practice, nice and noisy. Fog shrouded us most of the way. The Captain was worried about day and night fog, his cargo, and the risk of collision with Liberty ships which he regarded as more dangerous than submarines, saying angrily, "They try to handle them like a taxi." I didn't understand enough to be worried about anything and thought it a pleasant, interesting trip though not a barrel of fun, rather lacking in excitement. I kept skimpy notes, the last one is: "The voyage has been a fine rest cure."

I wouldn't willingly spend eighteen days afloat ever again but if the choice was between a cruise ship and a dynamite ship, I'd have no trouble in choosing.

And then there's Bali, a name of guaranteed glamour, known to all. Before the Second World War, I had heard of incomparable Bali from aristocrats of travel—those who could pay for the expensive journey—and plenty of picture books proved the beauty of tiny deadpan temple dancers with fingernails like quills, handsome native houses of woven mats and carved wood, a landscape of exotic elegance. Oddly enough I had no interest in seeing Bali, very odd considering my interest in seeing almost anywhere. I'm not sure why; perhaps I imagined it as a museum island, boringly exquisite, filled with poor beautiful people being stared at by rich beautiful people. But Bali was a transcendent experience for me too, in rare circumstances: the Japanese surrender.

This momentous occasion took place in March 1946. The reason for the delay, so long after the Japanese defeat, was that no one had time to get around to Bali. A single warship was assigned to handle the peculiar D-Day. For two nights we waited on deck, crammed with troops, in heat, dirt, thirst, everyone asking aloud and bitterly what we were waiting for. Then the great day dawned and we swarmed down nets into landing craft. The welcoming committee of Jap officers could be seen on the black sand beach and in order not to lose face we were supposed to make a ceremonial approach, all landing craft in line abreast. There followed a scene of glorious confusion; landing craft scurried like maddened water beetles, if two got in line, the others strayed. The troops became increasingly browned-off as well as seasick. We were pitched about inside these uncomfy steel jobs while the impassive Japs watched, no doubt wondering how our side won the war.

Finally someone in command, outdone by this display of anti-seamanship, bellowed to get ashore and the hell with it, so we straggled in to land. Whereupon Jap officers surrendered swords, as if giving away fountain pens. A Jap photographer from Domei sprang around clicking his camera as though this were a fashionable first night. I laughed myself into uncontrollable hiccoughs, further stimulated by seeing the neat composed Jap officers drive ahead in fine cars which we followed in ratty old trucks. When the troops caught sight of bare Balinese breasts, they cheered. Breasts were covered at once throughout the island.

My notes on that week are as meaningless as if written in Sanskrit. Place-names, people-names, problems, politics, Balinese festivities, descriptions of scenery, kampongs, conditions under Japanese rule. All I remember is laughter, joy in life.

I think I had the best of Bali, better than the stylish pre-War travellers and much better than the hordes who now invade the island which has become a hippy haven as well as providing high-class international beach resorts. Rumour says that the gentle Balinese are as skilful at gouging tourists as everyone else in the mysterious East. It sounds like an Oriental Capri, and worth avoiding.

Yes indeed, what bores whom? The threshold of boredom must be like the threshold of pain, different in all of us.

EDWARD HOAGLAND

Born in New York City in 1932, Edward Hoagland is the author of thirteen books of essays, fiction, and travel, including Notes from the Century Before, African Calliope, *and* Seven Rivers West. *His most recent book,* Heart's Desire, *is a collection of essays. He lives in Vermont, where he teaches at Bennington College. In the following piece, when the travel writer meets up with a young woman who goes further than he in "courting a catastrophe," his dispassionate account of her ordeal gives way to a subtle recognition that the two of them, each in their own ways, are not dissimilar.*

BALANCING ACT

There are writers like Evelyn Waugh, Graham Greene, and V. S. Naipaul who seem to go looking for bad journeys, for various reasons—political rage, an edgy personality, an appetite for satire or disaster—to our profit, indeed. But there are others who can be counted upon to make no ado at all about a bad trip—Marco Polo, John Muir, T. E. Lawrence—because their agendas and their virtues are different.

My own questing instinct tends toward a tolerant, patient, almost trusting viewpoint, and I don't find people suspect or dislikable by clan or race. I've experienced racism as a white man in Africa, and religious prejudice as a Christian in Israel and Yemen, and of course have recognized such vices within myself also. But I find that the balancing act by which I make my way among personalities and groups at home is not so unlike getting along with strangers abroad.

Arriving in Dar es Salaam or Cairo on a night plane without

reservations a decade ago—or when stranded on the wrong end of Kodiak Island during a perpetual rain—I've had some bad times. I've been lonely in Vienna and London, too; have worried about possible gunfights between militia bands along the Red Sea; and have felt panicky or stranded in blizzards north of the Arctic Circle. Yet all these interludes worked out pretty well eventually, as my optimism beforehand had expected them to.

Though, in shaky planes flying out of Fairbanks, or in Land-Rovers crossing dessicated patches of the Sahel, I was not such a fool as to think no mishap might befall the particular aircraft or vehicle carrying me, none did. And although I'm a lifelong New Yorker, I've never been mugged—or assaulted elsewhere in the world—and the tumors which doctors have discovered in me have been thus far benign, not malign, knock on wood.

This, perhaps, is my luck. In Mexico and the southern Sudan I've seen whimpering hunger. In Casablanca and Chicago I've seen people viciously clubbed. I know that life is an abyss, among other things, and like other travel writers, I enjoy wire-walking a bit, courting, in a sense, a catastrophe. Yet otherwise I believe in a deity—not one that will choose to protect me in a crunch, but one that makes the story of life, when grasped as a whole, a rhapsody. Nor would my dying slowly in the broken fuselage of a bush plane some day refute this idea, really.

But to come back to Dar es Salaam and a story: An Englishwoman, whom I had met in Nairobi, and I, after a certain amount of fuss, located a place to eat and sleep after our night arrival and much rushing about the black streets afoot, shouldering our baggage. Then for several days we contented ourselves with the pleasures of the small port and capital city. My friend had been raped on a beach on Lamu, an island off Kenya, shortly before joining forces with me. She had not been physically injured, however, and had waded into the surf in the aftermath to wash herself. But now she wanted to go swimming at an isolated beach south of "Dar," which we had heard was dangerous. I said it was a foolish notion and wouldn't, but she went alone, and, in this old slaving center, again was raped by a leggy, vigorous, Swahili-speaking man—nearly the first who noticed her lying on her beach towel—who, like the other rapist, wanted to penetrate but not use his knife on her. So again, she was free to wade into the Indian Ocean and douche afterwards, and return to the hubbub of Tanzanian bus stations, market bazaars, and expatriate Greek restaurants alive.

Why, oh why, I asked her, when her flood of tears had partly subsided. She said, in effect, that she had wanted to trust Tanzanians, as she had wanted to trust Kenyans, not behave like the British who didn't. I was massaging her neck and scalp as we talked, to comfort her, and there discovered an astounding dent under her hair, in the top of her head, for which she had no explanation that she could remember. She said only, with hesitance, that her mother had told her that her father had clobbered her with a frying pan when she was little— an incident absent from all recollection, which she now discounted as a subsequent influence.

As a matter of fact, this new misadventure, too, she managed to throw off, and we went on to have a good further tour of the country. But suppose she hadn't been able to throw it off? Would her Bad Trip, versus my Good Trip, be the result of having a horrendous father? John Muir's father almost killed him, also; yet Muir was a Good Trip man. I'm scarred with a stutter from my childhood's contretemps that is a much more visible mark than her dent, but my travels are quite devoid of nightmares—are comparatively mundane, but as cheerful as Marco Polo's. And ought one to conclude that T. E. Lawrence was a happier man than V. S. Naipaul because his travels sound nicer?

What *makes* a trip bad, in other words? Well, crashing on the tundra just as dusk fell might do it. Or breaking down in the desert without enough water. But Felix Krull and I: we do okay in third-class rail travel. And I'll sleep in a station with my feet on my luggage in reasonably good humor for lots of hours. In feverish delirium, I'll tend to doze in my hotel room instead of telephoning the U.S. ambassador. In my mind's eye I haven't become an Important Personage. Within the limits of my present experience, a bad trip is likely to be an organized trip with officious organizers, not a trip where reality intrudes its snaky head. I like both snakes and reality.

PART TWO

WRITERS AND THE FEAR OF FLYING

When it comes to flying, I am a nervous passenger but a
confident drinker and Valium-swallower.

—Martin Amis

PAULETTE JILES

Paulette Jiles was born in Missouri in 1943 and has lived in Canada since 1969. She worked in the Arctic and Sub-arctic, mainly with native communication groups, and then taught writing in Nelson, British Columbia, where she now lives. Her second book, Celestial Navigations, *won the Governor General's Award for poetry. Other books include* Sitting in the Club Car Drinking Rum and Karma-Kola, The Jesse James Poems, *and* Blackwater. *Her latest book, a collection of works for radio, is* Song to the Rising Sun.

··

NIGHT FLIGHT TO ATTIWAPISKAT

We are flying directly into darkness, the
dim polestar rides on the starboard wing, Orion
and his blue gems freeze in the southwest.

Our rare and singular lives are in the hands of the
pilot; after him the radar and one engine. There were
two engines when we started out but the other one
died. We watch

the starboard propeller feather in slow, coarse
revolutions. The pilot says we will make Attiwapiskat or
some place.
             Icarus, our pilot and our downfall.

Two thousand feet below dim lakes pour past as if
on their way to a laundromat. How could we have
sunk so low?
At times like this I consider life after death
as if it were a binary system, there are
no half-lives. We track cautiously down
the Milky Way, home of nebulae and Cygnus.

We are footloose in the corridors of the aurora.

The long stream of my life is flying out behind
this airplane like skywriting on the subarctic
night, fluttering, whipped with urgency. Each
episode was always cut off from the last, I used
to find myself a series of hostile strangers, startled
in doorways. Now they

gather themselves up, the wives, daughters, friends,
victims, perpetrators, the one with the pen and the
other carrying a blank mask, another at present
at the cleaners.

They catch up and slam together like
a deck of cards, packed into the present
moment. Is there a soul in there, a queen?
I draw one out; it's the ace of airplanes.
The radar repeats a fixed,

green idea. The pilot feels for the radio touch
of Thunder Bay.

At a thousand feet we make quick decisions
about our loyalties, the other engine might fail,
the suitcases of our hearts might be opened with

all that contraband, the jewels and screams, we
might have things to declare;
> the observable universe is my native country
> poetry is my mother tongue
> the ideas I have purchased on this side of the
border don't amount to more than a hundred dollars.
What comes after this?

What do you mean, what comes after this?
This is it.
Attiwapiskat approaches, a Cree village
on a cold salt coast, flying patchwork quilts in
several more colours than are found in nature,
shining with blue-white runway lights.

We will sleep in the guesthouse tonight, that
refuge of displaced persons. The pilot will
go down and repair the valve and say nothing happened.
(We flew into darkness at the rim of the world,
where distant lights broke through and something
failed us. Then at the edge when we were stamped
and ready to go through we were turned back.) We
can unload and forget it. But I will remember
and then go back and forget again.
This is Attiwapiskat, everything is as it should be.
We slide down to the airstrip through salt fogs
from Hudson Bay that slip through the night like
airborne bedsheets.
We get off, still life with sleeping bags.
Approaching us is an earthman,
speaking Cree.

TIMOTHY FINDLEY

As a young man Timothy Findley established himself as an actor in London and New York, as well as at the Stratford Festival in Ontario. He gained a wide literary reputation in 1977 with the publication of The Wars *and consolidated his success with his subsequent novels,* Famous Last Words, Not Wanted on the Voyage, *and* The Telling of Lies, *and with the story collections* Dinner Along the Amazon *and* Stones. *His recent memoir is* Inside Memory. *He is a past winner of the Governor General's Award for fiction, a script writer for film and radio, and an active supporter of P.E.N. Born in Toronto, he now lives in Cannington, Ontario.*

······································

AN UNFORGETTABLE JOURNEY
TO RUSSIA

The journey I am about to describe took place at a time when I was still an actor and working in the U.K. This was in November of 1955. I was twenty-five years old.

Peter Brook's all-star production of *Hamlet*, with Paul Scofield playing the title role, had been invited to the Soviet Union, where we would be the first English-speaking company of actors to play in Moscow since the Revolution of 1917. I had been cast as Osric, the kind of small, flashy part young actors kill for—though, luckily, in this case no corpses had accumulated.

Having rehearsed in London, we opened and played in Brighton and Oxford before the historic journey took place. Everyone, including Scofield—normally *Mister Cool* himself—was riddled with nerves. We were all about to be part of a momentous theatrical event and the prospect overwhelmed us. For one thing, this was before the age of commercial jets, and the distance to Moscow, in terms of hours alone, was vast. It called for one-and-a-half days of air travel, with stops in Berlin and Lithuania.

Another factor creating tension was the Cold War climate in which we had to make the trip. In the West, we were locked into an American-dominated foreign policy, syndicated by that coldest warrior of all, John Foster Dulles. As for the Soviet Union, the ghost of Joseph Stalin—dead for two years—hung like a pall over the Presidium. And making matters worse, the 1951 defections of British diplomats Guy Burgess and Donald Maclean were still a major source of embarrassment between the U.K. and Russia. It was not, by any means, the easiest time to be made the representatives of cultural détente. It was, however, a most exhilarating time.

The initial part of the journey, from London to Berlin, was made aboard a *BOAC* airliner of enormous size—the pre-jet version of a 747. We left mid-afternoon, arriving over Germany a good deal later than had been expected. The delay was caused by an encounter over the Lowlands with a storm that seemed determined to blow us back to England. There was also a display of thunder and lightning worthy of Steven Spielberg and, at one moment, the airliner fell eighty feet through an airpocket. The jolt at the bottom of this fall was almost lethal and I can still recall the sound of the bang it caused, and the sound of rattling bolts and screws as the aeroplane began, we were certain, to come undone around us. At this point, being a novice flyer, I turned around to look at my fellow passengers, most of whom were experienced air travellers, to see how they were reacting.

I should not have done this. . . .

Everyone on the plane was pale with fear—and it didn't help when, with something of a shock, I noticed for the first time the grim, silent features of the man who was seated four rows behind me on the other side of the aisle. His presence, I cannot really tell you why, was somehow unnerving. Perhaps this was only because my catching sight of him had come as a surprise. But why was he with us? What was he doing on board our aeroplane?

It was Graham Greene.

••••••••••••••

No one had told us Graham Greene would be joining our excursion. After all, we were on a chartered flight, which meant he had to be "one of us." He had, in that moment, the grey appearance of a "stowaway" and, when he saw me looking at him, his expression begged me not to draw attention to his presence. He was so intent upon not being recognized that I had to look away. Settling back into my fear of flying, I was able to take a little solace from the fact that Graham Greene had obviously been as frightened by our fall through the air as I had been. His knuckles, just like mine, were bone white and rigid. I also derived some comfort from the longshot hope that maybe God took "special care of special people." Surely He would not destroy that all-star cast of *Hamlet* and their newly revealed companion, the starry author of *Brighton Rock* and *The Power and the Glory*. Could God afford the headlines?

I suspect that, more than likely, most of us were making up those headlines for the next three-quarters of an hour as our wounded aeroplane slowly made its escape from the storm: SCOFIELD, WYNYARD, CLUNES, URE, BROOK ALL VICTIMS OF FIERY CRASH! My version added: BODY OF FAMOUS AUTHOR ADDS MYSTERY TO AIR DISASTER!

When, at last, the image of West Berlin presented itself below us—the Kurfürstendamm ablaze with lights—a cheer went up that might have come from a ship-wrecked crew when land has been sighted. Emerging from the plane at Tempelhof, several of us touched the ground with trembling, grateful fingers, swearing we would never fly again. But, of course, we still had the flight to Moscow before us, no one guessing what a nightmare that would prove to be.

••••••••••••••

We stayed for most of the night on the Wansee shore in one of those grand hotels where marble is mixed with neon to produce a kind of kitsch peculiar to Berlin. No one slept. Everyone drank a great deal and waited nervously for four A.M. This was the hour when the cavalcade of official limousines would arrive to take us away under cover of darkness deep into the East German countryside. Somewhere out there was the military airport from which we would make our departure for Moscow.

I remember all the tastes and smells of that night—of Turkish coffee, brandy, and of German cigarettes, and the warm aroma of *Knize Ten* cologne which have remained for me the signals of oncoming intrigue. The company sat en masse at a congregation of little tables spread beneath potted palms in the large café adjoining the hotel lobby. This, in spite of the fact that all of us had been assigned the comfort of beds and bathrooms. Nobody wanted to sleep for fear of missing a second of the great adventure.

I looked for Graham Greene and spotted him sitting with two male strangers beyond the palms, locked in a conversation that might, for all I knew, have been about the weather. On the other hand, because he was Graham Greene, I supposed the subject of their talk to be espionage. There had long been speculation, because of the tales in some of his books, that Greene was in the employ, one way or another, of the British Secret Service. Or perhaps he was tracking down another murderous Harry Lime. Certainly, he couldn't possibly have tagged along just to see the sights. Graham Greene a tourist . . . ? Never.

I was also intrigued by the fact that, although he had never once approached nor been approached by any one of the acting company's leading lights, I had nonetheless caught a glimpse of him in an upper corridor of our hotel engaged in a deeply serious conversation with one of the company's walk-on players. This was a woman whose presence in the company, while entirely welcome, had been somewhat mysterious because of her utter lack of acting talent. Still, since the theatre overflows with such people, no one had given it a second thought. This charming woman was with us—and that was that. Or rather, that was that until I saw her with Graham Greene in the corridor of that Berlin Hotel. And, when she finally came downstairs to join us in our café, passing Graham Greene without a flicker of recognition, I was quickly made aware that, if this lady couldn't act on stage, she could act the socks off every one of us in real life. What else could she be but a government spy?—an agent whose job, once Moscow had been achieved, would turn out to be some sort of secret mission. After all, besides Peter Brook himself, she was the only member of our company whose Russian was impeccable.

················

At four A.M. on the dot, the limousines arrived and we were divided into groups of six and eight and required to sit in the cars with the blinds drawn tight. Each of the vehicles was driven by a military driver and, after we had been locked in place in the back, a dark-suited gent got in up front and said, in Russian: "*Move!*". It was all very strange. But it was also funny, because our hosts were doing precisely what all the Cold War movies had told us they would do. The only thing they didn't do was call us *Comrade*.

We seemed to be in the cars for a very long time—even as long as an hour-and-a-half—before the official silence was broken. I have often wondered since if we were driven any real distance at all. Or was it an exercise in disorientation and were we only driven around in circles? At any rate, there came a moment when, still in transit, the dark-suited figure turned around and said, in English: "*You must raise curtains now.*" And when we did so, what was revealed was a flattened rural landscape, lighted by sunrise, showing much distressing evidence of the war: the skeletons of blasted houses and the absence of trees. Also, in spite of the early hour, there were endless lines of men and women setting out on foot along the roads on their way to work.

This landscape with its depressed population made it all too obvious how spoiled we had been in the West with our relatively quick recovery from the war. Everything there was as dark and as bleak as I remembered it being at home in the late 1940s—a bleakness from which we had emerged in the 1950s, into a Rinso-white and over-polished version of prosperity now called "the Eisenhower Era." But there in Eastern Europe, ten years after the war had ended, the people seemed unable to escape from its hardships. Inside the cars, we all fell silent.

————

The airport, once we got there, was set behind a double row of high wire fences. Soldiers—all of them shockingly young and armed with equally shocking sub-machine guns—strode up and down and watched our arrival with a mix of boylike curiosity and adult wariness. It appeared, in every way, still to be a war zone and we, though nothing overtly malicious happened, were treated for the moment more like prisoners than as guests.

"*Do not be looking*," someone said, as we were escorted into an aeroplane hangar. "*Do not be looking and do not be speaking. Thank you.*"

But looking and speaking were the only two things that any of us wanted to do. Where the hell were we? And where the hell were the washrooms? Where the hell were the aeroplanes that were going to fly us to Moscow?

The sight of all of us standing there must have been odd for the soldiers and officers in charge of us. We were not exactly "ordinary" looking. Actors—in those days, at any rate—always looked like actors: standing straighter, with more self-awareness; wearing their clothes with a sense of theatrical style; presenting themselves as if they were really there and not pretending they wanted to hide. Added to this was the fact that Diana Wynyard and Mary Ure had been dressed for the tour by the front rank of British designers—their clothes being advertisements for English chic. Not that chic was an issue in Russia, back in the days before Raisa Gorbachev, but the press of the Western world was covering our excursion and the British government had decided it was a perfect opportunity for showing off the best of British haute couture. The only problem was, not many people hang around military installations wearing Hardy Amies' cocktail suits and Norman Hartnell clutch coats. Or, for that matter, stiletto heels. . . .

Speaking of actors and haute couture, we had in the company one of the theatre's true eccentrics, the late and entirely delightful Ernest Thesiger. Mister Thesiger's eccentricities began with what nature had given him: a long, rather horselike face with a long, tilted nose. He was also tall, thin, and angular and his hands, which had been badly damaged in the First World War, were also long and thin and angular. In order to regain his use of them after they had been crushed during a bombardment on the Western Front, he had learned to do needlepoint and had become so proficient in this art that he was taken up by Queen Mary as her sewing companion. In fact, the widow of George V and

Ernest Thesiger bore a strong resemblance to one another—each of them squint-eyed—each of them dedicated to Edwardian dress—and each of them employing the same hairdresser, who turned them out in identical mauve-rinsed, marcelled waves with curl-framed foreheads. The thought of them together, bent above their sewing frames, scandal-hopping through Debrett's Peerage, conjures the image of a high-class act in turn-of-the-century Music Halls: "MA'AM AND ERNIE—THE TAT-TING TATTLERS!"

Ernest's other notable eccentricity also stemmed from the fact of his damaged hands. Convinced they were unbearable to look at (they weren't) he had begun wearing rings on every finger and, sometimes, even on his thumbs. These rings were often very large—and most of them were antiques. Some had once belonged to historical figures such as Napoleon and Marie Antoinette. His prize possession was a poison ring that had actually been *used* by Lucretia Borgia. I can still hear him saying: "*Used*, my dear—if you get my *drift!*"

It was Ernest Thesiger who, when he had been asked to describe his impression of the Western Front, first uttered the famous line: "*Oh, the noise, my dear! And the people!*" And it was Ernest who sported our company's only fur coat on our journey to Moscow. He had longed all his life to wear a fur coat and now he had the perfect excuse. Turning up his luxurious collar against the wind that invaded our hangar, Ernest surveyed the NKVD agents who were acting as our shepherds and said to me: "*You know what we should do the minute we get to Moscow, dear boy? We should march straight off to the Kremlin walls and write, in the biggest letters we can make:* BURGESS LOVES MACLEAN!"

"*But we don't have any chalk,*" I said.

"*Not to worry,*" said Ernest: "*I've brought a whole box.*"

And he had.

···············

When, at last, they paraded us out of the hangar and onto the tarmac, all we could see by way of aircraft were two or three DC-10's, a cargo plane the Americans had used in the war. Large numbers of these had been sold to the Russians for the same purpose. Now, they had the apperance of old tin traps, long past their youth and long past salvaging.

"*Thank heavens we don't have to fly in those!*" we all thought. But then, with a dreadful determination, our shepherds turned on the tarmac and started to lead us directly toward the DC-10's and—all hearts sinking— we realized these derelict crates were to be our transport to Moscow.

Our scenery and stage crew had preceded us. Now, the actors and the costumes were boarded and the engines were started. Everything shook and the propellers screamed. Inside the plane, we were seated in rows down either side of the fuselage—one row on the left, two rows on the right: death rows, we were certain. Taxiing down the snowy, ancient runway we were given such a ride that I realized for the first time what it was like to see the world through the eyes of Carmen Miranda: *one-and-two-and-three . . . LURCH! One-and-two-and-three . . . Bang!*"

Et cetera, et cetera, until we took off.

It was a flying nightmare.

Somewhere in the Baltic States (I think it was in Vilna) we stopped to have lunch. In the meantime, we had flown over Poland, which, in winter at any rate, had much the same appearance as parts of Ontario where it broaches the Manitoba prairie. There were a lot of small lakes below us, many trees and occasional farming communities. It was all very beautiful and somewhat reassuring. At least, if we fell, I would feel at home, which, of course, could not be said for anyone else.

Lunch was wonderful. We ate at huge round tables spread with pure white cloths and all around us there were other tables where various military personnel were eating—all of us being served by women dressed entirely in layers of thick white clothing. The soldiers and the airmen came from every region of the Soviet Union: exotic Mongols and flat-faced Slavs, black-haired Armenians, blond Ukrainians, and red-faced Muscovites, and all their varied languages gave the room the feel of Babel. Once, when the sun came out, all of us paused and, after a moment's silence, all said: "*aaaah!*" The effect of this was such a pleasant surprise that everyone laughed. Even Graham Greene was laughing, tucked in a private corner sitting alone at a small, white table. I wondered what would become of him now that we were about to depart on the final leg of our journey. I wondered if, at last, he would break his silence and speak with us—or would he maintain his distance and disappear, once we'd arrived.

················

As the afternoon wore on and the early winter darkness swept all sight of the earth away below us, we were offered Russian tea by our stewardess. This tea, which is both unique and delicious, is drunk with lemon zest and broken lumps of sugar from tall, thin glasses in silver holders. But, as the stewardess brought it around, it became quite clear that her supply of glasses and silver holders was somewhat more than slightly limited. In fact, she had only four of each and, consequently, only four passengers could be served at a time. No explanation was ever offered for this, but I cannot believe that, in all of Russia, they could not have found enough glasses to serve more than four of us at once. The reason, I am more inclined to suspect, had to do with the fact that we had entered, about the time the tea was first offered, a blizzard whose proportions were vaster and more violent than any blizzard I have experienced here in Canada. And that is saying a very great deal. Ernest told me that, in broken English, the stewardess had admitted to him: *"Now there is some possibleness we shall not be able to be landing. . . ."*

"Oh?" I said—white.

What, I wondered, would we do instead?

················

Increasingly, as the flight wore on, it became apparent that we really were in trouble. It became very cold in the plane. Everyone put on an overcoat. Blankets were offered. The pilot was attempting to climb above the storm, but he was failing to achieve his goal. The snow, apparently, went all the way to heaven.

Nobody spoke, which is the way of people in jeopardy, it seems. Neighbours retreated into private thoughts. We turned very slightly away from one another. The DC-10 began to shake and shudder. I thought how young we all were—even Ernest in his seventies. It is always too soon to die, I guess.

Moscow was at last achieved. At least, the sense of it was achieved,

56

straining somewhere out there trying to be heard on our radio. The stewardess came out of the cockpit at one point and beamed at everyone and just said: "Yes!"—and then turned around and disappeared again. But the city was there. We could feel it.

Sometime later, the plane began its descent and all at once—the same as over Berlin—the lights of the city began to wink at us one by one through the blowing snow. First, you would see them, then they would be wiped away, and then they would return, closer, more of them, multiplying like insects. Finally, searchlights appeared, finger-beams probing the blizzard. Everyone sighed.

But we were not down, yet.

Round and round and round the airport we flew in circles and as each circle was completed, the pilot banked the plane a little more until—as the circles were beginning to make us all dizzy—the plane was literally flying on its side and those of us on the "up-side" were holding on for dear life. And all the while, the searchlights seemed to be holding us up in a cat's cradle of crossed beams.

The stewardess made another appearance and told us—practically standing on her head to do so—that: *"There is no need to worry, please. Our pilot was in war planes and is best we have!"*

I'll bet!

Then, the moment came when we had been cleared to land and the plane levelled off. Now, the whole storm rushed past our tiny windows and all we could see was its white and incandescent light. When the wheels touched the earth, we still could not see what was there below us.

················

Once the plane was stilled and sitting in its designated place, everyone applauded. The stewardess smiled and waved as if she had done it all alone. In fact, I think we all felt as if we had done it alone: kept the whole world alive. It was a wonderful moment.

Then the door was opened and the sound of the storm swept in with a burst of snow—and everyone laughed. We all lined up to make our departure. And it was only then that we became aware we were not alone.

Racing over the great, wide field of the airdrome, a hundred people and more came running through the beams of light and the streaming snow—and they were all like small round balls of fur being blown toward us—jubilant in thick black coats and round black hats—and all of them, every one of them, carrying armfuls of flowers. And, as each of us stepped from the plane, a dozen hands reached out and thrust red roses, carnations, snapdragons, tulips, lilies into our chests and we were virtually embraced by all these flowers, and then we were swept away through the snow and the lights and the people toward the warmth of lounges, bars, and cafés that awaited us.

Only then did we realize who all these people were. They were all the actors of all the theatres in Moscow. I doubt that anyone could ask for a better ending to a journey than that. Someone very wise had known that the language of kind—of actors and of theatre people everywhere—is universal.

···············

As for Graham Greene, he chose that moment to slip away as I had thought he might. He did not return with us—and I don't know how his journey ended. But if, as I suspected, he had come for some liaison, for whatever reason, with Burgess and Maclean—then we held one thing in common. I, too, met Guy Burgess during that month in Moscow. But that is very much another story—not to be told until I'm old. The real adventure was in getting there.

STUART STEVENS

Malaria Dreams, Stuart Stevens' second book, is an account of his amusingly difficult, three-month trans-Sahara trek from the Central African Republic north to Algiers, accompanied by an ex–fashion model. He seems to specialize in hard journeys alleviated by interesting companions. In his first travel book, Night Train to Turkistan: Modern Adventures along China's Silk Road, *he tells of his attempts to retrace the famous journey Peter Fleming made in 1936. On Stevens' journey, in 1986, he is accompanied by a six-foot female rower in Lycra stretch gear, and fellow travel writer Mark Salzman. In the following passage, having reached Kashgar by bus, train, and donkey cart, he now hopes to return by plane to Peking. Stevens, who grew up in Jackson, Mississippi, now lives in Connecticut and New York City, where he is a political consultant and a journalist.*

----

from NIGHT TRAIN TO
TURKISTAN

During our third day waiting at the airport, the PLA security detail decided to test the metal detector. The procedure began with a large Hami melon removed from a crate labeled XINJIANG TREASURES. The guards placed the melon in the X-ray machine. They observed the results gravely, nodding to each other like consulting surgeons. They then opened the machine and plunged a long, gold-handled dagger—the kind of knife all Muslims in Kashgar carried—into the melon. This was X-rayed. Several more daggers were embedded into the melon and X-rayed.

When the melon finally fell apart, the guards ate it, using the plate of the machine as a table.

After three days waiting for a plane, the Kashgar airport was beginning to feel like home to us. Each morning at seven we loaded our bags into a taxi and rode to the airport. Although we arrived in the dark, there was always a crowd of Chinese already in line at the ticket counter. Each day we stacked our bags in line. Since our status was strictly stand-by, position was critical. A large chalkboard proclaimed that the flight would leave at eleven o'clock. Though written in chalk supposedly for ease of alteration, this departure time was never changed.

Each day we would wait as the lobby filled with expectant passengers. The eleven o'clock departure time came and went. We waited all day. And then, around seven P.M., when no planes had arrived or departed, we returned to the hotel.

By the third day, I had begun to suspect that the airport was in truth a prop for some elaborate deception, no more useful than the plywood docks and destroyers the Allies employed to trick German intelligence about D-day preparations.

The scene certainly had a military feel. Young Han troops drilled on the tarmac from dawn to dusk. These teenagers carried wooden rifles and were the happiest group I'd seen in China. They appeared to revel in the discipline, working hard to please their lean, handsome drill sergeants. In the latrine on the edge of the runway, the only toilet at the airport, the recruits admired each other's uniforms, fingering the thick green wool, the shiny metal buttons. They wore white gloves of a rough cotton, like gardener's gloves, and brown fur hats mounted with a red star.

The airport looked like a bus station, with no visible signs—like radar or control tower—normally associated with the movement of planes. The only sign that it might be a place visited by planes— apparently rarely—was the long stretch of asphalt where the troops drilled. After their afternoon drilling, the troops were issued shovels and they hacked away at the ice lining the edges of the runway.

While we waited, there were no announcements, but, hourly, rumors buzzed around the waiting room, which had begun to look like a refugee camp. The lack of information created some tension between Mark and me. My need to ask questions battled against his inclination to wait. "I think we'll know if a plane comes," he replied when I badgered him to help me find someone who might know what was happening. On the second day, I met a young official who spoke a little English. He hung out in a back room with his pals, smoking cigarettes and perusing aviation magazines. (I feared this might be their only contact with planes.) They welcomed a new face and, in a tortured way, we discussed the merits of different aircraft. They were very disappointed when I told them that the Concorde was narrow and uncomfortable and made a lot of noise.

Toward the end of the third day, the plane arrived. There was no announcement. The faint throb of the distant engines electrified the crowd. After a stunned pause, there was a mad dash toward the check-in counter. Though I scrambled along with everyone else, I didn't understand the logic of the rush. Since all prospective passengers had placed their luggage in a long line winding from the counter, one's place in line had been already established.

But not so. While some people did take a position next to their luggage, most used this point as a staging ground for valiant assaults toward the front. I felt like I had been caught in a fire-crazed crowd fleeing toward an exit.

The roar of the plane thundered through the building, adding to the panic. Windows shook. I could feel vibrations through the floor, and for a moment I thought the pilot had erred and the plane would crash into the waiting room.

As the plane landed, a semblance of order returned to the line, like a major battle that had subsided with continuing skirmishes on the edges. An official appeared behind the counter. This really is going to happen, I thought. Then, everyone started to drift toward the exits. I had heard no announcement. That sickening feeling of being the last one to know anything—a feeling that had become very familiar—returned.

A few minutes later, we learned what everyone else seemed to know telepathically—the flight would not leave today. It was too late, and the pilot did not like to fly after dark.

We slunk back to the JOINT BUILDING-HOTEL WITH CIVILIZATION.

···············

It was the most wonderful flight of my life. I reclined in the plane in a happy daze, occasionally glancing out the window just to remind myself of the distances we were traveling. No one had spit on my feet or vomited next to me. It was warm. The seat was soft. Then, the plane dipped down out of the clear sky into clouds. We were landing in Ürümqi, just an hour and a half after leaving Kashgar. This was heaven.

And then I heard Fran scream. I looked at her across the aisle. She was staring out the window with a terrified look.

The plane had broken through the cloud cover. We were over a city; something was wrong.

"Oh my God," Fran said. "Those smokestacks—"

"What?"

"They're higher than we are—"

The plane jerked upward, back into the clouds. A little murmur of fearful laughter rolled through the cabin.

"I was looking *up* at the smokestacks," Fran said. "I promise you, I was."

We flew around in the clouds for a long time, circling and occasionally dipping down like a wounded pigeon. Next to me, a woman vomited into the paper bag CAAC had provided. She also appeared to be crying. Her husband looked on disgustedly.

"Did I ever tell you what CAAC stands for?" Mark asked. He was reading Stephen King and appeared quite content.

"No."

"Chinese Airlines Always Crashes."

The plane nosed into a steep dive. We broke through the clouds and plopped down almost instantly onto a runway. Tires screeching, the Russian plane skidded to a stop.

"Thank God," Fran murmured. I felt the same way. We started to get up but were waved down by one of the stewardesses.

We sat on the runway for over an hour. No one complained. No one explained. The stewardesses passed out little plastic packages containing combs and toothbrushes. This smacked of an extended delay of the overnight variety and made me very nervous. I looked at Mark, hoping he would ask one of the stewardesses how long it might be before we could get off, but he was buried behind *Salem's Lot*. Rising to use the bathroom, I was gently pushed back into my seat by a stewardess.

It was all beginning to feel like a polite hijacking.

We sat there for another hour. Children urinated on the floor and the smell was appalling. Finally, a particularly impressive-looking cadre-type said something to one of the stewardesses.

"No mistake was made. The weather was just bad," she told him curtly.

It hit me then. We weren't in Ürümqi. We had landed at the wrong town.

This panicked Fran. "You mean we'll have to do all that over again?"

"All what?"

"Take off, land."

"What we've got to do," I told Mark, "is find out how close we are to Ürümqi. If we're not far, let's demand they let us off and we can take a bus the rest of the way."

"You've got to be kidding."

The engines started. The high voice of the stewardess came over the loudspeaker. Mark relaxed.

"We're going to Ürümqi," he said, looking relieved.

"We'll just have to see," I said, pulling out a compass. "I'm not sure I believe them. If we head west back to Kashgar, call the stewardess and demand to go back."

"I think I'm going to kill you."

We quit talking after that, amazed at what we were seeing. Apparently troubled by the overcast, the pilot decided to fly under the clouds all the way to Ürümqi. These clouds were very low. Often, we appeared to be skimming the ground. I looked out the window and realized that we were following a road. I could see drivers in their trucks; some stuck their heads out of the window and gazed up, panic-stricken. Others swerved off into the desert, convinced, understandably, that the plane was going to land, or crash, on the blacktop. The woman beside me opened her mouth wide in a silent scream. She had bad teeth, like broken rocks.

When we landed, no one moved until the stewardesses insisted we were in Ürümqi and the flight was over.

At the plane's door, the head stewardess gave me a little pin of wings emblazoned with CAAC! I wore it like a medal.

MARTIN AMIS

Born in Oxford in 1949, Martin Amis was educated in Britain, Spain, and the United States before attending Exeter College, Oxford, where he earned a formal First in English. Primarily a novelist, whose works include Money, Other People, Success, Dead Babies, The Rachel Papers *(which won the 1974 Somerset Maugham Award), and* Einstein's Monsters *(short stories), he is also the author of* The Moronic Inferno and other Visits to America *and has contributed to* Vanity Fair, Granta, The Observer, *and* The New Statesman. *The following essay basks in the good fortune of the bad trip it describes. As the narrator in his latest novel,* London Fields, *writes, "The letter with the foreign postmark that tells of good weather, pleasant food and comfortable accommodation isn't nearly as much fun to read, or to write, as the letter that tells of rotting chalets, dysentery and drizzle."*

....

EMERGENCY LANDING

When it comes to flying, I am a nervous passenger but a confident drinker and Valium-swallower. And although I wasn't exactly goosing the stewardesses or singing "Viva España" (this was a BA flight to Málaga), I was certainly in holiday mood. In fact I had just called for my second pre-lunch cocktail—having enjoyed, oh, I don't know, a good three or four on the ground—when I began to sense that something was up.

Suddenly withdrawing the half-dozen meal-trays she had just laid

out, the flustered blonde stewardess told me that the bar-service had
been suspended. In answer to my very anxious enquiries, she told me
that the bar-service would soon resume. I was still grumbling to myself
about this when the Captain's voice came on the public-address system.
"As you have probably noticed," he began (I hadn't), "we have turned
full circle and are heading back to Gatwick. For technical reasons."

Now I saw that the sun had indeed changed places, and that we
were flying north over France towards the Channel. Unworriedly I
resigned myself to the usual frustrations: the six-hour wait, the free
orangeade, the bun-voucher. Now I saw also that the stewardesses were
systematically searching the overhead compartments. So. A bomb scare.
But this bomb didn't scare *me*.

The Captain came on again. In a bored voice he levelled with
us about the "alert"; then, more urgently, he added that, in view of
the time factor, it was now thought necessary to make an emergency
landing, at Dinard. At this point, still feeling no more than mildly
devil-may-care, I took the second half of my Valium 5, helping it down
with a swig of duty-free whisky. I offered the bottle to the girl in the
window seat, whose clear distress I began, rather grandly, to pooh-pooh.
The bottle was taken from my hand by the stewardess and fondly restored
to its yellow bag. We speared down on Dinard, not in the cruising,
wallowing style that aeroplanes usually adopt for landing, but with steep
and speedy purpose.

*Seats upright. Place your forehead on the back of the seat in front
of you. There will be more than one bump. Don't be alarmed by the
reverse thrust. Leave all your hand-baggage. Move as quickly as you can
to the exits and slide down the escape-chutes. When you are on the
ground—run.*

I glanced, for the first time in my life, at the benign cartoons of
the safety-procedure card. Then I hunkered down for the final seconds.
I thought of my wife and eight-month-old son, whom I was flying out
to join. I had escorted them to Gatwick ten days previously, on the
same morning that the Air India jumbo had been blown to pieces (or
so we then thought) over the seas of south-west Ireland. My apprehension at Departures that day had been far more intense than anything I
was feeling now. What I was feeling now was, mainly, relief that my

wife and child weren't with me. Had they been, everything would now be different. For a start, I wouldn't be drunk. I placed my wallet on my lap (I had no jacket), and waited.

The 737 landed like a skimmed stone, like a bomb itself, like a dam-buster. The reverse-thrust came on with such preternatural power that the tail seemed to lift, as though the whole aircraft were about to start toppling end over end. In this weird squall of gravity and inertia, my wallet shot off my lap and slithered along the floor, four or five rows away. Now the plane was quenched of its speed; seatbelts clicked, and immediately a pressing queue had formed in the aisle.

My paramount concern at this point was, of course, to find my wallet. Coolly lingering in a vacant three-pack, I was well placed to watch the passengers flee past me to the end of the aeroplane. As they awaited the stewardess's order (the doors had to open, the chutes had to inflate), the passengers pressed forward, four or five women—perhaps those with children—in the forefront. Physically they showed no more agitation than, say, people in fairly desperate need of a bathroom. But their voices contained an edge of panic. In those few seconds I remember only one word being spoken, and often repeated. "Please . . . Oh please." Soon the stewardesses were urgently shooing them down the aisle. I waited. Then, grumbling and swearing, I crawled around in search of my wallet and scattered credit cards, which had themselves been torn loose by the G's.

At last I strolled to the door. "Sit and jump," said the stewardess. Those elongated dinghies are a lot less stable than they look, but down I went—wheee!—and jogged away from the aircraft, which, I saw, had reached the very brink of its runway and had jarred to a halt midway through a ninety-degree turn. Five yards from its nose lay the edge of a lumpy brown field.

Around me was being enacted the formless drama that perhaps invariably succeeds every incident of mass crisis or jeopardy. I can only describe it as a scene of peculiar raggedness, with sights and sounds somehow failing to coordinate. A man keeled over in the grass, clutching his heart and moaning loudly. A girl with a sprained ankle was being helped away three-legged to safety. Busily the stewardesses gave comfort where they could. I myself—with, no doubt, egregious nonchalance—attempted to console a weeping woman. There was a good deal of crying

66

in the air, brittle, exultant. Soon the French security guards were shepherding us tenderly across the field to the terminal.

After a shock (I later learned), the body needs a lot of sweet tea. But the drinks were on BA, and most people drank a lot of brandy, which (I later learned) is the very thing the body needs least. I compromised by drinking a lot of whisky, and remained in capital fettle throughout the five-hour wait. The evening soon became an exercise in maximum *esprit de corps*, with the passengers informally dividing into two camps: those who were saying, "I've never been so scared in my life," and those who were saying, "You think this was bad? This was nothing. Let me tell you about the time I . . ." My position was, I suppose, unusual. I had not felt fear; but I knew that fear would have been an appropriate feeling.

Now, all writers secretly maintain a vampiric attitude to disaster; and, having survived it, I was unreservedly grateful for the experience. Here I sat, not in Gatwick but in Dinard, enjoying a good free dinner and pleasant camaraderie. And when I flopped into bed at five the next morning—replacement aircraft (the original was later searched, fruitlessly), baggage identification on the dark tarmac, the incident-free completion of the journey—I felt like a returning hero, a man who had come through a testing time, without a scratch, without a wince.

And I was wrong. For the next few days, although outwardly cheerful enough, I was pretty sure I was dying—and of natural causes, too. My body was subject to strange tinglings. Throughout my tragic siestas I lay there trembling and boiling, as if a tram station or a foundry had established itself beneath the bed. I watched the world through veils of helplessness. This was no hangover. This was old age.

My wife suggested that I was suffering from delayed shock—which, I admit, gave me quite a turn. Although I had privately diagnosed a brain tumour, I was still reluctant to identify the malaise as an after-effect of something that had bothered me so little. My body, however, continued to insist on the truth. Hoaxers and other operatives in the terror business will be relieved to learn that, when it comes to fear, there's no such thing as a free lunch, or a free dinner.

So much, then, for my valour on the fields of Dinard. I emerge from the incident with another new experience, and no credit whatever. I was as brave as a lord, as brave as a newt. Chemically numbed at the time, my fear—of which there had clearly been plenty—had just burrowed deep and waited. I had sneaked out of the restaurant without settling the bill. The body's accountants had redressed the ledger, with interest. And for nearly a week I was wearily picking up that tab.

PART THREE

WRITERS AS TOURISTS

Life on board the Oceanien *was like some terrible bed-sitting-room marriage. Almost everything formed grounds for divorce: the conch in the bathroom, the bad food, the way the waiters threw down the plates then completely disappeared, because they had gone to sea for adventure and were sick of finding themselves waiting all the time, the peeling, yelling Australians, the cynical French, the argumentative, prick-proud Germans, the lolling sea, the timelessness. I was either in a stupor or furious.*

—Hugo Williams

HUGO WILLIAMS

Hugo Williams was born in England in 1942 and educated at Eton. At twenty-one he set out to travel around the world, publishing an account of his two-year journey in All the Time in the World *(1966), from which the following chapter was taken.* Williams *has been associated with* London Magazine *and has written frequently for* The Times Literary Supplement. *His books of poetry include* Self-Portrait With a Slide, Selected Poems, Writing Home, Love-Life, Some Sweet Day, Sugar Daddy, *and* Symptoms of Loss. *He lives in London.*

LA FOLIE ANGLAISE

Next day the *Oceanien* was flying the Blue Peter and at five o'clock a bell rang on board, signalling our departure. It was not sad. Too many people were laughing and crying and waving to ward off their home-sickness. The whole of Papeete seemed to have left their shops and bars to see us off. There were more people there than on the quay at Sydney, but instead of streamers, it was necklaces of shells and garlands of flowers they threw to one another.

We had taken on a lot of Tahitians and their necks were com-pletely hidden under huge collars of seashells and hibiscus. I circled about taking pictures of them as they leant over the rail throwing back their necklaces like broken promises. In the middle of the crowd below was a little knot of white-clad nuns, their white faces like snowdrops among the tulips. People who had never met and would never meet were waving and blowing passionate kisses to one another.

Most of the new passengers were "metropolitan" civil servants returning to France with their Tahitian wives and girlfriends. But there were also some young Tahitian boys leaving home for the first time. Since 1958, all eighteen-year-olds have had to do two years military training in France. It is all part of de Gaulle's plan for integration and assimilation. After two years the young men return to their island completely Gallicized and Tahiti is a little more part of France than it was before. So far the results have been sad. The young men come home dissatisfied and uncertain. They no longer feel part of Tahiti and yet they know that they can never be true Europeans.

There was one Tahitian on board who was making the journey to France for the second time. He had been to France on National Service and while he was there he had married a French girl. The girl wanted to go back to Tahiti with him, so when he came out of the army he took her there and they tried to settle down. Things soon began to go wrong. He found he couldn't make as much money as the Frenchmen living on the island and yet they found that they spent most of their time with the French, trying to keep up, but succeeding only in alienating both their Tahitian and French friends. In the end they decided to give France another try. They had scraped together the cash and booked a passage on the *Oceanien.*

There was no separation of the two races on board, as there might have been on an English ship. Perhaps that was why, being English, I was given a French family to share my cabin. It was the end of my isolation. Maître Pompier Toulemonde et Fils had come to stay. Madame Toulemonde was on the other side of the boat in the Women's Quarters, but soon after we sailed she came round to introduce herself and help her husband unpack. As soon as she knew I spoke French she started to pour out her heart to me. For two years in Tahiti she had had to put up with Madame So-and-So and her daughter and now she found herself sharing a cabin with them on the way home. It was too much. She added that there was some terrible island girl who kept combing her scurf about everywhere and speaking to men in the doorway. Also there was no room for her clothes in the wardrobe and one of the women had already left some dirty knickers in the bathroom.

"Well, you'd better move into our spare bunk," I said jokingly.

"Oh, thank you, thank you," she said. "I was so hoping you would understand. You are too kind." A minute later the bunk was unfolded from the wall and that night we had the only openly mixed Tourist cabin on board.

I took it as a bad sign. The cabin was already tiny and there is something much more voluminous about women than men. It is to do with their bottles and a tendency to put up clothes lines. I was immediately sure that Madame Toulemonde would always be in the bathroom washing out her husband's underclothes and ranging them over the bathtub. She had already set a phalanx of ointments and pill boxes against the three-sided mirror, making it a one-sided mirror. Her husband seemed almost as dismayed as I was and shrugged his shoulders at me as she stooped over their young son, who was suffering from seasickness. She was in the process of administering a suppository to him. He gave a sudden yelp as it was plunged home, and burst into tears. I went up on deck and walked around looking for someone to grumble to. But I soon got used to the idea and in the end it turned out for the best. Madame Toulemonde was so grateful for my unconditional surrender that she decided to look after me from the start. She seemed to never cease washing and ironing for me and bringing me back pieces of fruit and cheese from her table because she thought I was too thin. She would sit and look at me as I ate to see the effect of it on me. She had big round eyes which blinked when she agreed with you or laughed, and when she said "no" she always held up one finger and shook it briefly. She was a real Marseillaise and never stopped chatting and roaring with laughter at her own jokes.

I might have really got to like the Toulemondes, but for one thing. This was a seashell which they kept in the soap dish in the bathroom. It was very large and lifeless and every time I leant over to clean my teeth I smelt its powerful cat stench. I am usually rather fiery about such things, but my previous concessions and seasickness made me phlegmatic and all I did was ask after it from time to time. I naturally assumed that it was a rare specimen, but Monsieur soon told me that no, it was not particularly rare, but extremely venomous, that is to say "mortelle," highly dangerous. Once I suggested boiling it in water so that the animal would melt and run out. But they had already thought of that and decided that it would spoil the colour. I got to know it well over the weeks that followed. It actually had a big crack in it and was not at all beautiful. I believe it wielded some strange power over its benefactors. I may even have come under its influence myself during the weeks which followed.

One day I went to the cabin after lunch and found the door locked. I knocked and then crept off feeling rather stupid. After that it was accepted that I stay on deck a couple of hours at that time of day. I used to take up a pad and a pen and try to write home. It was usually no good. I would just lie there, my mind as empty as the clear blue sky, knowing that one day, some day, it would all have to be described, but grateful that I felt unable to do it at the time.

I believe I shall be writing home about this trip for the rest of my life. I think I may easily develop a mania to be heard out and may well be seen, years from now, still recollecting, like an old white hunter, shadowy images to an empty fireplace, far into the night.

······

Life on board the *Oceanien* was like some terrible bed-sitting-room marriage. Almost everything formed grounds for divorce: the conch in the bathroom, the bad food, the way the waiters threw down the plates then completely disappeared, because they had gone to sea for adventure and were sick of finding themselves waiting all the time, the peeling, yelling Australians, the cynical French, the argumentative, prick-proud Germans, the lolling sea, the timelessness. I was either in a stupor or furious. Life was like an uneasy sleep constantly interrupted by the drunk friends of one's flat-mate stumbling over one's inert body in the middle of the night. There was nowhere to go to escape. All one could do was remain anonymous and go to the commissaire every day at three o'clock to make deflated complaints about the service and food. What a clever move to have a special complaining time. The idea has unpleasant memories of queueing up to be punished. We expect you to come, it says, being foreigners you won't understand, so you'd better all come together and get it over with. But by the time an hour had elapsed after lunch one was either asleep or pacified.

I once made the fatal error of calling one waiter a cretin and from then on I was the villain. Later in the trip someone got so angry with him he challenged him to a fight in the next port, but it never came off.

At four o'clock every afternoon there were taped concerts in the First Class Music Room and I used to creep in there to read in the air-conditioned salon. But there was one woman in there who resented my tourist ears on her First Class music. She had a huge book which she was always marking and when I entered the salon she would lift pointed steel eyes in my direction, knit me a little, and drop me where I stood. I always waved a smile as a white flag, but she never relented and in the end I grew to admire her as one admires a cliff or a crater. I admired her loneliness, for she never smiled or spoke much, even when the Australians played with her little girls by the swimming pool. She seemed to display more energy and intelligence on her own than all the other enthusiasts playing quoits and deck golf and scrabble around her. She was like Queen Victoria.

Energy of any kind for anything was hard to conserve from the hours and hours of unpolarized sunshine which fell every day upon the deck, melting the very muscles in one's fingers. There was no escape. Even the cabins were constantly wobbling with the brilliant, reflected light from the sea. It was like being a desert reptile without any eyelids.

Just an hour on deck was enough to turn everyone a shade darker—redder, browner, or blacker—each day and most people concentrated their attention without much subtlety to this end.

•••••••••••••

We had crossed the International Dateline and the waiters were even more mutinous because they were working an eight-day week.

To mark the occasion there was to be a Fancy Dress Ball. "Travestis Recommandés" said the invitation, so six of us dressed up as CND beachcombers with placards saying "SAVE TAHITI FROM THE BOMB" and "NON À DE GAULLE"—the reverse of the most common propaganda slogan to be found in the French Pacific. When the time came to go into the party we discovered that we were the only ones to have dressed up, so our entry was more like a cabaret act and as a cabaret it fell rather flat. It was another case of "La folie Anglaise" the French passengers were saying in their neat, round-shouldered suits and dresses, having never for a moment considered wearing anything else. "Ils font ça sur les bateaux anglais," said one woman sitting near us, excusing the lunatics. Another, sitting not far off, had made a small concession to the occasion by pinning one of the artificial orchids from the tourist bar to her bun, à la Tahitienne. It was worn in such a way that the large phallic stamen seemed to be poking out of her ear, which we all took to be the "travesti" of the evening.

All of us were soon outshone by a host of little vahinés who came swaying on to the floor in grass skirts and shell necklaces to dance an exciting Tamourré. This is a modernized version of the old Hula Hula. Instead of going round and round, as with a Hula Hoop, the hips flick from side to side, faster and faster as the dance progresses. In the euphemisms of a brochure "The Tamourré is a dance designed to quicken the heartbeats of the menfolk." Nowadays "menfolk" get away with all kinds of things ordinary men go to prison for.

Only one of the dancers was not Tahitian. This was the beautiful young daughter of a French fonctionnaire returning home from Tahiti. I had admired her across the deck for more than a week, but had only spoken to her the day before at Bingo, and hadn't expected to find her so young. She was sixteen, but her parents had obviously zealously protected her from Tahitian ways during the four years she'd lived there and she had a tantalizing innocence. On the dance floor, among the Tahitian girls, she was all at sea. I suppose her parents must have jollied her into it but she was terribly shy and embarrassed at the hot rhythms and absurd necklaces, with the result that she looked completely naked and thereby memorable. It was the sort of traumatic experience parents let their children in for out of sheer goodwill, unknowingly hastening their own dispensability.

There was a small Scottish contingent among the First Class passengers, who for some reason took objection to the sexy dancing. They voiced their opinions and kept craning their scrawny old necks upwards and away from it all to glimpse an eclipse of the moon which was going on prettily enough, if somewhat inevitably, overhead. But it was the eclipse which was eclipsed in the end.

Next day, the Tahitian men and women were strumming and laughing as usual in their corner of the deck. But as the days took us further from Tahiti, their hibiscus garlands and their lilting songs seemed to grow more feeble and to fade. Soon they were to be subdued and Westernised, perhaps forever.

ALBERTO MANGUEL

Born in Buenos Aires in 1948, Alberto Manguel grew up in Israel, where his father was the Argentine ambassador. He later lived in Argentina, where he was a young friend of Jorge Luis Borges, and in several other countries, including France, Germany, and Tahiti. In Canada, where he settled, he is a critic, translator, and anthologist, the editor of such collections as Black Water: The Anthology of Fantastic Literature, Other Fires: Short Fiction by Latin American Women, *and* The Oxford Book of Canadian Ghost Stories. *He is the coauthor of* The Dictionary of Imaginary Places *and translator of Marguerite Yourcenar's* Oriental Tales. *His forthcoming novel is entitled* News from a Foreign Country Came.

THE FARTHER WE'RE FROM ENGLAND

The year of the Beatles' last LP I was living in London, sharing a house with three other guys and paying £5 a week. My Argentinian passport made it impossible for me to get a work permit in Europe, so I made a living selling painted leather belts, which I hawked on Carnaby Street and later in a store called "Mr. Fish." My hour of glory came when Mick Jagger Himself bought one of my belts and wore it on stage during a concert. Life was never that magnanimous again.

But we trifle with Fortune. On the spur of the moment, I accompanied a friend to Paris, spent a few days nursing a coffee at the Café de Flore, and then, having visions of irate clients storming beltless up and down Piccadilly, I decided it was time to get back to London. The cheapest fare was a combination of bus, ferry, and bus. I bought my ticket and set off for Calais in the late afternoon.

Crossing what the egocentric British like to call the English Channel is, as everyone knows, a sickening experience, unrelieved by the sight of the white cliffs of Dover which, in the pale moonlight, greet the nauseated traveller like huge piles of slightly-off cottage cheese. I walked unsteadily down the gangplank and waited in line for passport control.

The officer behind the passport desk looked very much like Peter O'Toole in *Lawrence of Arabia*. He cast pale blue eyes on my passport, raised them to look at me, looked back at the passport, and once again at me. What he saw seemed to make him immensely sad.

I was dressed in the style appropriate to Carnaby Street at the time. My sandals and flowing white cotton shirt were Indian, my cerise-coloured trousers had bell-bottoms, I was wearing a belt of my own design on which I had painted *Leda and the Swan* in the exact style (if I say it myself) of Poussin. My hair curled coquettishly over my shoulders.

"What is the purpose of your visit?" asked Peter in a low, pained voice.

Suddenly I realized that, just as if I'd been confronted by his namesake in heaven above, I had to give Peter a good reason to let me into his green and pleasant land. My brain made a quick deduction. This man was a bureaucrat. Bureaucrats are impressed by officialdom. My father had been, fifteen years earlier, the Argentine ambassador to Israel. There are few people more official than ambassadors. In my best pseudo-Argentine accent (which I recognized, years later, as identical to that of Manuel in *Fawlty Towers*) I told him that I had come to meet my father, the ex–Argentine ambassador.

Peter's eyebrows arched ever so slightly.

"And where are you to meet the . . . ehm . . . ambassador?"

Again, my brain desperately scrambled for an answer. Once I had stayed at a Salvation Army Hostel in London, just across from (what seemed to me at the time) a very chic hotel. I remembered the name.

"At Hotel St. James'," I said.

(Years later I found out that the St. James' is what the French call *un hotel de passe*, lodging an inordinate number of Mr. and Mrs. Smiths.)

"Have you got a reservation at the . . . ehm . . . St. James'?" asked Peter.

"I think . . . father of I did reservation."

"Let us phone then, shall we?" said Peter.

By now the other passengers had drifted past and the busdriver was getting restless. After waiting another few minutes, he shrugged his shoulders and waved goodbye. I had no idea how I'd get from Dover to London. I had 10 francs and £2 in my pocket. Hitchhiking in England didn't have a good reputation.

Peter put the phone down.

"At the St. James' they have no reservation for . . . ehm . . . Ambassador Manguel."

Another officer joined us. The hint of a smile appeared on Peter's face, dispelling some of the sadness.

"This gentleman says his father is an Argentine ambassador and that he is to meet him in London, at the St. James'."

"At the St. James'?"

The other officer's eyes rolled up and down.

"I see."

"But they have no reservation. Perhaps we should call the Argentine Embassy."

I argued that there would be no one in at this hour. It was shortly before midnight.

"We'll try, shall we?" said the other officer.

He tried and someone answered who obviously only spoke Spanish. The other officer handed me the phone.

"Ask him whether he knows your father and will vouch for you."

I asked, in Spanish, whom was I speaking to.

"This is José," said the voice.

"José," I said. "Whoever you are, will you please tell the officer that you know my father, ex-Ambassador Manguel?"

"Sure," said José.

I silently blessed the Argentine sense of camaraderie and passed the phone back to the other officer.

"He'll tell you," I said.

The other officer listened to José's declaration in Spanish.

"I don't understand what you're saying. Can you try repeating it in English? Aha. Yes. And what is your position at the embassy, sir? I see. Thank you."

He put down the phone.

"I'm afraid that the janitor's vouching for you isn't sufficient," he said.

In the meantime, Peter was going through my rucksack with keen interest. He opened my tube of toothpaste, squeezed some out and tasted it. He flicked through my copy of *Siddhartha*. He sniffed at my joss-sticks. Finally he found my address book. He disappeared with it inside the office. When he re-emerged, he had a smile on his face, like that of Lawrence after the capture of Khartoum.

"It seems that you failed to tell us you were sharing a house in London. One of your friends there told me that you work selling knick-knacks on Carnaby Street. I assume you haven't got a work permit? Now why would the ambassador's son do that?"

I was taken to a small white room with a cot and told that I'd have to wait there until the first ferry next morning, when I would be sent back to France. All night long I thought about what I was about to lose: my room, the books I had collected, my artistic career which had received the blessings of Mick Jagger. Ever since I had started to read, London had been, in my mind, a sort of Garden of Eden. The stories I liked best took place there; Chesterton and Dickens had made it familiar to me; it was what to others are the North Pole or Samarkand. And now, because of two pesky, prissy officials, it had become just as remote and unattainable. Bureaucracy, unfair immigration laws, power given to blue-eyed employees who are allowed to squeeze other people's toothpaste seemed to me then (and now) despicable abominations.

And that is how, in November of 1969, I became a moderate anarchist.

P . K . PAGE

P. K. Page was born in England in 1916 and came to Canada as an infant. It is as a poet that she established her reputation with such books as Cry Ararat! *and* The Glass Air. *But she is also an accomplished painter (under the name P. K. Irwin) and a script and fiction writer. Her husband, Arthur Irwin, was Canadian High Commissioner to Australia from 1953 to 1956, duing which time the two of them traveled widely down under—as they would do again during their ambassadorial stay in Brazil from 1957 to 1959, recounted in her book* Brazilian Journal. *She has also lived in Mexico and the United States and now resides in Victoria, British Columbia.*

....

ON THE ROAD AGAIN
THE AUSTRALIAN OUTBACK,
JUNE 1956

It was early morning but already brazen when A., the Inspector, and I set forth once again into the familiar vastness of flat grassland with its underpainting of Venetian red. Overhead, the insistent blue almost hurt. We said our final goodbyes to our hosts and the aborigines who had gathered to see us go, and we climbed into the small, stifling Chevy. I was sorry to leave; I had grown to like these people. Parting *is* sweet sorrow. I leaned out the car window and waved until the little group was no more than a collection of tottering ninepins in the moiréd air.

Once under way, A. casually asked the Inspector what biting insects there were in the area, as he had been bitten in the groin the previous afternoon, and the bite was beginning to be troublesome. Probably a bull ant, the Inspector replied. It could give a nasty, but in no way serious, sting. This was the first I'd heard of it as A. and I had been separated for two nights—I in a single bed in a small room, A. on the verandah with the men.

We were headed for Tennant Creek, a mining town, a day's drive distant. It was insufferably hot, jammed into that tight little Chevy— the hottest day we'd had on the road. At first the country was similar to what had gone before—flat and treeless. We stopped for morning coffee at a bachelor station, where the only women were the abos who worked about the house. A gentle accountant greeted us; the other bachelors were all setting up camp at the Race Track. A lubra brought us tea and crackers and the accountant talked of the absent manager whom he admired with a totally uncritical admiration. This invisible paragon, whom we had met at the race track the day before—a small wiry man dressed entirely in navy blue despite the temperature—neither smoked nor drank. Tireless as a man half his age, he rose each morning before the heat of the day to water the trees he had planted as a youth and which now provided his property with a leafy shade. He trained racehorses as a hobby, plaited their harnesses and bridles. He had tried to leave the outback once—his sister in Melbourne wanted him to join her and he felt that perhaps he should. But how could he be happy in a city? the accountant asked us. How could he possibly leave all this? And he waved a hand at the dry surroundings as if at the Garden of Eden.

The tropical cedars and rain trees were aflutter with zebra finches as we left—such a fragile flowering of plants and birds from that biscuit-fired tableland!

Each station where we stopped was like an oasis in the desert. Yet to use the word desert is false. Desert, in this country, is where the scrub grows. And these endless miles of perennial mitchell grass are grazing land—anything but desert. As the day wore on, instead of being oppressed by the land's sameness, as I had been, I found a lovely lyrical quality in the blonde tufted grass under that unending blue sky and regretted not having been able to see it this way sooner.

We saw a pelican on a lagoon—its size a tremendous surprise.

Bigger than a swan. Immense and white with its great beak, it floated on the water.

Lunched at Frewena.

Half-blind from the light, we walked into the sprawling corrugated shed which is Frewena. Were met by the owner—young, black-bearded, in dirty white ducks and a B.V.D. top. The incongruous, absurd, and inexplicable sight of women in hats sitting at small tables and reading magazines as if in an airport waiting-room, absorbed my attention so fully that, for a moment at least, I forgot the heat. But not for long. This was the worst so far. The mere act of walking was like forcing your body through hot brine.

We ordered beer and drank it with the Sautelles. He, a film director who made *Jedda*, is currently working on a series of shorts for BBCTV. With his wife and two young men, he is on his way to film the Picnic Races. Odd to sit down in the middle of the heat in the middle of the Territory and talk film over a beer.

The wife of the young man who met us took our orders for lunch. She was cook and waitress. Straight dirty hair hung about a pasty unmade-up face. She wore a filthy cotton dress and tucked into its belt, an even dirtier—in fact, absolutely black, handkerchief. Dough-colored legs, scabbed and reddened with bites, appeared below the dress. I asked her for the ladies' room (what a euphemism!) and she led me down great corridors in the corrugated shed, past incredibly primitive over-night accommodations—the beds still unmade at lunchtime—and de-posited me at an unsavory-looking door, saying in the prettiest and most educated of voices that she hoped I would excuse its untidiness, that she had not had time to get at it today. Days are evidently long at Frewena. I have never, anywhere, seen such a bathroom. I clad my hand in the hem of my skirt in order to turn on the tap. Surely the very water itself was dirty. There are no words to describe the lavatory. I suppose if one were half-blind as well as short of water one might get into that state. But even then, only with a will to do so.

Perhaps because of ladders in the untidy corridor, an ironing board with assorted clothing spread over it, and odd men standing about, I had the illusion of being backstage during a theatrical production. Of what? God knows. Maugham? Conrad? The latter, perhaps. Certainly that young man with the beard . . . And then, a quick cut to the airport waiting room again, and those women in hats!

We had little appetite for lunch, prepared and served by that filthy girl—a new bride—one of the trio that ran the pub. The second man, we saw later, naked to the waist, drinking in the bar. He and the bearded young man were "mates."

Outside, the leaves of the tropical trees were like maidenhair. Fragile. Light. Freckling the bare earth with shade. Under that still weight of heat—a slab of metal.

··············

Between Frewena and Tennant Creek golden wattle blazed on the roadside. A half-dozen or so miles from Tennant we passed the bore from which its bathing water was transported by truck. Comforting to know there would be water. We saw the monument to Flynn of the Inland—that extraordinary unloved man who had transformed the interior with his Flying Doctor Services. And then—we were there, at Tennant, in the blare of its wide main street, with the red earth of its lawns and gardens gaping at us, the brass sun clanging, and its one hotel set, plumb, on the burning sidewalk.

Our bedroom and the Inspector's were next door to each other, but closer even than such proximity suggests. In order to achieve maximum circulation of air, the builders had separated the rooms by partitions which stopped well short of the ceiling. Two large louvered areas flanked our door to the hall, while the outside wall opened onto a verandah separated from its neighbours by partitions low enough to climb over. A. and I unpacked in the swithering heat and talked in whispers. We shared a room again—but with the whole hotel!

As we undressed for showers I took a look at A.'s bite—a raised white platform, high in the groin, about three inches in diameter with three scarlet spots where the sting or nippers had pierced the skin. It was surrounded by an inflamed red area that extended to his knee. He said that he felt slightly dizzy, but otherwise all right and that the sting proper was unpleasant but not causing actual pain. It looked nasty but as he didn't seem sick and the bite had occurred some twenty-four hours earlier I didn't think of it as serious. In fact I even forgot about it in my fight with the Tennant water supply.

The washing facilities were at the end of the hall. The shower was a small cubicle where the only hook on which you could hang your dressing gown and towel was directly in the line of the spray. I suppose that should have told me something. The only tap was marked COLD. I turned it on. Nothing. I waited for one slow drop to swell and grow and finally fall from the faucet. Minutes passed. No drop formed. I contemplated a sponge bath in the small handbasin in full view of all visitors to the lavatory, telling myself I'd have no more privacy on a Canadian train. But I wouldn't have been as hot and dirty either. Then a tiny dribble began. Eagerly I twisted and turned beneath it, diligently soaping each small area as it became wet. I had just reached my waist when the water stopped. I gave the pipe a bang, hoping it might release just enough more for me to wash off the soap. When nothing came out I dusted off the dried soap and gave up, wondering how people live without water, realizing how spoiled I had been all my life.

A., meanwhile, had shared his shower with the Inspector, who had commented as he saw him naked, "That's no bull ant bite. You'd better see a doctor." So we dressed, still whispering and, if not clean— at least changed—drove to the hospital, a bungalow-style building on the edge of town. The Inspector spoke to one of the nurses and came back with the information that the doctor had gone off to the country on a call. She suggested we return to the hotel and have dinner and that the doctor would phone as soon as he returned.

The dining room of the hotel was an inside room without windows. Oppressively dark. Two oleos of mountain lakes in some pseudo-Canada decorated our corner of the room. A shy young married couple shared our table with us and showed no willingness to join the ranks of talkative, friendly, informal Australians. There was one other couple—a rather brassy-looking blonde and her man, about whom the Inspector made disparaging remarks.

After dinner, on the advice of a telephone call, we returned to the hospital. The doctor had phoned, giving instruction for A. to have an injection then return to the hotel and lie down. A. was duly closeted in a room with a nurse—too nice a girl to look at the bite—who gave him a shot of something and told him the doctor would call at the hotel at nine.

The heat had made us deadly sleepy so, fully dressed, we stretched out on the only good beds we had had since Darwin, and under the glare of the bare overhead bulb, fell into a hot and stupefied sleep. At ten I wakened with a lurch, alarmed. A. still slept. Was it a toxic sleep? Had the injection knocked him out? Was he perhaps really ill? And why had the doctor not arrived? Or had he come and been unable to find us?

I decided to look for the Inspector. The hotel was silent, dark, and hot. There were no public rooms where he might be found, nor was he hanging around in the warm black air of the street. The car was useless to me as the ignition was locked. And inside, the only phone was in the locked front office. Had the hospital rung, there would have been no one to hear, let alone answer.

Like a shade moving through the dim corridors, I went upstairs again, hoping that A., if awake, might have some bright suggestion, or at least assure me that he was not ill. As I passed the Inspector's room I heard a gentle snoring through the louvers. Stooping, I called his name, knocked gently, listened; called again. It seemed very late indeed. But for a muted giggling coming from the room with the blonde and her boyfriend and the Inspector's rhythmic snores, everything was quiet. I continued to knock and call, louder each time, until I felt the whole hotel must wake to protest and blame. There were moments when so many elements of Kafka converged that I could have believed myself in a dream of *The Trial*.

At last I heard the Inspector move, saw his light switch on, heard him stumble to the door in his stocking feet. The door opened to a totally strange man.

How extraordinarily helpless one can feel. And how often parents must feel like this—in no way protected, as I had thought as a child, by the magic of the phrase "grown up." This sleep-swaddled stranger, shaking his head and blinking, was the only person in all of Tennant Creek who could help me at that moment. Yet all I could do was ask his forgiveness for waking him (why does it seem such a crime to rouse a sleeper?) and inquire if he knew where I could find the Inspector. He didn't. I had a horrid mental picture then of my own hands, very huge and helpless, and this image seemed to come between me and any intelligent thought.

Perhaps if I walked I might find a public phone on the street. I went aimlessly downstairs again. And there, by the darkened window of the office, was a young man in a tweed jacket moving his hand rather as if he were trying to hit a nonexistent bell. He asked if the place was shut or was it possible to raise anyone. I asked if he wanted a room. "No, the Canadian High Commissioner," he replied. And then we were going upstairs very fast. I don't remember speaking. I remember opening the door, the dimensionless look of the room in that flat light, and the doctor's voice, conciliatory but guarded. "I'm awfully sorry, sir, that you've had such bad luck."

Bad luck! He had not even seen the bite. And then it became clear. Somewhere between the first report given by the Inspector to the nurse and the appearance on the scene of the doctor, the bite had become that of a red-backed spider. Its sting is not necessarily fatal but it is serious. And the doctor planned to do what the book said and administer morphine at once. He was a young Englishman from a London hospital who had been in Australia exactly three weeks! A. was not having any morphine. And the doctor, not unreasonably, was taking no chances. If A. was refusing morphine then he must go to the hospital for observation. The bite looked very angry and A.'s pulse rate was high.

So we trailed through the dark corridor, three of us this time, and squeezed into the ambulance. It was a clumsy, somber-looking vehicle, most likely with a jeep engine for outback calls—the sort of medical lorry that looked as if it should be moving off to the front lines. The doctor, by now, seemed really rather pleased to see us and the encounter was rapidly changing from medical to social. By the time we drew up in front of the hospital he had decided it would be a good idea for A. to have a cup of tea at his place before checking in for the night.

A neat-featured, pretty girl, rather stockily built and wearing a grey blouse covered with red dust, was setting a table as we came in. The house, presumably furnished by the administration, was unspeakably awful—the worst kind of undress Victorian barracks with, here and there, on the cheap wooden furniture, a black Wedgwood half-draped woman—or a white one. In this so obviously impersonal house, what in the name of heaven were these fragile formal figures doing on tabletop and bookcase?

The doctor's wife, after being introduced, unlaid the table and began again, this time setting it for four and using the "good" silver. We were offered a beer and when we refused the doctor said he would let us in on a secret—that he didn't drink, or rather, as he didn't think he could afford it, he was starting out in this new community as *if* he didn't. He wondered how it would work. So, indeed, did I. I joined his wife in the kitchen, where she was cutting a potato into hunks with a very blunt knife. I asked what I could do and she gave me a can of soup to open. That finished, I offered to continue with the potato. It appeared that we were all going to have dinner. After much protesting and exclaiming it was finally agreed that A. and I would only have tea. They, it appeared, had had no dinner—the doctor's wife had taken the baby out for a drive in the bush and got stuck in some sand. The doctor, finding her not back by six-thirty, had gone after her. So, as she carved the dried meat off a scrawny chicken and gouged great chunks of lard out of a tin can for frying, I peeled potatoes and cut them up for the deep fat, or gave the soup a stir, and learned of her adventure.

She had set out to explore—the country was all new to her. An Australian, she had spent the past two years in London, where she had met her husband. No, she had not been working in London. She had at first, but found English wages so low, it was much better to live on an allowance from home. But she had missed Australia and so had persuaded her husband to emigrate and they had come here. They brought nothing of their own with them except the Wedgwood and the silver, which they had bought together in England. They both loved Wedgwood figures.

That afternoon, she had taken her baby and set out in the car. Miles into the bush she had got stuck. Had she been frightened? No, not of being stuck. She had tried to get out without success, but knowing that her husband would ultimately turn up, she looked hopefully about for some signs of wild life to distract her. She was just about to go to sleep when she saw two hawks circling overhead. And then she *was* frightened. They were looking ominously at her baby. But was it an open car? I asked. No, but she was afraid they would come right through the glass.

When we finally bore in the dinner—the Wedgwood tea set prominent on the table—the two men were poring over a map and the doctor had a too bright light in his eye. He was altering the whole climate and culture of Australia, pumping water uphill from the Gulf of Carpentaria into the Territory, and so, ending the Dry and bringing a new life to the continent. His dream was to save the money spent on beer and racing and put it back into the land; to breed a race of disciplined idealists who would act as though they would live forever. Kindness and self-sacrifice would save the world. But did he not complain that the soup was not hot enough? Nicely, mark you, quickly adding that it didn't matter. Smiling. Forgiving, forgiving. But not before the thorn had found the soft flesh.

We bombarded them with questions: had they seen much of the country around Tennant? Not yet, but soon it would have offered up all its little secrets. Was it expensive to live there? Food was expensive, yes, but they were planning to start a garden. Electricity was expensive too, so they never used the electric stove, only the wood range. Didn't that make it hot? Yes, very, but it was too expensive to use the electric. What about the water shortage? Well, it didn't bother them too much because they couldn't afford to heat the water for showers, anyway, so they didn't take them.

But now it was time for the patient to go to the hospital, and A. went—although at this point neither of us believed there was any such need. At midnight the doctor and I clambered into that high ambulance and drove back to the hotel, lumbering through the wide and empty streets of Tennant Creek, the headlights occasionally lighting a strip of naked earth the color of blood. I thought of A. in the hospital surrounded by a world I had not seen and would never know, and this strange young man who sat beside me, his keeper and guardian, checking his pulse and temperature through the starched, cosmeticed, feminine extension of himself—the nurse on night duty.

The hotel was silent and empty and black. I went upstairs like a conspirator, past the Frigidaire wheezing on the landing where the misty water bottles stood—cursing that I had no glass with me and that I must make the trip along that dark corridor twice more for water to clean my teeth.

The blonde and her boyfriend were quiet now. The Inspector or his roommate snored heavily. I turned out the light at the door of our room and through alien space felt my way to bed.

It was a restless night. To the far edges of town you could hear the wind tugging and teasing at bits of litter in untidy yards; and near at hand, all the louvers blowing, rattling, banging. The room was designed like a windmill to catch every breeze. But now, one's bed among the vanes, it offered a clanking and cold sleep.

I was wakened early by the drop in temperature and the sound of louvers blowing. I shut everything as tight as possible and dressed without too much regard for cleanliness, turning my back on the unreliable shower with its tap marked COLD. Impossible already to remember the heat of yesterday.

During breakfast a message came from the hospital that the patient could leave, and as the Inspector rescued A. from the smell of iodoform, I watched the morning queue forming outside—ginns with their picaninnies—milk chocolate–colored babies with blond hair, in the arms of their black mothers.

Eager to be off, A. and I returned and packed in what was now a bright silver bedroom—the rainy sky having invaded the room. Like something out of Rousseau, a golden lioness entered from the verandah, rubbed against my leg, bit my foot, leapt onto the bed among the articles to be packed, explored them all with a swift inquisitive movement of muzzle and paw and settled down among my underwear—square shoulders and square paws perfectly synchronized—rhythmically pumping and purring.

ANITA DESAI

Anita Desai was born in 1937 in Mussoorie of a Bengali father and a German mother. When she graduated from Delhi University in 1957, she was already writing short stories in English. Among her eight novels are Clear Light of Day, Fire on the Mountain, In Custody, *and* Baumgartner's Bombay. *She has twice been short-listed for the Booker Prize, and* The Village by the Sea *won the* Guardian Award for Children's Fiction *in 1982. She is married with four children and divides her time between Massachusetts, where she teaches, and Delhi. She is a Fellow of the Royal Society of Literature in London.*

....

FROZEN IN FRØYA

No, it was not till I was forced onto and into the boat that bucked violently upon the waves as if equally reluctant to have me, that I realized exactly what I had done. It had all seemed alluring rather than alarming as long as I was airborne, looking down from the plane onto the snowy mountainscape of northern Norway that gave off the silent lunar radiance released by snow at night, in places inked by the shadows of massed forests and in others startlingly illuminated by electricity along the ski slopes. What an adventure, I had said to myself, smugly congratulatory: here I am, in Norway, in the dead of an Arctic winter— what could have been further from my wildest dreams? The opportunity had been provided by an invitation from the UN to participate in a programme devised by some eccentric genius to celebrate the Decade of Women. Six women writers from the West were invited to visit

countries in the East, and write about the women they met there, and
six women writers from the East were to go to the West and examine
the state of womanhood there. It seemed like a game we were to play—
with plenty of opportunity for fun. The diabolic genius at the UN then
chose the month of February in which the game of cat's cradle was to
be played. At that very moment women writers from the howling canyons of New York, of London, and Oslo were on their way to Kenya,
to Indonesia, to India, and I—I was let off the plane into the Arctic
night at the edge of a coastal town that twinkled and winked bravely in
the snow. I crunched through the ice crystals, surrounded by my own
cloud of vapour, into the heat and crush of the small airport terminal
where I was met, fitted out with a fur coat, cap, and boots, driven
through the icy darkness and raging winds, then lifted gently but firmly
onto the boat set for the island of Frøya.

Then, then at last I knew I had been had. Once you are on board
a small steamer in the midst of a winter gale, and sent down a fjord
with the waves flinging you up on the crest of one wave and dashing
you down the abyss of another, and the cold and the dark and the storm
and the sea keep you down in the soggy hold with the other three or
four travellers in their polar bear and wolf furs, you realize you are
caught: there is no getting off, no turning back, no rescue nor retrieval
to be had for all the crying you can do. I tried to sit upright on a bench,
disregard the sight of maniacal waves dashing against the portholes,
leering at me and howling, close my eyes and concentrate on some
spirit level that must surely exist within us all and remain sane, even,
resistant to being tipped and swung violently by the elements. It was
very clear there was no such thing, that whatever I contained was being
heaved to the rhythm of the waves. If only there was a rhythm—but
if I braced myself for a lurch to the left, the boat invariably swung to
the right, and if I prepared myself for being flung forward onto my face,
then the waves contrived to hurl me upward to the ceiling or dash me
onto the floor. After a while I found myself lying full-length on the
bench, clutching it as if it were a log adrift in the sea—and for all the
water sloshing beneath it, the penetrating cold and the wild wetness
raging around us, it might have been just that. Sometimes I raised my
head in desperate appeal. Sometimes I saw oily yellow lights swing

past—rescue boats or another coastal town? But they would vanish in the dark. Such dark that could not be created by one element alone, had to be the result of all the elements conspiring together, conspiring surely to drown me in a fjord in northern Norway, never allow me to set foot on land again, or see the island of Frøya.

But Frøya I was destined to see. Someone was tugging at me, forcing me to release my hold on the bench. Someone—a laughing man with a frost-bitten face and arms like a butcher's—was lifting me out of the boat, throwing me over its edge onto the quay. I suppose it was a quay. Down by a dark shed was a huddle of figures in great boots and hats. One of them detached itself and dashed up to me, crying "From India? The lady from India? Then come—you are for me!" I realized dimly it was a woman, she was my hostess, I her guest. So I allowed her to bundle me into her car—at least it stood on ground, not water, I thought as I squeezed into it, clutching to me the bedraggled coat and cap, but once we set off, my driver hallooing and whooping with what I could not tell was delight or bravado, it was actually hard to tell what we stood, or moved, upon. Darkness, certainly, such darkness as I had never encountered before—but if it was wet or dry, I could not tell. Everywhere were whoops, howls, wails, roars, and crashes— and through it all the little vehicle rode across what must have been a blasted heath beneath a blasted storm.

Then the headlights picked out some stones, rocks, more stones. We bumped along what might have been a lane, or a drive of sorts, and stopped short in the shelter of a wall. The driver plunged out of the car, pulled me out with cries of encouragement, and dragged me and my bag through the wind that stood about us as solidly as a wall, found in it a doorway, and swung me through it.

But had we arrived at shelter at last? Was it to light, warmth, and comfort we had come? No, no, this was Frøya and it was not to be. My hostess—Maria we shall call her—worked desperately at the switches on the wall—on, off, on, off—but to no avail. "Electricity's gone—pah!" she spat, throwing down my bag in the dark where it landed with a disconsolate thump. "Candles then—where are the candles?" She crashed around while I stood dripping in a pool of water, trying to see through the dark. "This is not my home," she explained, "my house is on the other side of the island. It is my friend's house. Where does he keep his candles?" She did eventually find one and even managed to light it in spite of the draughts that swept through the abode (not being able to see, I could not tell if it were hut, house, cottage, or castle) but naturally could not get the electric stove to provide us with food or warmth. "Tcha! Let us sit then. Come, come near the candle. You want bread? You want cheese?" I let her pull me down onto what must have been a couch but could not contemplate food: the thought of swallowing anything *down* made my insides rise *up* as they had been taught by the boat to Frøya. So we huddled there by the candle, and she shouted through the noise of the storm information of the places I was to visit and the people I was to meet the next day. "I am journalist. I look after you. You interview me, I interview *you*, ja?"

But we proceeded no further with our discourse for there was a hammering at the door, distinct from the rattling of the storm, and up sprang Maria to run and let in, along with air like a barrel of ice, a man with his cap and boots and leather jacket awash with water. "My friend! My friend has come!" she screamed as theatrically as an opera singer, a mezzo-soprano who achieves in one triumphant moment the high-register trill of a soprano, and thumping him on his leather-jacketed back, she sent him promptly down into the cellar with a candle. We heard him plunging around there, clattering and clanking the switches on and off, and then—lo, there was light.

But I was no longer there to see. Just as my insides had heaved up against the forcing down of food, so now my inner darkness refused the light, and I found myself pitching forward onto my face to blot it out. Then I was being dragged up by the armpits and hauled up the stairs, my heels bumping on each one by turn, and heaved at last into bed. Having achieved this riddance, Maria flew down the stairs to her friend, to light, to company, singing an aria of joy. And I, I lay in bed. I assumed I was in a bedroom but could not rise and explore. I could not even rise to pull off my coat or cap or boots. Fully clothed, I lay stiffly under the covers, and nothing, nothing short of a fire would have made me move a finger outside them. At the window the storm raced and hurtled. Draughts whistled from corner to corner, shaking and banging all the loose wood and metal in and around the house. The noise was deafening. The cold was as clamorous. Or perhaps it was my teeth and bones that rattled so. I could do nothing about it. I was too fatigued, too frozen, too appalled to stir.

....

When I went downstairs to the kitchen in the morning, Maria was waiting, glowing like a fire from the night before. She was taking me to see her friend's factory. Then another factory. Then a shop. Then a school. Then a ship. Then—but we must leave, we must fly. I turned to the window, desperately hoping to draw her attention to the storm that would make any such expeditions impossible, but the sky was as clear as a piece of mockery, neither sleet nor snow to body forth its malice, only the gale that hurled its ghoulish laughter against the walls and doors and, at the end of the road, dashed great glassy waves to pieces upon the rocks.

It was not enough to stop Maria. Bundling me into the car, slamming the door shut on me, she pelted across the island, merrily battling the winds that buffeted the little car as if about to lift up a tin cup and toss it into the sea. Bleakly I looked upon the landscape of Frøya—bleakly it looked back at me: windblown, saltsown, a few bedraggled firs clinging by their roots to the thin soil, and outcroppings of lichened rocks but nothing more. Here and there a few desolate shacks stood, unadorned by any sign of life, human or animal. Maria assured me that in the summer the earth bloomed, the sun shone, holidaymakers sailed up from the mainland to sport in seasonal balminess. It was hard to picture.

"You like?" shouted Maria, nodding enthusiastically first at the landscape and then at me. So I nodded too. "Is nice, hah? You will remember Frøya?" "Oh yes, yes," I assured her with passion, "always." Then added, out of some shred of scruple of which the winds had not divested me, "I think wherever you go becomes a part of you somehow." Maria took that in, then shouted, enigmatically, "Hah!"

At the factory, a great tin hangar on the rocks at the edge of the sea, the friend from the night before greeted us, smiling. He was helping his workmen unravel great lengths of blue plastic twine from one end of the hangar to the other. They stood together in the centre of that echoing place, knotting it into nets. The friend described to me how the nets formed cradles for young salmon when lowered into the sea, securely tethered to the shore so that when they were of sufficient size the fishermen could haul in the nets and do with them what is done to salmon from the sea. Would I like to go out and watch? There were some nets in the bay right outside the factory. Hastily I declined. Truthfully I explained it was women I had come to see, not fish. Ah, women. Women? Luckily amongst them was one who had not had to be away on account of a baby teething or a husband sick. They closeted me with her in the office, where we sat amongst the boots and raincoats for sale to fishermen, and I asked all the questions I imagined the UN wished me to ask: How much education had she? Had she held other jobs? How did this one compare with others? How much was she paid—less or more than the men? Was she married? Had she children? Who looked after them while she . . .

I listened carefully and noted her answers conscientiously. But after that I found myself repeating the same questions and receiving the same answers at every halt. One at a fish-packing factory where hearty women in aprons stood at long tables, slapping and cutting and chopping the fish they lifted out of tubs of brine so they could be processed and packed into tins and boxes exported to lands less favoured by fish than Frøya. ("Eat, try," said one smiling woman, extending a knife to me with a shred of bloodied flesh at its tip.) Then, at the local school where they rushed about the engineering section till they found me one girl student who happily swung a wrench and said she enjoyed motor mechanics; unfortunately we found no boy in the domestic science section who could say the same for changing diapers or washing dishes. So we climbed—gingerly—onto a boat where students learned to sail fishing boats out to sea like their fathers, but the one girl student I had been promised on board was absent that day, alas, so—gingerly we climbed down again, green and giddy from that brief reminder of the night before. Finally, as a surprise, we drove miles down a deserted road across the deserted land to a petrol pump, behind which stood a fashion shop and there met women in red dresses and with painted fingernails who sold fashion garments to—to whom? I could not tell.

When we emerged from there, the sun was gone, the sky was

pale at the rims, and the wind now seemed to be driving darkness onto us in great pouring waves that met no obstacle on that barren land. Even Maria's driving took on the desperation of an escape as we fled back to the house where her friend awaited us. He had shed his leather jacket and cap; he stood at the stove in shirtsleeves, whistling as he fried great platters of fish. "You like?" He winked at me as he held up a forkful. "I like," I assured him and did not add I'd like anything hot, solid, and filling. "Is good," he agreed, throwing another handful of fish into a pan of sizzling oil. Maria ran about the house, fetching glasses and bottles. Soon we sat at table in the bright kitchen and a plate of fish was passed to me. "You like?" Maria asked. "I like," I cried and crammed some into my mouth. "Is good?" they asked together, watching. "Is good," I sputtered, nodding. Then, triumphantly, the lid was whipped off a large pot to release a cloud of steam. "You know this?" they asked. I peered in. "Potatoes," I nodded, "yes." "You have seen?" they asked incredulously, "in *India*?" "Oh yes, in India," I assured them, growing a little sharp in my impatience. "What, potatoes in *India*?" they asked, exchanging looks of incredulity. Then the friend shook his head. "Potatoes in India," he said and ruminated awhile before bringing out, generously, "Then I will come to India." And Maria laughed, I laughed, and potatoes were piled on my plate and I ate. "Is good?" they asked. "Is good." "You like?" "I like." They ate too and lifted their elbows and filled the glasses with fiery spirits that washed down all the salt and fat. At last every crumb was gone, the plates were empty. I laid down my fork and rose to my feet, swaying. I did not feel I could stay upright a moment longer. Maria and her friend tilted back their chairs and refilled their glasses and hardly noticed when I sidled out of the room and up the stairs. There the winds still howled like a lunatic in an asylum, and the doors and windows shook and rattled but added to their sounds were those of the merriment below, laughter and song. Climbing into bed, I pulled the covers over my head and deafened myself to both.

················

In the morning there was no smell of coffee, no sound of life below, but I went down as I had a boat to catch back to the mainland and to

Trondheim. The room downstairs looked as if the storm had blown right through it at night. The radio muttered on a shelf above the cold stove, and Maria sat at the table as if she had sat there all night. She was clutching her dishevelled head in her hands. Raising her face out of her fists, she looked at me red-eyed and wailed, "Ach, my head, my head—it is *killing!*" Then her friend appeared, slowly edging his way down the stairs as if all his bones ached. He gave me a lopsided smile. "I have come to take you to the ferry," he said, "but first we must listen to the weather report on the radio—" and he went over to it to catch its mutter. What he heard made him shake his head gloomily. His face had darkened. "It is saying no ferry today. . . ."

"Ooh, my head, my head," shrieked Maria, rolling her eyes about in appeal.

Her friend bit his lip and decided, "I take you anyway. We will go and see."

Certainly I had no alternative. Fetching my bag, I climbed into his car, wondering where I would go if the ferry did not appear. To the fish factory? The fashion shop by the petrol pump? Where would I find shelter on Frøya? But the idea of staying another night in the gale was not to be tolerated and I kept my eyes peeled for a sign of the boat on the surging seas by the road to the docks. No, no ferry today, the sign clearly read. "Come," shouted my companion, "I know of another place," and we swept down the whole length of the island to its very tip as if blown by the gale itself, and there, miraculously, was a ferry—a large, flat boat that would carry me away from Frøya. It tossed upon the waves, it stank of oil, and water sloshed ankle-deep everywhere—but I threw in first my bag, then myself, and waved to Maria's friend, who had lowered his head and pulled down his cap and run back to the car. As the boat pulled away, I saw it scurrying along the stony road, then disappear into the barrenness that was suddenly swallowed up by the boiling sea.

I sat alone on a bench in the hold, the sole passenger that day, abandoning myself to the horrors of a seasick journey over the sea. But all the boat seemed to do was swing itself slowly around and when it had done that, it had crossed the narrow strait and arrived at the mainland and deposited me in a town of which I had never heard since no one had told me. Moreover it was totally sunk in the deep snow that held the mainland in thrall. I stood up to my knees in it and would have slowly turned to ice had a young man with red hair not leapt off a truck waiting at the dock gates and come to me at a run. "You come from Frøya? Going to Trondheim?" he shouted, and lifted me up into the cabin of his great blue truck.

In no time we were out of the nameless town and up in the great mountains that were like billowing clouds of snow, deep and soft and pure. We drove up twisting roads, higher and higher into the mountains, through forests of blue spruce and expanses of white wildness. The sun dropped over the hills and vanished; the shadows on the show turned first blue, then violet. The truck driver, silent all the way, might have been carrying me to wherever Norwegian bandits go in the winter— ice palaces or bears' caves, I had no idea. I sat in silence too, stupefied by the snow, the scene. It was when the stars came out in the sky that we suddenly rounded the crest of a hill and saw below us the sparkle of city lights in the valley below, to which we coasted as if on skis. It was Trondheim.

"You see that building?" said the truck driver, pointing. "It is the UN office. You go in there."

·············

Several months later I was sent a package of newspaper clippings regarding the UN project on the Decade of Women. Amongst them was a translation of an article in a Frøya newspaper, signed by Maria. An account of our expedition ended with the words: "When she left, she said a part of her would be forever left behind on Frøya."

ROHINTON MISTRY

Rohinton Mistry has published Swimming Lessons and
Other Stories from Firozsha Baag, *which was nominated
for a Governor General's Award. He was born in Bombay
in 1952 and emigrated to Toronto in 1975, where he worked
in a bank for ten years before devoting himself full-time to
his writing. He lives near Toronto, where he has just finished
working on a novel entitled* Such a Long Journey.

....

RUNNING WATER

It was still raining when we stopped outside Hotel Bhagsu. I took my
socks off the taxi's corroded chrome door handles, where they had hung
to dry for almost four hours, and pulled them over my clammy feet.
The socks were still soggy. Little rivulets ran out of my shoulder bag
as I squelched into the lobby. The desk clerk watched with interest
while I fastidiously avoided a trail of water that ran from the leaky
umbrella stand to the door. Why, with the shoes already sopping wet?
he must have wondered. I was not sure myself—perhaps to emphasize
that I did not generally go about dripping water.

As I signed the register, shaking raindrops from my hands, the
desk clerk said that candles would be sent to my room before dark.
Candles, I asked?

He had assumed I would know: "There is a small problem. Electricity workers are on strike." Worse, the strikers were sabotaging the
power lines. No electricity anywhere, he emphasized, in case I was
considering another hotel: not in Upper Dharmsala, not in Lower
Dharmsala, nowhere in Kangra District.

I nodded, putting out my hand for the room key. But he held on to it. With that circular motion of the head which can mean almost anything, he said, "There is one more problem." He continued after a suitable pause: "There is no water. Because of heavy rains. Rocks fell from the mountains and broke all of the water pipes."

He seemed surprised by the lack of emotion with which I greeted his news. But I had already glimpsed the handiwork of the pipe-breaking avalanches during my four-hour taxi ride. The car had laboured hard to reach McLeod Gunj, up the winding, rock-strewn mountain roads, grinding gears painfully, screeching and wheezing, negotiating segments that had become all but impassable.

Perhaps a bit disappointed by my stolidity, once again the desk clerk assured me it was the same in Upper and Lower Dharmsala, and in all of Kangra District; but management would supply two buckets of water a day.

So there was no choice, the hotel would have to do. I requested the day's quota hot, as soon as possible, for a bath. He relinquished my room key at last. Its brass tag had Hotel Bhagsu engraved on one side. "What is Bhagsu?" I asked him, picking up my bag.

"In local language, means Running Water," he said.

······

The room had an enormous picture window. The curtains, when thrown open, revealed a spectacular view of Kangra Valley. But I could not linger long over it, urgent matters were at hand. I unzipped the bag and wrung out my clothes, spreading them everywhere: over the bed, the chair, the desk, the doorknob. Wet and wretched, I sat shivering on the edge of the bed, waiting for the hot water and remembering the warnings to stay away from Dharmsala while it was in the clutches of the dreaded monsoon.

······

When the Dalai Lama fled Tibet in 1959, just hours before the Chinese conducted a murderous raid on his palace in Lhasa and occupied the country, he found refuge in India. For months afterwards, other Tibetans followed him, anxious to be with their beloved spiritual leader.

The pathetic bands of refugees arrived, starving and frostbitten—the ones lucky enough to survive the gauntlet of treacherous mountain passes, the killing cold, and, of course, Chou En-lai's soldiers. Each arriving group narrated events more horrific than the previous one: how the Chinese had pillaged the monasteries, crucified the Buddhist monks, forced nuns to publicly copulate with monks before executing them, and were now systematically engaged in wiping out all traces of Tibetan culture.

The Dalai Lama (whose many wonderfully lyrical, euphonious names include Precious Protector, Gentle Glory, and Ocean of Wisdom) spent his first months of exile in anguish and uncertainty. Faced with unabating news of the endless atrocities upon the body and soul of Tibet, he eventually decided that Dharmsala was where he would establish a government-in-exile. Perhaps this quiet mountain hamlet in the Himalayas reminded him of his own land of ice and snow. Soon, a Tibetan colony evolved in Dharmsala, a virtual country-within-a-country. Visitors began arriving from all over the world to see Namgyal Monastery, Tibetan Children's Village, the Dalai Lama's new temple, or to study at the Library of Tibetan Works and Archives.

As a child, it always struck me with wonderment and incredulity that I should have an uncle who lived in Dharmsala. In this remote mountain hamlet he ran the business which has been in the Nowrojee family for five generations. To me, a thousand miles away in Bombay, this land of mountains and snow had seemed miraculously foreign. Photographs would arrive from time to time, of uncle and aunt and cousins wrapped in heavy woollens, standing beside three-foot-deep snow drifts outside their home, the snow on the roof like thick icing on a cake, and the tree branches delicately lined with more of the glorious white substance. And in my hot and sticky coastal city, gazing with longing and fascination at the photographs, I would find it difficult to believe that such a magical place could exist in this torrid country. Now there, somewhere in the mountains, was a place of escape from heat and dust and grime. So, to visit Dharmsala became the dream.

But for one reason or another, the trip was never taken. Those old photographs: snow-covered mountains and mountain trails; my cousins playing with their huge black Labrador; uncle and aunt posing in the *gaddi* dress of native hill people, a large hookah between them: those old black and white photographs curled and faded to brown and yellow. Years passed, the dog died, my cousins got married and settled elsewhere, and my uncle and aunt grew old. Somehow, the thousand miles between Bombay and Dharmsala were never covered. There was always some logistical or financial problem, and travelling third class on Indian trains was only for the foolish or the desperate.

Then, by a quirk of fate I undertook a different journey, a journey ten thousand miles long, to Canada, and I often thought about the irony of it. So this time, back in Bombay to visit family and friends, not monsoon rain nor ticket queues nor diarrhoea nor avalanches could keep me away from Dharmsala.

Thus twenty-eight hours by train first class brought me to Chakki Bank, in Punjab. It was pouring relentlessly as the first leg of the long journey ended. "Rickshaw, *seth*, rickshaw?" said a voice as I stepped off the train. I quickly calculated: there could be a big demand for transportation in this weather, it might be prudent to say yes. "Yes," I said, and settled the price to Pathankot bus station.

Outside, auto rickshaws—three wheelers—were parked along the station building in a long line. Enough for everyone, I thought. They had black vinyl tops, and plastic flaps at the side which could be fastened shut, I noted approvingly. I followed my man.

And we came to the end of the line. There, he placed my bag in a pitiful cycle rickshaw, the only one amidst that reassuringly for-midable squadron of auto rickshaws. The cycle rickshaw had open sides; and old gunny sacks tied to the top of the frame formed a feeble canopy. I watched in disbelief, appalled by my bad luck. No, stupidity, I cor-rected myself, for it was clear now why he had come inside the station to solicit a fare. That should have made me suspicious. Once upon a time it would have.

The cycle rickshawalla saw my reaction. He pointed pleadingly at the seat, and I looked him in the face, something I never should have done. I am trusting you, his eyes said, not to break our contract. The auto rickshaws taunted me with their waterproof interiors as I stared longingly after them. Their owners were watching, amused, certain I would cave in. And that settled it for me.

Within seconds of setting off, I was ruing my pride. The gunny sacks were as effective as a broken sieve in keeping out the rain, and despite my raincoat I was soon drenched. The downpour saturated my bag and its contents—I could almost feel its weight increasing, minute by minute. The cycle rickshawalla struggled to pedal as fast as he could through streets ankle-deep in water. His calf muscles contracted and rippled, knotting with the strain, and a mixture of pity and anger confused my feelings. I wished the ride would end quickly.

In Pathankot, he convinced me a taxi was better than a bus in this weather. Afterwards, I was glad I took his advice: on the mountains, buses had pulled over because the avalanches, the pipe-breaking avalanches, had made the roads far too narrow. Meanwhile, I waited as the rickshawalla and the taxi driver haggled over the former's commission.

And four hours later I was draping my underwear, socks, shirts, and pants over the doorknob, armchair, lampshade, and window. There was a knock. The houseboy (who doubled as waiter, I discovered later in the restaurant) staggered in with two steaming plastic buckets, one red and the other blue. He looked around disbelievingly at my impromptu haberdashery. "All wet," I explained. He smiled and nodded to humour the eccentric occupant.

I wondered briefly where the water in the buckets came from if the pipes were broken. My guess was a well. In the bathroom, I splashed the hot water over me with a mug.

················

Dharmsala is a collection of settlements perched across the lower ridges of the Dhauladur range. The Dhauladur range itself is a southern spur of the Himalayas and surrounds the Kangra Valley like a snow-capped fence. McLeod Gunj, at seven thousand feet, is one of the highest settlements. I had passed others on my way up by taxi: Lower Dharmsala and Kotwali Bazaar, the main commercial centre crowded with hotels, shops, and restaurants; Forsyth Gunj, a one-street village; and, of course, the huge military cantonment, which was the beginning of everything, back in the British days.

Early in this century, the British were considering making Dharm-

sala their summer capital; they found the plains unbearable in the hot
season. But an earthquake badly damaged the place in 1905, and they
chose another hill station, Simla, a bit farther south. (Later, my uncle
would describe it differently: the official in charge of selecting the capital
was travelling from Dalhousie to Dharmsala when he caught dysentery
on the way, reached Dharmsala, and died. The idea of Dharmsala as
summer capital was promptly abandoned.)

I wanted to see more of McLeod Gunj and Upper Dharmsala.
But first I was anxious to meet my aunt and uncle. Next morning, I
telephoned them at their general store, and they were delighted to hear
my voice. The line was so bad, they thought I was calling from Bombay.
No, I said, Hotel Bhagsu, and they insisted I come immediately, their
place was only a five-minute walk away.

It was still drizzling. Along the side of the hotel, under every rain
spout, was a plastic bucket. My red and blue were there as well. The
houseboy was standing guard over them, watching them fill with the
run-off from the roof. He looked away guiltily at first when he saw me.
Then he must have decided to put the best face on things, for he
acknowledged me by smiling and waving. He seemed like a child caught
red-handed at mischief.

························

My uncle and aunt were sorry for the way my visit had begun. "But
didn't anyone tell you? This is not a good season for Dharmsala," they
said. I had been warned, I admitted, but had decided to come anyway.
They found this touching, and also confusing. Never mind, Uncle said,
perhaps half our troubles would soon be over: the military cantonment
had dispatched its men to find and repair the sabotaged power lines.
The only snag was, as soon as they mended one, the strikers snipped
through some more.

As for water, said my aunt, not to worry, their supply had not
been affected, I could shower there.

Not affected? How? Just then, customers arrived, asking for candles. My aunt went to serve them and my uncle told the story.

During the devastation of the 1905 earthquake, the Nowrojee
store was practically the only structure that survived. Uncle's grandfather

had handed out food and clothing and blankets from store supplies till proper relief was organized by the British District Commissioner. When McLeod Gunj was back on its feet, the District Commissioner wanted to show his gratitude to the family. He gifted a mountain spring to them, and arranged for direct water supply from the spring to their house. That private pipeline was still operating after eighty-odd years and had survived the present avalanches.

I promised I would use their shower in the evening. Then more customers entered, and he had to assist my aunt. Local people were inquiring if the newspaper delivery was expected to get through to Dharmsala. Foreign tourists in designer raincoats were seeking out the sturdy black umbrella which, locally, was the staple defense against the rains. The tourists were also laying in a stock of Bisleri mineral water.

There was a lull in business after this surge. My aunt suggested that Uncle take me around Dharmsala for a bit, she could hold the fort alone. So we set out for a walk.

At first the going was slow. Almost every person we passed stopped to exchange a few words, mainly about the weather, and which roads were closed and which were still passable. But it was heartening to see the Tibetan monks, in their crimson robes, always smiling joyfully. For a people who had suffered such hardships and upheavals, struggling to start life over again in a strange land, they were remarkably cheerful and happy. Perhaps this, and their Buddhist faith, is what sustained them. They had the most wonderful beaming, smiling faces. Just like their spiritual leader, whom I had watched some time ago on *60 Minutes*, whose countenance seems to radiate an inner well-being.

Exchanging *namaskaars* with everyone we met (the folded-hands greeting, which translates into: I greet the God in you, common to Hindus and Buddhists), we arrived at a tall gold-crowned structure at the centre of a group of buildings. It was a *chorten*, a religious monument, dedicated to the memory of all those suffering under Chinese occupation in Tibet. The faithful were circling round it, spinning two rows of prayer wheels and reciting mantras.

We left the little square and the buildings which housed Tibetan handicraft shops, restaurants, and hotels. Farther down were the Tibetan homes: shacks and shanties of tin and stone, and every window was adorned with flowers in rusty tin cans. Faded prayer flags fluttered in the trees overhead.

The road climbed steeply. Before I knew it, the buildings and the *chorten* were below us. My uncle turned and pointed. There used to be a beautiful park there, he said, at the centre of McLeod Gunj, but it had to go when the refugees came.

During our walk I gathered he loved the Tibetan people, and had done much to aid them. I could hear the respect and admiration in his voice when he talked about the Dalai Lama, whom he had helped back in 1959 to acquire suitable houses and properties where the Tibetans could start rebuilding their lives. But now as my uncle told the story of Dharmsala and the arrival of refugees, I could not help feeling that there was also some resentment toward these people who had so radically changed and remade in their own image the place where he was born, the place he loved so dearly. My aunt, who likes the hustle and bustle of big cities and gets her share of it by visiting relatives periodically, said he would pine away if she ever insisted they leave Dharmsala.

We continued to climb, and on the mountain spur that dominates the valley rose the golden pinnacles of Thekchen Choeling, the Island of Mahayana Teaching, the complex which was the new residence of the Dalai Lama. His cottage had a green corrugated roof, and the temple was a three-story lemon-yellow hall topped by gold spires. On a low verandah surrounding the temple, a woman was performing repeated prostrations. She was making a circuit of the temple, measuring her progress with her height.

We removed our shoes and went inside. The main hall had a high throne at one end: the Dalai Lama's throne, on which he sat when he gave audiences and preached. There would be no audiences for the next few days, though, because he was away in Ladakh to deliver the Kalachakra—Wheel of Time—Initiation. Behind the throne was a larger-than-life statue of the Buddha in the lotus position. The Buddha was locked in a huge glass case. Myriads of precious and semi-precious stones formed a halo around the Buddha's solid gold head, and hence the locked glass: things had changed in Dharmsala; the increase in population and the tourist traffic forced the monks to take precautions.

The changes were having other effects, too. The mountain slopes were being rapidly deforested by the poverty-stricken population's hunger for firewood. And, as elsewhere in the world, the disappearance of trees was followed by soil erosion. My uncle had pointed out the gashed and scarred hills on our climb up. He said that so many mudslides and rockfalls were unheard of in the old days; and there was less and less snow each year.

I thought of those photographs from my childhood. Their memory suddenly seemed more precious than ever. The pristine place they had once captured was disappearing.

Inside the temple, at the throne's right, more statues were displayed. One of them had multiple heads and arms: Chenrezi, the awareness-being who symbolizes compassion in the Tibetan pantheon. The legend went that Chenrezi was contemplating how best to work for the happiness of all living things, when his head burst into a thousand pieces as he realized the awesome nature of the task. The Buddha of Limitless Light restored him to life, giving him a thousand heads to represent the all-seeing nature of his compassion, and a thousand arms to symbolize the omnipresence of his help. But now Chenrezi, along with other statues bedecked with gold and jewels, was locked behind a floor-to-ceiling collapsible steel gate.

The rain finally ceased. My uncle wished the mist would clear so he could show me Pong Lake in the distance. When the moon shone upon the water, he said, it took one's breath away. But the mist sat over the valley, unmoving.

Descending the temple road, we saw several monks, prayer beads in hand, walking a circular path around the complex. They were simulating the Lingkhor, the Holy Walk circumscribing the Potala, the Dalai Lama's palace in Tibet. Round and round they walked, praying, perhaps, for a time when he would be back in his palace, and they treading the original Lingkhor.

Inside: the woman, making a mandala of her prostrations around the temple. Outside: the monks, creating circles of prayer around their beloved leader's residence. Circles within circles. The Wheel of Time.

Back at the general store, bad news awaited: the taps were dry. The Tibetan refugees (everyone, Tibetans included, used that word, despite their having lived here thirty years; perhaps clinging to this word kept alive the hope of returning to their Land of Snows) had discovered that the Nowrojee pipeline still held water. They had cut it open to fill their buckets. Strangely, my uncle and aunt were not too upset. It had happened before. They just wished the people would come to the house and fill their buckets from the taps instead of cutting the pipe.

Later that night, I found my way back to Hotel Bhagsu with a borrowed flashlight. My uncle accompanied me part of the way. Near the incline that led to the hotel, where the road forked, there was a little lamp in an earthen pot, sitting at the very point of divergence. How quaint, I thought. A friendly light to guide the traveller through the pitch-black night. But my uncle grabbed my arm and pulled me away. He said to tread carefully to the right of the lamp, by no means to step over it.

What was it? Something to do with Tibetan exorcism rites, he answered. Did he believe in such things? He had lived here too long, he said, and seen too much, to be able to disbelieve it completely. Despite my skepticism, he succeeded in sending a shiver down my spine. It was only the setting, I explained to myself: a pitch-dark mountain road, the rustling of leaves, swirling mists.

Back at the hotel, the desk clerk apologetically handed me the stubs of two candles. Dharmsala was out of candles, what remained had to be strictly rationed. I asked for water.

One more day, I decided, then I would leave. There was not much to do. The avalanches had closed the roads farther north, and the side trips I had planned to Dalhousie, Kulu, and Manali were not feasible. The houseboy knocked.

He was carrying the red bucket. "Where is the blue?" He shook his head: "Sorry, not enough rain. Today only one bucket."

The electricity was back next morning, I discovered thankfully. Around nine, I went to the empty restaurant and ordered tea and toast. Afflicted with a bad stomach, I had been virtually living on toast for the past three days. The houseboy in the persona of waiter took my order cheerfully and left.

Thirty minutes later I was still waiting. The door marked EM-

PLOYEES ONLY was ajar, and I peered into the kitchen. It was empty. The backyard beyond the kitchen window was deserted too. I went to the front desk. No one. Finally, I ran into the night watchman, who had just woken. "What is going on?" I asked him with manufactured testiness, remembering long-forgotten roles and poses. "Waiter has disappeared, no one in the kitchen, no one on duty. What has happened? Is this a hotel or a joke?"

He studied his watch and thought for a moment: "Sunday today? Oh yes. Everyone is watching *Ramayan*. But they will come back. Only five minutes left."

The *Ramayana* is one of the two great Sanskrit epics of ancient India. The other is the *Mahabharata*, which recently found its way in translation onto Western stages in Peter Brook's production. But when the *Ramayana*, the story of the god Rama, was made into a Hindi TV serial, sixty million homes began tuning in every Sunday morning, and those who did not own TVs went to friends who did. In the countryside, entire villages gathered around the community set. Before the programme started, people would garland the TV with fresh flowers and burn incense beside it. Classified ads in newspapers would read: Car For Sale—But Call After *Ramayan*. Interstate buses would make unscheduled stops when the auspicious time neared, and woe betide the bus driver who refused. Ministerial swearing-in ceremonies were also known to be postponed.

The series ended after seventy-eight episodes, which, however, were not sufficient to cover the entire epic. In protest, street sweepers went on strike and there were demonstrations in several cities. The Ministry of Information and Broadcasting then sanctioned a further twenty-six episodes in order to bring *Ramayan* and the strike to their proper conclusions.

But the story does not end there. Not satisfied with burning incense and garlanding their television sets on Sunday mornings, people began mobbing the actor who played the role of Rama, genuflecting wherever he appeared in public, touching his feet, asking for his blessing. To capitalize on the phenomenon, Rajiv Gandhi's Congress Party enlisted the actor-god to campaign for their candidate in an upcoming election. The actor-god went around telling people that Rama would give them blessings if they voted for the Congress Party, and how it was the one sure way to usher in the golden age of Rama's mythical kingdom of Ayodhya.

At this point, the intellectuals and political pundits sadly shook their sage heads, lamenting the ill-prepared state of the masses for democracy. Suspension of disbelief was all very well when watching television. But to extend it to real life? It showed, they said, the need for education as a prerequisite if democracy was to work successfully.

When it was time to vote, however, the masses, despite the actor-god and the shaking heads of the intellectuals, knew exactly what to do. The Congress candidate went down in a resounding defeat, and the actor-god became sadly human again.

My waiter returned, promising immediate delivery of my tea and toast. I threw my hands in the air and pretended to be upset: How long was a person supposed to wait? Was this a hotel or a joke? In response to my spurious annoyance, he affected a contrite look. But like me, his heart was not in it. Like the voters and the actor-god, we played out our roles, and we both knew what was what.

In Bombay, at the beginning of the trip, I had listened amusedly when told about the power of the serial. Intriguing me was the fact that what was, by all accounts, a barely passable production lacking any kind of depth, with embarrassingly wooden acting, could, for seventy-eight weeks, hold a captive audience made up not only of Hindus but also Muslims, Sikhs, Parsis, Christians—cutting right across the religious spectrum. Could it be that under the pernicious currents of communalism and prejudice, there were traces of something more significant, a yearning, perhaps, which transcended these nasty things, so that the great Sanskrit epic of ancient India, a national heritage, could belong to all Indians?

I had not expected to receive a personal demonstration of the Sunday morning power that *Ramayan* wielded. Least of all in this faraway mountain hamlet. In a way, though, it was fitting. Everywhere, *Ramayan* brought diverse communities together for a short while, to share an experience. But in Dharmsala, the native population and the refugees have been sharing and living together for many years. Even the electricity saboteurs cooperated with the show. Of course, shortly after *Ramayan* the region was once again powerless.

MARK SALZMAN

Mark Salzman was graduated Phi Beta Kappa, summa cum laude from Yale in 1982, with a degree in Chinese Language and Literature. Between 1982 and 1984 he lived in Changsha, Hunan, where he taught English at Hunan Medical College. Iron & Silk *is his narrative of the variety of people he met abroad during that period. While in China he continued his study of the martial arts, and in 1985 traveled back to China to participate in the National Martial Arts Competition and Conference in Tianjin. He has recently completed a novel entitled* The Laughing Sutra.

----

from IRON & SILK

Changsha stayed hot and humid through the early part of November. By then I had developed a painful case of athlete's foot and started looking around for some medicine. None of the local stores carried anything for it, and none of my doctor students was familiar with the symptoms. At last someone acquainted with diseases of the skin had a look at me. He recognized the problem right away, but was unable to treat me. Athlete's foot, he told me, had been declared successfully driven out of China, and therefore could be contracted only if one left the Socialist Motherland or had contact with foreigners. For this reason it was now called "Hong Kong Foot," and no medicine was available for it. He advised me to have someone send medicine from the States.

I wrote to someone in Hong Kong and he put a few tubes of medicine, along with some candy bars and brownies, in a small cardboard box and mailed it to me right away.

A few days later a pick-up notice addressed to me showed up in our mailbox. I walked over to the post office and handed it to a young woman behind the counter. She snatched it out of my hand, marched into the back room, came out with my package—torn open, its contents in disarray—dropped it on the counter, slapped a bill in front of me, and barked, "Sign and pay!" She seemed to be in terrible humor and refused to look me in the eye, choosing to glare at the clock on the wall instead. I looked at the bill and saw that it imposed on me a tax that surpassed the value of the package's contents.

I took a deep breath and risked all by asking the woman to explain the tax. Her face turned white and her nostrils flared. "Import tax for Foreign Friends! Hurry up!" I began to get annoyed, because I had been told repeatedly by the Foreign Affairs Bureau that this tax was waived for foreigners living and working in China. It was supposed to be levied only on foreign travelers, who presumably are all rich and don't mind being exploited. When I explained this to the young woman, she yelled, "Then let the Foreign Affairs Bureau pay the tax!" shoved my box to the far side of the counter, and refused to pay attention to me anymore.

I stalked over to the Foreign Affairs Bureau office, calming myself by anticipating the satisfaction of thrusting an official document bristling with angry red seals under that woman's nose. She would have to surrender my box or be sent to a labor camp. But when I told Comrade Hu at the bureau about the problem, instead of giving me an official document he told me not to worry, that the Foreign Affairs Bureau would "research the matter" for me. In Chinese bureaucratic language, "researching the matter" means putting it aside until it solves itself or just goes away, so I pressed him for a better answer. He said he understood the need for expediency and smilingly agreed to "look into the matter," which is usually better than "researching the matter."

A few days later I visited the Foreign Affairs Bureau again to see if my medicine had been released.

"Oh yes," Comrade Hu said, smiling, "it is a very simple problem. You see, this tax is imposed on foreigners who import things into China that China already has. China is a developing country, but nevertheless has medicine and food of its own. For someone to import medicine and food insults our country and the government assumes that foreigners wish to exploit Chinese people by selling foreign goods to them at high prices, saying that their foreign goods are better than Chinese goods. Of course, we know that you wouldn't do anything like that! You are a friend of China! But, unfortunately, we don't control the regulations!"

"Yes, Comrade Hu, I understand that, but I was told that this import tax applied only to foreigners traveling in China, not to those living and working in China."

After a pause and a few words with Group Leader Chen, Comrade Hu smiled again.

"Yes, exactly. But the Postal Customs officials in Canton get confused. Apparently they don't have your name on their list of foreign residents. So why don't you just pay the tax. We will examine the matter for you, and Canton will reimburse you in no time."

Not wishing to let responsibility for the matter shift to Canton, I tried something else.

"Since this is an internal matter, Comrade Hu, why doesn't your office pay the tax, and then have Canton reimburse you?"

After another pause, and a few more words with Group Leader Chen, Comrade Hu smiled and answered, "Our office, I am sorry to say, is not authorized to disburse funds. If you like, though, we can look into the possibility of having the Health Office of the medical college pay the tax for you. It might take some time for us to determine exactly which channels to go through, however."

Knowing that I had been defeated, I said I would think about it and let them know later. They smiled, and Comrade Hu told me that anytime anything came up I should feel free to come see them. That way, even if we couldn't solve a problem right away, we could come to understand it.

I felt I had had enough of the matter for the time being, and decided to pay the tax the next day. At dinner that night the wife of an American doctor doing research at our hospital mentioned to me that she had a package of mine. She brought it out and indeed it was my medicine and chocolates—she had seen it on the counter at the post office in the afternoon, saw that it was for me, and innocently walked out with it. Our little American community cheered this small victory over the forces of evil, and I went to bed a happy man.

The next day we received no mail. The day after that, we again received no mail. The third day without mail I went to the post office.

I walked straight to the counter where the young woman worked and stood there until finally she hissed, "What do you want?" I answered as quietly as possible that we had not been getting any mail recently, was there a problem? Without looking up she pointed at a pile of mail in the far corner of the room, on her side of the counter—all international mail. I asked if I could pick it up, and once more she slapped the tax bill on the counter. I paid up without a word, and that afternoon we got a big pile of mail.

Several weeks after I had taken my receipt to the Foreign Affairs Bureau, Canton announced that Postal Regulations had changed, and all related debts owed to foreigners had become void.

UMBERTO ECO

Umberto Eco's best-selling novels include The Name of the Rose *and* Foucault's Pendulum. *He is a professor of semiotics at the University of Bologna, a distinguished historian, philosopher, and aesthetician. The following passage is from a section called "Enchanted Castles" in a long essay from 1975, "Travels in Hyperreality" (collected in a volume of the same name). Commenting in a preface, Eco writes: "In these pages I try to interpret and to help others interpret some 'signs.' These signs are not only words, or images; they can also be forms of social behavior, political acts, artificial landscapes." He lives in Milan.*

---

from TRAVELS IN HYPERREALITY

Winding down the curves of the Pacific coast between San Francisco, Tortilla Flat, and Los Padres National Park, along shores that recall Capri and Amalfi, as the Pacific Highway descends toward Santa Barbara, you see the castle of William Randolph Hearst rise, on the gentle Mediterranean hill of San Simeon. The traveler's heart leaps, because this is the Xanadu of *Citizen Kane*, where Orson Welles brought to life his protagonist, explicitly modeled on the great newspaper magnate, ancestor of the unfortunate Symbionese Patricia.

Having reached the peak of wealth and power, Hearst built here his own Fortress of Solitude, which a biographer has described as a combination of palace and museum such as had not been seen since the days of the Medicis. Like someone in a René Clair movie (but here reality far outstrips fiction), Hearst bought, in bits or whole, palaces, abbeys, and convents in Europe, had them dismantled brick by numbered brick, packaged and shipped across the ocean, to be reconstructed on the enchanted hill, in the midst of free-ranging wild animals. Since he wanted not a museum but a Renaissance house, he complemented the original pieces with bold imitations, not bothering to distinguish the genuine from the copy. An incontinent collectionism, the bad taste of the nouveau riche, and a thirst for prestige led him to bring the past down to the level of today's life; but he conceived of today as worth living only if guaranteed to be "just like the past."

Amid Roman sarcophagi, and genuine exotic plants, and remade baroque stairways, you pass Neptune's Pool, a fantasy Greco-Roman temple peopled with classical statues including (as the guidebook points out with fearless candor) the famous Venus rising from the water, sculpted in 1930 by the Italian sculptor Cassou, and you reach the Great House, a Spanish-Mexican–style cathedral with two towers (equipped with a thirty-six-bell carillon), whose portal frames an iron gate brought from a sixteenth-century Spanish convent, surmounted by a Gothic tympanum with the Virgin and Child. The floor of the vestibule encloses a mosaic found in Pompeii, there are Gobelins on the walls, the door into the Meeting Hall is by Sansovino, the great hall is fake Renaissance presented as Italo-French. A series of choir stalls comes from an Italian convent (Hearst's agents sought the scattered pieces through various European dealers), the tapestries are seventeenth-century Flemish, the objects—real or fake—date from various periods, four medallions are by Thorvaldsen. The Refectory has an Italian ceiling "four hundred years old," on the walls are banners "of an old Sienese family." The bedroom contains the authentic bed of Richelieu, the billiard room has a Gothic tapestry, the projection room (where every night Hearst forced his guests to watch the films he produced, while he sat in the front row with a handy telephone linking him with the whole world) is all fake Egyptian with some Empire touches; the library has another Italian ceiling, the study imitates a Gothic crypt, and the fireplaces of the various rooms are (real) Gothic, whereas the indoor pool invents a hybrid of the Alhambra, the Paris Métro, and a Caliph's urinal, but with greater majesty.

The striking aspect of the whole is not the quantity of antique pieces plundered from half of Europe, or the nonchalance with which the artificial tissue seamlessly connects fake and genuine, but rather the sense of fullness, the obsessive determination not to leave a single space that doesn't suggest something, and hence the masterpiece of bricolage, haunted by *horror vacui*, that is here achieved. The insane abundance makes the place unlivable, just as it is hard to eat those dishes that many classy American restaurants, all darkness and wood paneling, dotted with soft red lights and invaded by nonstop music, offer the customer as evidence of his own situation of "affluence": steaks four inches thick with lobster (and baked potato, and sour cream and melted butter, and grillled tomato and horseradish sauce) so that the customer will have "more and more," and can wish nothing further.

An incomparable collection of genuine pieces, too, the Castle of Citizen Kane achieves a psychedelic effect and a kitsch result not because the Past is not distinguished from the Present (because after all this was how the great lords of the past amassed rare objects, and the same continuum of styles can be found in many Romanesque churches where the nave is now baroque and perhaps the campanile is eighteenth century), but because what offends is the voracity of the selection, and what distresses is the fear of being caught up by this jungle of venerable beauties, which unquestionably has its own wild flavor, its own pathetic sadness, barbarian grandeur, and sensual perversity, redolent of contamination, blasphemy, the Black Mass. It is like making love in a confessional with a prostitute dressed in a prelate's liturgical robes reciting Baudelaire while ten electronic organs reproduce the *Well-Tempered Clavier* played by Scriabin.

But Hearst's castle is not a *unicum*, not a *rara avis*: It fits into the California tourist landscape with perfect coherence, among the waxwork Last Suppers and Disneyland. And so we leave the castle and travel a few dozen miles, toward San Luis Obispo. Here, on the slopes of Mount San Luis, bought entirely by Mr. Madonna in order to build a series of motels of disarming pop vulgarity, stands the Madonna Inn.

The poor words with which natural human speech is provided cannot suffice to describe the Madonna Inn. To convey its external appearance, divided into a series of constructions, which you reach by way of a filling station carved from Dolomitic rock, or through the restaurant, the bar, and the cafeteria, we can only venture some analogies. Let's say that Albert Speer, while leafing through a book on Gaudi, swallowed an overgenerous dose of LSD and began to build a nuptial catacomb for Liza Minnelli. But that doesn't give you an idea. Let's say Arcimboldi builds the Sagrada Familia for Dolly Parton. Or: Carmen Miranda designs a Tiffany locale for the Jolly Hotel chain. Or D'Annunzio's Vittoriale imagined by Bob Cratchit, Calvino's *Invisible Cities* described by Judith Krantz and executed by Leonor Fini for the plush-doll industry, Chopin's Sonata in B flat minor sung by Perry Como in an arrangement by Liberace and accompanied by the Marine Band. No, that still isn't right. Let's try telling about the rest rooms. They are an immense underground cavern, something like Altamira and Luray, with Byzantine columns supporting plaster baroque cherubs. The basins are big imitation-mother-of-pearl shells, the urinal is a fireplace carved from the rock, but when the jet of urine (sorry, but I have to explain) touches the bottom, water comes down from the wall of the hood, in a flushing cascade something like the Caves of the Planet Mongo. And on the ground floor, in keeping with the air of Tyrolean chalet and Renaissance castle, a cascade of chandeliers in the form of baskets of flowers, billows of mistletoe surmounted by opalescent bubbles, violet-suffused light among which Victorian dolls swing, while the walls are punctuated by art-nouveau windows with the colors of Chartres and hung with Regency tapestries whose pictures resemble the garish color supplements of the Twenties. The circular sofas are red and gold, the tables gold and glass, and all this amid inventions that turn the whole into a multicolor Jell-O, a box of candied fruit, a Sicilian ice, a land for Hansel and Gretel. Then there are the bedrooms, about two hundred of them, each with a different theme: for a reasonable price (which includes an enormous bed—King or Queen size—if you are on your honeymoon) you can have the Prehistoric Room, all cavern and stalactites, the Safari Room (zebra walls and bed shaped like a Bantu idol), the Kona Rock Room (Hawaiian), the California Poppy, the Old-Fashioned Honeymoon, the Irish Hills, the William Tell, the Tall and Short, for mates of different lengths, with the bed in an irregular polygon form, the Imperial Family, the Old Mill.

The Madonna Inn is the poor man's Hearst Castle; it has no artistic or philological pretensions, it appeals to the savage taste for the amazing, the overstuffed, and the absolutely sumptuous at low price. It says to its visitors: "You too can have the incredible, just like a millionaire."

Translated from the Italian by William Weaver

JOHN METCALF

*John Metcalf was born in England in 1938 and came to
Canada in 1962, where he now lives in Ottawa. A novelist,
critic, and editor, he is best known for his short fiction,
collected in* The Lady Who Sold Furniture, The Teeth of
My Father, *and* Girl in Gingham. *His latest collection of
stories and novellas,* Adult Entertainment *(1986), is as
much interested in the metaphorical as the geographical direction of its main work, "Travelling Northward." The following extract from the same collection is taken from "The
Nipples of Venus," a story set in Italy.*

······················

from ADULT ENTERTAINMENT

No, I told Helen on Sunday morning, not the Forum, not the Colosseum, not the Capitoline, the Palatine, or the Quirinal. I wanted to
be lazy. I wanted to be taken somewhere. But not to monuments. Trees
and fields. But not *walking*. I didn't want to *do* anything. I wanted to
see farmhouses and outbuildings. What I wanted—yes, that was it
exactly—a coach tour! I wanted to gaze out of the window at red-and-
orange roof tiles, at ochre walls, poppies growing wild on the roadsides,
vines.

At ten A.M. we were waiting in a small office in a side street for
the arrival of the coach. The brochure in the hotel lobby had described
the outing as Extended Alban Hills Tours—Castelli Romani. Our coach
was apparently now touring some of the larger hotels picking up other
passengers. The whole operation seemed a bit makeshift and fly-by-
night. The two young men running it seemed to do nothing but shout

denials on the phone and hustle out into the street screaming at drivers
as coach after coach checked in at the office before setting out to tour
whatever they were advertised as touring. Commands and queries were
hysterical. Tickets were counted and recounted. And then recounted.
Coaches were finally dispatched with operatic gesture as if they were
full of troops going up to some heroic Front.

As each coach pulled up, we looked inquiringly at one or other
of the young men. "This is not yours," said their hands. "Patience. Do
not fear. When your conveyance arrives, we will inform you," said
their gestures.

We were both startled by the entry of a large, stout man with a
shaved head who barged into the tiny office saying something that
sounded challenging or jeering. His voice was harsh. He limped, throwing out one leg stiffly. Helen sat up in the plastic chair and drew her
legs in. Something about his appearance suggested that he'd survived
a bad car crash. He leaned on an aluminum stick which ended in a
large rubber bulb. He was wearing rimless blue-tinted glasses. His lip
was permanently drawn up a little at one side. There was a lot of visible
metal in his teeth. He stumped about in the confined space shouting
and growling.

The young man with the mauve leather shoes shouted "no" a lot
and "never" and slapped the counter with a plastic ruler. The other
young man picked up a glossy brochure and, gazing fixedly at the
ceiling, twisted it as if wringing a neck. The shaven-headed man pushed
a pile of pamphlets off the counter with the rubber tip of his aluminum
stick.

A coach pulled up and a young woman in a yellow dress got
down from it and clattered on heels into the office. They all shouted
at her. She spat—*teh*—and made a coarse gesture.

The young man with the mauve leather shoes went outside to
shout up at the coach driver. Through the window, we watched him
counting, pulling each finger down in turn.

. . . five, six, *seven*.

Further heart-rending pantomime followed.

Still in full flow, he burst back into the office brandishing the
tickets in an accusatory way. Peering and pouting into the mirror of a

compact, the girl in the yellow dress continued applying lipstick. They all shouted questions at her, possibly rhetorical. The horrible shaven-headed man shook the handle of his aluminum cane in her face.

She spat again—*teh*.

The bus driver sounded his horn.

The other young man spoke beseechingly to the potted azalea.

"Is that," said Helen, "the Castelli Romani coach? Or isn't it the Castelli Romani coach?"

There was silence as everyone stared at her.

"It *is*, dear madam, it *is*," said the horribly bald man.

"Good," said Helen.

And I followed her out.

We nodded to the other seven passengers as we climbed aboard and seated ourselves behind them near the front of the coach. They sounded American. There were two middle-aged couples, a middle-aged man on his own, rather melancholy-looking, and a middle-aged man with an old woman.

"Here he comes goosewalking," said Helen.

"*Stepping*," I said.

The shaven-headed man, leg lifting up and then swinging to the side, was stumping across the road leaning on the aluminum cane. His jacket was a flapping black-and-white plaid.

"Oh, *no!*" I said. "You don't think *he's* . . ."

"I told you," said Helen. "I told you this was going to be awful."

The shaven-headed man climbed up into the bus, hooked his aluminum cane over the handrail above the steps, and unclipped the microphone. Holding it in front of his mouth, he surveyed us.

"Today," he said with strange, metallic sibilance, "today you are my children."

Helen nudged.

"Today I am taking you into the Alban Hills. I will show you many wonders. I will show you extinct volcanoes. I will show you the lake of the famous Caligula. I will show you the headquarters of the German Army in World War II. Together we will visit Castel Gandolfo, Albano, Genzano, Frascati, and Rocca di Papa. We will leave ancient Rome by going past the Colosseum and out onto the Via Appia Antica completed by Appius Claudius in 312 before Christ."

He nodded slowly.

"Oh yes, my children."

Still nodding.

"Before Christ."

He looked from face to face.

"You will know this famous road as the Appian Way and you will have seen it in the movie *Spartacus* with the star Kirk Douglas."

"Oh, God!" said Helen.

"Well, my children," he said, tapping the bus driver on the shoulder, "are you ready? But you are curious about me. Who *is* this man?, you are saying."

He inclined his shaved head in a bow.

"Who am I?"

He chuckled into the microphone.

"They call me Kojak."

Cypresses standing guard along the Appian Way over sepulchres and sarcophagi, umbrella pines shading fragments of statuary. Tombs B.C. Tombs A.D. Statuary contemporaneous with Julius Caesar, of whom we would have read in the play of that name by William Shakespeare. It was impossible to ignore or block out his voice, and after a few minutes we'd come to dread the clicking on of the microphone and the harsh, metallic commentary.

You will pay attention to your left and you will see . . .

A sarcophagus.

You will pay attention opposite and you will see . . .

"Opposite what?"

"He means straight ahead."

"Oh."

. . . to your right and in one minute you will see a famous school for women drivers . . .

Into view hove a scrap-metal dealer's yard mountainous with wrecked cars.

You will pay attention . . .

But despite the irritation of the rasping voice, I found the expedition soothing and the motion of the coach restful. The landscape as it passed was pleasing. Fields. Hedges. Garden plots. The warmth of terra-cotta tiles. Hills. White clouds in a sky of blue.

The Pope's summer residence at Castel Gandolfo was a glimpse through open ornate gates up a drive to a house, then the high encircling stone wall around the park.

Beech trees.

In the narrow, steep streets of the small town, the coach's length negotiated the sharp turns, eased around corners, trundled past the elaborate façade of the church and through the piazza with its fountain by Bernini.

The famous Peach Festival took place in June.

At Lake Albano we were to stop for half an hour.

No less, my children, and no more.

The coach pulled into the restaurant parking lot and backed into line with more than a dozen others. The restaurant, a cafeteria sort of place, was built on the very edge of the lake. It was jammed with tourists. Washrooms were at the bottom of a central staircase and children ran up and down the stairs, shouting. There was a faint smell of disinfectant. Lost children cried.

In the plastic display cases were sandwiches with dubious fillings, tired-looking panini, and slices of soggy pizza that were being reheated in microwave ovens until greasy.

The man from our coach who was travelling with the old woman sat staring out of the plate-glass window which overlooked the lake. The old woman was spooning in with trembling speed what looked like a huge English trifle, mounds of whipped cream, maraschino cherries, custard, cake.

Helen and I bought an ice cream we didn't really want. We stood on the wooden dock beside the restaurant and looked at the lake which was unnaturally blue. There was a strong breeze. White sails were swooping over the water. I felt cold and wished we could get back in the coach.

"So this was a volcano," said Helen.

"I guess so."

"The top blew off and then it filled up with water."

"I suppose that's it."

The man from our coach who was on his own, the melancholy-looking man, wandered onto the other side of the dock. He stood holding an ice cream cone and looking across the lake. He looked a bit like Stan Laurel. We nodded to him. He nodded to us and made a sort of gesture at the lake with his ice cream as if to convey approval.

We smiled and nodded.

The engine of the coach was throbbing as we sat waiting for the man and the old woman to shuffle across the parking lot. The stiff breeze suddenly blew the man's hair down, revealing him as bald. From one side of his head hung a long hank which had been trained up and over his bald pate. He looked naked and bizarre as he stood there, the length of hair hanging from the side of his head and fluttering below his shoulder. It looked as if he'd been scalped. The attached hair looked like a dead thing, like a pelt.

Seemingly unembarrassed, he lifted the hair back, settling it as if it were a beret, patting it into place. The old woman stood perhaps two feet from the side of the coach smiling at it with a little smile.

And so, my children, we head now for Genzano and for Frascati, the Queen of the Castelli . . .

We did not stop in Genzano, which also had Baroque fountains possibly by Bernini in the piazzas and a palazzo of some sort. Down below the town was the Lake of Nemi, from which two of Caligula's warships had been recovered only to be burned by the retreating Adolf Hitler.

The famous Feast of Flowers took place in May.

"Why do I know the name Frascati?" said Helen.

"Because of the wine?"

"Have I had it?"

I shrugged.

"I had some *years* ago," I said. "Must be thirty years ago now— at a wedding. We drank it with strawberries."

"Whose wedding?"

"And I don't think I've had it since. Um? Oh . . . a friend from college. I haven't heard from him—Tony Cranbrook . . . oh, it's been *years*."

"There," said Helen, "what kind of tree is that?"

I shook my head.

Frascati.

The wine was dry and golden.

Gold in candlelight.

The marriage of Tony Cranbrook had been celebrated in the village church, frayed purple hassocks, that special Anglican smell of damp and dust and stone, marble memorials let into the wall:

. . . departed this life June 11th 1795 in the sure and certain hope of the resurrection and of the life everlasting . . .

Afterwards, the younger people had strolled back through deep lanes to the family house for the reception. I'd walked with a girl called Susan, who turned out to be the sister of one of the bridesmaids. She'd picked a buttercup and lodged it behind her ear. She'd said:

Do you know what this means in Tahiti?

Late in the evening they'd been wandering about the house calling to us to come and eat strawberries, calling out that I had to make another speech.

Jack?

We know you're there!

Susan?

Jack and Su-san!

The larger drawing room was warm and quick with candlelight. In the centre of the dark polished refectory table stood a gleaming silver épergne piled with tiny wild strawberries. By the side of it stood octagonal silver sugar casters. The candelabra on the table glossed the wood's dark grain. Reflected in the épergne's curves and facets, points of flame quivered.

You will pay attention to your right . . .

Traffic was thickening.

Fisher!

The bus was slowing.

Susan Fisher!

. . . above the piazza. The Villa is still owned by the Aldobrandini family. You will notice the central avenue of box trees. The park is noted for its grottos and Baroque fountains.

"Doubtless by Bernini," I said.

"Is that a *palm* tree?" said Helen.

The Villa is open to tourists only in the morning and upon ap-

plication to the officials of the Frascati Tourist Office. If you will consult your watches, you will see that it is now afternoon so we will proceed immediately to the largest of the Frascati wine cellars.

The aluminum cane with its rubber bulb thumping down, the leg swinging up and to the side, Kojak led the straggling procession towards a large grey stone building at the bottom end of the sloping piazza. A steep flight of steps led down to a terrace and the main entrance. Kojak, teeth bared with the exertion, started to stump and crab his way down.

"Oh, look at the poor old thing, Jack," said Helen. "He'll never manage her on his own down here."

I went back across to where they were still waiting to cross and put my arm under the old woman's. She seemed almost weightless.

"I appreciate this," he said, nodding vigorously on the other side of her. "Nelson Morrison. We're from Trenton, New Jersey."

"Not at all," I said. "Not at all. It's a pleasure."

The old woman did not look at either of us.

"That's the way," I said. "That's it."

"She's not a big talker. She doesn't speak very often, do you, Mother?"

Step by step we edged her down.

"But she enjoys it, don't you, Mother? You can tell she enjoys it. She likes to go out. We went on a boat, didn't we, Mother?"

"Nearly there," I said.

"Do you remember the boat in Venice, Mother? Do you? I think it's a naughty day today, isn't it? You're only hearing what you want to hear."

"One more," I said.

"But she did enjoy it. Every year you'll find us somewhere, won't he, Mother?"

Inside, the others were sitting at a refectory table in a vaulted cellar. It was lit by bare bulbs. It was cool, almost cold, after coming in out of the sunshine. In places, the brickwork glistened with moisture. Kojak, a cigarette held up between thumb and forefinger, was holding forth.

The cellars apparently extended under the building for more than a mile of natural caves and caverns. In the tunnels and corridors were more than a million bottles of wine. Today, however, there was nothing to see as the wine making did not take place until September. But famous and authentic food was available at the café and counter just a bit farther down the tunnel, and bottles of the finest Frascati were advantageously for sale. If we desired to buy wine, it would be his pleasure to negotiate for us.

He paused.

He surveyed us through the blue-tinted spectacles.

Slowly, he shook his head.

The five bottles of wine on the table were provided free of charge for us to drink on its own or as an accompaniment to food we might purchase. While he was talking, a girl with a sacking apron round her waist and with broken-backed men's shoes on her feet scuffed in with a tray of tumblers. Kojak started pouring the wine. It looked as if it had been drawn from a barrel minutes before. It was greenish and cloudy. It was thin and vile and tasted like tin. I decided to drink it quickly.

I didn't actually see it happen because I was leaning over saying something to Helen. I heard the melancholy man, the man who was travelling alone, say, "No thank you. I don't drink."

Glass chinking against glass.

"No thank you."

A chair scraping.

And there was Kojak mopping at his trouser leg with a handkerchief and grinding out what sounded like imprecations which were getting louder and louder. The melancholy man had somehow moved his glass away while Kojak was pouring or had tried to cover it or pushed away the neck of the bottle. Raised fist quivering, Kojak was addressing the vaulted roof.

Grabbing a bottleneck in his meaty hand, he upended the bottle over the little man's glass, glugging and splashing onto the table.

"Doesn't drink!" snarled Kojak.

He slammed the bottle down on the table.

"Doesn't drink!"

He flicked drops of wine onto the table off the back of his splashed hand.

"*Mama mia! Doesn't drink!*"

Grinding and growling he stumped off towards the café.

He left behind him a silence.

Into the silence, one of the women said,

"Perhaps it's a custom you're supposed to drink it? If you don't, it's insulting?"

"Now wait a minute," said her husband.

"Like covering your head?" she added.

"Maybe I'm out of line," said the other man, "but in my book that was inappropriate behaviour."

"I never did much like the taste of alcohol," said the melancholy man.

His accent was British and glumly northern.

"They seem to sup it with everything here," he said, shaking his head in gloomy disapproval.

"Where are you folks from?" said the man in the turquoise shirt.

"Canada," said Helen.

"You hear that, June? Ottawa? Did we visit Ottawa, June?"

"Maybe," said June, "being that he's European and . . ."

"It's nothing to do with being European," said Helen. "It's to do with being rude and a bully. And he's not getting a tip from *us*."

"Yeah," said June's husband, "and what's with all these jokes about women drivers? I'll tell you something, okay? *My wife drives better than I drive.* Okay?"

He looked around the table.

"Okay?"

"I've seen them," said the melancholy man, "in those little places where they eat their breakfasts standing up. I've seen them in there first thing in the morning—imagine—taking raw spirits."

The old woman sat hunched within a tweed coat, little eyes watching. She made me think of a fledgling that had fallen from the nest. Her tumbler was empty. She was looking at me. Then she seemed to be looking at the nearest bottle. I raised my eyebrows. Her eyes seemed to grow wider. I poured her more and her hand crept out to secure the glass.

"*Jack!*" whispered Helen.

"What the hell difference does it make?"

I poured more of the stuff for myself.

June and Chuck were from North Dakota. Norm and Joanne were from California. Chuck was in construction. Norm was on a disability pension and sold patio furniture. Joanne was a nurse. George Robinson was from Bradford and did something to do with textile machinery. Nelson and his mother travelled every summer and last summer had visited Yugoslavia but had suffered from the food.

I explained to June that it was quite possible that I sounded very like the guy on a PBS series because the series had been made by the BBC and I had been born in the UK but was now Canadian. She told me my accent was cute. I told her I thought her accent cute too. We toasted each other's accents. Helen began giving me looks.

June had bought a purse in Rome. Joanne had bought a purse in Florence. Florence was noted for purses. June and Chuck were going to Florence from Rome. Helen had bought a purse in Florence—the best area of Florence for purses being on the far side of the Ponte Vecchio. In Venice there were far fewer stores selling purses. Shoes, on the other hand, shoe stores were everywhere. Norm said he'd observed more shoe stores in Italy than in any other country in the world.

Nelson disliked olive oil.

George could not abide eggplants. Doris, George's wife who had died of cancer the year before, had never fancied tomatoes.

Nelson was flushed and becoming loquacious.

Chuck said he'd had better pizza in Grand Forks, North Dakota, where at least they put cheese on it and it wasn't runny.

George said the look of eggplants made him think of native women.

Joanne said a little pasta went a long way.

Milan?

After Venice, Norm and Joanne were booked into Milan. What was Milan like? Had anyone been there?

"Don't speak to me about Milan!" said Helen.

"Not a favourite subject with us," I said.

"We got mugged there," said Helen, "and they stole a gold bracelet I'd had since I was twenty-one."

"They," I said, "being three girls."

"We were walking along on the sidewalk just outside that monstrous railway station . . ."

"Three *girls*, for Christ's sake!"

"They came running up to us," said Helen.

"Two of them not more than thirteen years old," I said, "and the other about eighteen or nineteen."

"One of them had a newspaper sort of folded to show columns of figures and another had a bundle of tickets of some sort and they were waving these in our faces . . ."

"And talking at us very loudly and quickly . . ."

". . . and, well, *brandishing* these . . ."

". . . and sort of grabbing at you, pulling your sleeve . . ."

"*Touching* you," said Helen.

"*Right!*" said Norm. "Okay."

"*Exactly,*" said Joanne. "That's *exactly* . . ."

"And then," I said, "I felt the tallest girl's hand going inside my jacket—you know—to your inside pocket . . ."

"We were so *distracted*, you see," said Helen, "what with all the talking and them pointing at the paper and waving things under your nose and being *touched* . . ."

"So anyway," I said, "when I felt *that* I realized what was happening and I hit this girl's arm away and . . ."

"Oh, it was *awful!*" said Helen. "Because *I* thought they were just beggars, you see, or kids trying to sell lottery tickets or something, and I was really horrible to Jack for hitting this girl . . . I mean, he hit her *really hard* and I thought they were just begging so I couldn't believe he'd . . ."

"But the best part," I said, "was that I probably wasn't the main target in the first place because we walked on into the station and we were buying tickets—we were in the line—and Helen . . ."

"I'd suddenly felt the weight," said Helen. "The difference, I mean, and I looked down at my wrist and the bracelet was gone. I hadn't felt a thing when they'd grabbed it. Not with all that other touching. They must have pulled and broken the safety chain and . . ."

"Of course," I said, "I ran back to the entrance but . . ."

I spread my hands.

"Long gone."

"With us," said Joanne, "it was postcards and guidebooks they were waving about."

"Where?"

"Here. In Rome."

"Girls? The same?"

"Gypsies," said Norm.

"Did they get anything?" said Helen.

"A Leica," said Joanne.

"Misdirection of attention," said Norm.

"Were they girl-gypsies?" I said.

"Misdirecting," said Norm. "It's the basic principle of illusionism."

"I was robbed right at the airport," said Nelson.

"It must be a national *industry*," said George.

"They had a baby in a shawl and I was just standing there with Mother and they pushed this baby against my chest and well, naturally, you . . ."

"I don't *believe* this!" said Norm. "This I do not *believe*!"

"And while I was holding it, the other two women were shouting at me in Italian and they had a magazine they were showing me . . ."

"What did they steal?"

"Airplane ticket. Passport. Traveller's cheques. But I had some American bills in the top pocket of my blazer so they didn't get that."

"Did you feel it?" said Joanne.

He shook his head.

"No. They just took the baby and walked away and I only realized when I was going to change a traveller's cheque at the cambio office because we were going to get on the bus, weren't we, Mother?"

"A baby!" said June.

"But a few minutes later," said Nelson, "one of the women came up to me on her own with the ticket and my passport."

"Why would she give them back?" said Helen. "Don't they sell them to spies or something?"

"I paid her for them," said Nelson.

"Paid her?" said June.

"*Paid her!*" said Norm.

"*PAID!*" said Chuck.

"Ten dollars," said Nelson.

"They must have seen you coming!" said George.

"They must have seen *all* of you coming," said Chuck.

Nelson poured himself another murky tumbler of Frascati.

"It wasn't much," he said. "Ten dollars. She got what she wanted. I got what I wanted."

He shrugged. Raising the glass, he said,

"A short life but a merry one!"

We stared at him.

"I got what I wanted, didn't I, Mother? And then we went on the green-and-red bus, didn't we? Do you remember? On the green-and-red bus?"

The old woman started making loud squeak noises in her throat.

It was the first sound we'd heard her make.

She sounded like a guinea pig.

"It's time for tinkles!" said Nelson. "It's tinkle time."

And raising her up and half carrying her to the door of the women's malodorous toilet, he turned with her, almost as if waltzing, and backed his way in.

BOB GELDOF

*Bob Geldof was born in Ireland in 1954. A rock singer with
the Boomtown Rats, he became internationally renowned
for organizing Band Aid and then Live Aid, which played
to hundreds of millions of TV viewers around the world on
July 13, 1985. From Wembley Stadium in London and
J.F.K. Stadium in Philadelphia, he and other musicians
raised tens of millions of dollars for the starving in Ethiopia,
where he also helped to administer these funds. In 1974, at
loose ends, he had been a music writer for* The Georgia
Straight *in Vancouver. Twelve years later he published his
peripatetic autobiography,* Is That It? *He has recently released his second solo record album,* The Vegetarians of
Love.

----

from IS THAT IT?

I was delighted to be in Bangkok again. I loved the contrasts of South-
East Asia, at their most extreme in this city. The smells of traffic,
orchids, open sewers, frangipani, the extremes of heat on the street or
cold in the buildings, the violence of the crowd, the gentleness of an
individual, the snarling sounds of traffic by day and the almost soothing
insect, jungle noises at night, the openness of the people's character
and the closed nature of the political systems. I strolled down to the
Thai equivalent of Soho or Times Square, the Patpong, named after
Mr. Patpong, who owns the two streets that make up the area. There
are a hundred bars and a hundred girls in each one. I pushed open the
door of one and we sat down. To my astonishment the girls were dancing
on the tables to one of my songs, "When the Night Comes."

They were beautiful creatures, blank-eyed and indifferent, and, almost naked, they spun on tabletops like tiny hummingbirds oblivious of everything but the loud beat. When the Clash came on, a man who had been drinking alone in the corner stood up to dance by himself. He was like something out of *Apocalypse Now*; bald, no eyebrows, no arm hair, like an uncracked egg on permanent R & R. He stood in front of the big video screen and danced in slow, murderous karate moves, scissoring outwards in rigid, rhythmic precision to the 4/4 beat of the strobe system. The girls danced unenthusiastically on either side of him on small platforms beside the screen. No one danced with him. The spinning lights just caught the emptiness of his eyes. He was everywhere else but here, deep in the heart of nowhere. He never looked at the girls, or the boys for that matter. No one pestered him for a drink like the girls were doing to the other customers. No one suggested he spend the night with them. No one paid him attention. They understood blankness and they knew better than to trouble it. He stayed out there for four or five songs, then stopped dead. He moved a bit sideways. Behind him Mowgli rode an elephant and two girls did the Bangkok Hustle. Then he said very loudly, "What sort of fuckin' dump is this, eh?" Nobody could be bothered to answer. "You know something," he said, "fuck you!"

I had become quietly unsober. A man said, "You want girls?"

"No."

"You want boys?"

"No."

Now I was silently locked into my movie. Now I wanted to see all these things I'd read about in these places. I imagined if we went down far enough we'd find the Russian roulette scenes from *The Deerhunter*.

"You want donkey, animals?"

"No, no. Something else, show us something else." Show me something that makes me wonder why I want to see it, something that makes me sick and sad for us all, show me something where the other side of us is made real, except we don't have to live it or die it.

He took us through varying degrees of human degradation. How far down does it go, I wondered. "Something else," I said.

He took us to a tiny door in the side of a white-walled building.

137

It was hot and there was a smell of damp and dirt as we walked down a narrow passage with stone walls. It opened out into a tiny bar in a small unevenly shaped room with stained concrete walls. At the bar, beneath the neon, sat four totally emaciated opium addicts, their eyes blank.

Behind the bar stood an old woman with cold hard eyes and a face twisted with the malignity of a lifetime of exploiting the hopeless addicts whom she supplied. We were the only customers besides the junkies in the stinking room. She spoke English. "You want drink?" she snapped. Assuming that the water would not be safe to mix with the whisky, I asked for a Scotch and coke. She called to the back room and a naked girl with the same vacuous look in her eyes came out. She stood before me, put one leg up on the bar stool, stuck the Coke bottle into the lips of her vagina, and opened the bottle. The old woman clapped her hands and shrieked again and from the back came another girl with the same wasted look, carrying a filthy rug, which she put down on the floor. She was naked and very ugly. She lay down on it with her feet toward us and then threw her legs over her head so that her genitals stuck out toward us. She produced a packet of cigarettes and stuck two into her behind and three into her vagina. She lit them. We watched as she smoked them down to the end. I had an attack of giggling nausea. Afterward she rose, and with the same blank expression, produced two stubby candles, lit them, and dripped the hot wax onto her breasts. When the wax had formed a solid layer she took the candles and stuck them into the wax so that each one protruded from a breast. They dripped melted wax into her stomach. With them still balanced there, she opened her legs and drew a string of razor blades out of her vagina. Tricks of violence. The magic of self-loathing. I was beginning to get afraid. I was afraid of the physical danger if we continued our journey into degradation, but I was more afraid of the mental danger.

"You want to see more?" asked the woman. "Girl cut herself with knife."

"I want to go," I said. Sometime later we went back to the hotel. I think we'd have found those *Deerhunter* scenes if we'd wanted. Who needs it?

JOHN UPDIKE

Prolific author of novels, stories, criticism, poems, and memoirs, John Updike was born in 1932 in Shillington, Pennsylvania (as the dust jackets of his books frequently inform us), an American writer who has traveled to many parts of the world—twice to Venezuela—as an eloquent ambassador for American literature. In 1973 he traveled in Africa as a Fulbright Lecturer, and five years later published The Coup, *set in the imaginary, sub-Saharan country of Kush. "The purity of Kush is its strength," says its proud ruler and narrator Colonel Ellelloû. "In the lands of our oppressors the fat millions have forgotten how to live and look to the world's forsaken to remind them. . . ." Updike has lived in Massachusetts since 1957.*

VENEZUELA FOR VISITORS

All Venezuela, except for the negligible middle class, is divided between the Indians (*los indios*) and the rich (*los ricos*). The Indians are mostly to be found in the south, amid the muddy tributaries of the Orinoco and the god-haunted *tepuys* (mesas) that rear their fearsome mile-high crowns above the surrounding jungle, whereas the rich tend to congregate in the north, along the sunny littoral, in the burgeoning metropolis of Caracas, and on the semi-circular shores of Lake Maracaibo, from which their sumptuous black wealth is drawn. The negligible middle class occupies a strip of arid savanna in the center of the nation and a few shunned enclaves on the suburban slopes of Monte Avila.

The Indians, who range in color from mocha to Dentyne, are

generally under five feet tall. Their hairstyle runs to pageboys and severe bangs, with some tonsures in deference to lice. Neither sex is quite naked: the males wear around their waists a thong to which their foreskins are tied, pulling their penises taut upright; the females, once out of infancy, suffer such adornments as three pale sticks symmetrically thrust into their lower faces. The gazes of both sexes are melting, brown, alert, canny. The visitor, standing among them with his Nikon FE and L. L. Bean fannypack, is shy at first, but warms to their inquisitive touches, which patter and rub across his person with a soft, sandy insistence unlike both the fumblings of children and the caresses one Caucasian adult will give another. There is an infectious, wordless ecstasy in their touches, and a blank eagerness with yet some parameters of tact and irony. *These are human presences*, the visitor comes to realize.

The rich, who range in color from porcelain to mocha, are generally under six feet tall. Their hairstyle runs to chignons and blow-dried trims. Either sex is elegantly clad: the males favor dark suits of medium weight (nights in Caracas can be cool), their close English cut enhanced by a slight Latin flare, and shirts with striped bodies but stark-white collars and French cuffs held by agates and gold; the females appear in a variety of gowns and mock-military pants suits, Dior and de la Renta originals flown in from Paris and New York. The gazes of both sexes are melting, brown, alert, canny. The visitor, standing among them in his funky Brooks Brothers suit and rumpled blue button-down, is shy at first, but warms to their excellent English, acquired at colleges in London or "the States," and to their impeccable manners, which conceal, as their fine clothes conceal their skins, rippling depths of Spanish and those dark thoughts that the mind phrases to itself in its native language. They tell anecdotes culled from their rich international lives; they offer, as the evening deepens, confidences, feelers, troubles. These, too, are human presences.

The Indians live in *shabonos*—roughly circular lean-tos woven beautifully of palm thatch in clearings hacked and burned out of the circumambient rain forest. A *shabono* usually rots and is abandoned within three years. The interiors are smoky, from cooking fires, and eye diseases are common among the Indians. They sleep, rest, and die in hammocks (*cinchorros*) hung as close together as pea pods on a vine.

Their technology, involving in its pure state neither iron nor the wheel, is yet highly sophisticated: the chemical intricacies of curare have never been completely plumbed, and with their blowpipes of up to sixteen feet in length the Indians can bring down prey at distances of over thirty meters. They fish without hooks, by employing nets and thrashing the water with poisonous lianas. All this sounds cheerier than it is. It is depressing to stand in the gloom of a *shabono*, the palm thatch overhead infested with giant insects, the Indians drooping in their hammocks, their eyes diseased, their bellies protuberant, their faces and limbs besmirched with the same gray-brown dirt that composes the floor, their possessions a few brown baskets and monkey skins. Their lives are not paradise but full of anxiety—their religion a matter of fear, their statecraft a matter of constant, nagging war. To themselves, they are "the people" (*Yanomami*); to others, they are "the killers" (*Waikás*).

The rich dwell in *haciendas*—airy long ranch houses whose roofs are of curved tile and, surprisingly, dried sugar-cane stalks. Some *haciendas* surviving in Caracas date from the sixteenth century, when the great valley was all but empty. The interiors are smoky, from candlelit dinners, and contact lenses are common among the rich. The furniture is solid, black, polished by generations of servants. Large paintings by Diebenkorn, Stella, Baziotes, and Botero adorn the white plaster walls, along with lurid religious pictures in the colonial Spanish style. The appliances are all modern and paid for; even if the oil in Lake Maracaibo were to give out, vast deposits of heavy crude have been discovered in the state of Bolívar. All this sounds cheerier than it is. The rich wish they were in Paris, London, New York. Many have condominiums in Miami. *Haute couture* and abstract painting may not prove bulwark enough. Constitutional democracy in Venezuela, though the last dictator fled in 1958, is not so assured as may appear. Turbulence and tyranny are traditional. Che Guevara is still idealized among students. To themselves, the rich are good, decent, amusing people; to others, they are "*reaccionarios.*"

Missionaries, many of them United States citizens, move among the Indians. They claim that since Western civilization, with all its diseases and detritus, must come, it had best come through them. Nevertheless, Marxist anthropologists inveigh against them. Foreign experts, many of them United States citizens, move among the rich. They claim they are just helping out, and that anyway the oil industry was nationalized five years ago. Nevertheless, Marxist anthropologists are not mollified. The feet of the Indians are very broad in front, their toes spread wide for climbing avocado trees. The feet of the rich are very narrow in front, their toes compressed by pointed Italian shoes. The Indians seek relief from tension in the use of *ebene*, or *yopo*, a mind-altering drug distilled from the bark of the *ebene* tree and blown into the user's nose through a hollow cane by a colleague. The rich take cocaine through the nose, and frequent mind-altering discotheques, but more customarily imbibe cognac, *vino blanco*, and Scotch, in association with colleagues.

These and other contrasts and comparisons between the Indians and the rich can perhaps be made more meaningful by the following anecdote: A visitor, after some weeks in Venezuela, was invited to fly to the top of a *tepuy* in a helicopter, which crashed. As stated, the *tepuys* are supposed by the Indians to be the forbidden haunts of the gods; and, indeed, they present an exotic, attenuated vegetation and a craggy geology to the rare intruder. The crash was a minor one, breaking neither bones nor bottles (a lavish picnic, including *mucho vino blanco*, had been packed). The bottles were consumed, the exotic vegetation was photographed, and a rescue helicopter arrived. In the Cessna back to Caracas, the survivors couldn't get enough of discussing the incident and their survival, and the red-haired woman opposite the visitor said, "I *love* the way you pronounce '*tepuy*.' " She imitated him: *tupooey*. "Real zingy," she said. The visitor slowly realized that he was being flirted with, and that therefore *this woman was middle-class*. In Venezuela, only the negligible middle class flirts. The Indians kidnap or are raped; the rich commandeer, or languorously give themselves in imperious surrender.

The Indians tend to know only three words of Spanish: "*¿Como se llama?*" ("What is your name?"). In Indian belief, to give one's name is to place oneself in the other's power. And the rich, when one is introduced, narrow their eyes and file one's name away in their mysterious depths. Power among them flows along lines of kinship and intimacy. After an imperious surrender, a rich female gazes at her visitor with new interest out of her narrowed, brown, melting, kohl-ringed eyes. He has become someone to be reckoned with, if only as a potential source of financial embarrassment. "Again, what is your name?" she asks.

Los indios and los ricos rarely achieve contact. When they do, mestizos result, and the exploitation of natural resources. In such lies the future of Venezuela.

MURRAY BAIL

Murray Bail was born in Adelaide in 1941 and now lives in Sydney. He has traveled the world, living for a number of years in Bombay and London. He is the author of a collection of stories, The Drover's Wife, *and two novels,* Homesickness, *which won the National Book Council Award in Australia in 1980, and* Holden's Performance. *He is also editor of* The Faber Book of Contemporary Australian Short Stories. *What follows is a fictional account of a group of Australian tourists in New York, who—as in other foreign cities they visit in this epistemological novel— find it difficult to dissociate appearance and reality. Bail parodies the conventions of tourism and its naïve expectations, questioning the very idea of travel when it is governed by moral acquiescence.*

----

from HOMESICKNESS

Divided more or less into two: there were those who frowned in silence trying to hold and separate the constellation of impressions, mainly useless impressions; and those who cluttered it with words, any words, shattering the approximate form of things. The first were easily recognizable. In the foyer they pondered the carpet with their toes, as if they'd found a fleeting impression underfoot. The rest, comprising the hub, stood as a group distinguished by skipping head movements and voice, and light-coloured clothing. A surprising number stamped in the one spot, rubbing their hands. It wasn't cold. To fill in time they offered cracks, quips, comments, and isolated adverbs. Yes. For example,

Garry: "Did everyone bring their mosquito nets?" They received only casual acknowledgement, but were still appreciated. It was considered normal: mortar between the bricks.

They were finishing mugs of instant coffee—"good old nylon coffee"—a crack—and two or three, the ladies, had trouble fitting their mouths around the huge hero sandwiches. Many wore coats, furs, mufflers, and whatnot; and the early tea certainly added to the atmosphere. It was almost dark outside. The traffic had more of a distant night sound. Abruptly Doug Cathcart breathed on the pale blue eyes of his binoculars and felt for his handkerchief; Kaddok there had the leather-hooded telephoto lens protruding ready from his abdomen.

The tour organizer from the hotel hurried over. Natty, natty.

"Alright, gang," he said looking at his watch, "you're on. Good luck."

Good luck? What does that mean?

But the entrepreneur clapped Gerald on the back, smiling. Americans can do that: easy.

The Land-Rovers, long wheelbase models, were fitted with metal spades and spare cans of juice, spotlights and winches. Driving the front one a barrel-chested American had a scraggy silver beard, a scar on his forehead, and whisky on his breath. When he spoke he either swore or grunted in some Indian lingo—a nasty bastard. He was the Park Ranger. The second driver, his partner, never left the vehicle and only afterward when the party compared notes did they discover he was the Ranger's exact double. Both men also wore the same crumpled safari jacket equipped with sheath knife, a cartridge clip, and a water bottle. In this respect they were similar to their specially equipped Land-Rovers.

A practised forward-arching motion of his arm out the window; the Ranger then shoved into whining four-wheel drive and the convoy got going.

The Game Park was located in the central most unexpected part of New York, uneven terrain of abandoned benches, of bushes, rock formations, and small ravines.

The Ranger wasn't answering questions.

So Phillip North said to Sasha, "Well I'm told they have foxes, jack-rabbits, skunks, and owls. And of course the squirrels."

At that the Ranger let out a roar of a laugh and shouted over his shoulder: "You hear that, Charo? That's rich."

"Yes, bwana."

A black man in khaki shorts and bare feet crouched in the back; had to uncoil slightly to answer.

Muttering to himself the Ranger laughed again or rather hissed through his teeth. It sounded remarkably like the Land-Rover engine.

Wedged against him, Sasha glanced at North. He shrugged. Better leave him alone.

Turning into the Park, the headlights were switched off and Violet in the back was told to douse her cigarette. The Ranger drove carefully. Many of the trees had lost their leaves. The track wandered in and out; edges of dark branches tried to scratch and sprang back. Black bushes bulged like boulders, yet ordinary footpaths and stone benches were glimpsed at the sides. Before long the petroleum hum and horns of Detroit faded, the lights of the surrounding tall buildings almost all blotted out. The Land-Rover swung into a large bush; they were enveloped unexpectedly in leaves.

He switched the engine off.

All quiet then: the leaves rustled when anyone moved.

Quickly, they followed the Ranger out some thirty paces, all but Kaddok stumbling and tripping, the virtually invisible black man taking up the rear, lugging two wicker hampers under his arm like suitcases.

The Ranger shinned up a large Black Oak—remarkably agile for a man of his size and age. The pleat in his safari jacket opened to reveal a Colt .45 in its tan holster. Violet and Gerald were giggling and whispering, but a sharp word came from above among the vibrating bending branches. Gwen, the first to follow, found a wooden ladder. Doug began pushing his wife up. Heh, heh. The life of the party, Garry, bunted Sasha with his head, and she told him to stop; the others were glancing around furtively instead of laughing.

So subtle and naturally camouflaged was the panelled treehouse that they were inside it before they fully realized. In the moonlight they made out an upholstered bench around three sides, and sat down automatically, shoulder-to-shoulder.

The bearer too finally made the climb with the hampers, and

after giving him a playful pinch in the stomach the Ranger closed the door.

"You can speak normally," he said in his twang, "if you whisper."

They could hear him breathing heavily as he made space for himself by the slot which they now noticed opened like a window behind their necks. It explained the draught, the cold.

Staring outside into the dark the Ranger moved his hand and found the special switch.

"You've got to hand it to the Yanks," Garry whispered, the first words spoken.

Directly below, an ordinary-looking street lamp coruscated then lit up with unexpected vividness a typical intersection of footpaths which are found in the park. A bench and a casually placed trash bin set the scene, and the surrounding grass was pale green. A newspaper blew across and clutched the base of the lamp. Inside the specially constructed blind the same light illuminated their faces and shadowed the walls.

They looked around, interested. For some reason Gwen Kaddok and Atlas both smiled.

"I'm not liking this," Sasha whispered.

"They can't see us," the Ranger breathed. And he looked around at them, settled on Violet, then Louisa, before returning to the window. Those with cameras and binoculars set them up and waited.

The effectiveness of .357 Magnum rifles cropped up in a polite and professional conversation with Phillip North. On this the Ranger proved to be extremely knowledgeable. Elephant and aardvark entered the conversation. Single-syllable impressions of Africa.

"My herocs," Violet yawned. "How boring."

"Quiet, woman."

The Ranger glanced at his watch and took a swig from his hip flask. Soon after, the bearer opened the hampers for the others. It was good eating the ham sandwiches and coffee, steaming black. It all came in the price.

"Ever shot a red roo?" Garry leaned across. That reminded him. Ha, ha. Friend of his, Bill Smallacombe, last year—

"Bwana!"

The Ranger held up his hand to the others.

"Is that our decoy?" Garry enquired. He gave a low whistle.

"It should be an old man on crutches." The Ranger looked at his watch. "I knew he was late."

So they looked at the woman in the fur coat. She was young and paced up and down as if she waited for someone. They could see her white face.

"She shouldn't be there," the Ranger went on. He was being earnest. "She could get hurt."

"Not a bad decoy though," Garry laughed, a bit nervous.

The others went silent.

"A mob was sighted at dusk farther along. About five; all males. She's going to frighten them off or she'll get hurt. She'd better move on."

He took another swig and scanned the undergrowth behind and on either side of the woman. The street lamp formed a yellow canopy blurred at the edges, hundreds of moths circling the centre as the woman paced up and down.

"She's going to spoil everything."

"It is finished," said Charo. He stood up.

"No. Wait."

No one spoke. Experienced travellers, they made allowances. In the poor light Ken Hofmann could move his hand to touch the neck of Violet Hopper. Louisa had squeezed Borelli's hand.

"Capitalism," Borelli was saying to Gerald, "free enterprise, is by nature violent. It's structured on power, speed, and visibility. It relies on them. Visual differences and selfishness are promoted—"

"There has to be a winner," said Kaddok.

"No wonder those who are flung out to the edges feel the recourse is simply to grab."

"Survival of the fittest, the law of the jungle?" Kaddok threw in. Another platitude.

"But you're not political, are you?" Louisa whispered.

"Not especially, no. I've just been thinking."

Phillip North tapped the Ranger's arm. "Shouldn't we warn her, call out or something?"

"No, that would frighten them."

This being their last night in America, the Cathcarts took the opportunity to scribble messages on a pile of postcards.

"Bwana," whispered the bearer.

The woman had stopped walking. She swung around.

"No!" cried Sasha.

"Shut up," the Ranger hissed.

Puerto Ricans in leather, one white face among them, stepped out from the shadows, nonchalant-like, as dark and as silent as the shadows, surrounding her. The woman glanced one way, then the other. She held the neck of her coat.

"They're big," the Ranger breathed.

North shook the Ranger's arm. Leaning forward, watching intently, he didn't seem to feel it.

The woman tried running. She pushed against one and fell. They closed in around her, the circle. Rolling on her back she tried kicking, and lost a shoe. First, her handbag was pulled off her. She began sobbing.

"Somebody stop them!" Sasha cried. "The animals!"

The Ranger pulled her back from the window.

"You wanted to come. Now stay. The woman has committed an error in life. Nature takes its course. That's life." He turned to North, "You too, sit!"

Poor woman, her white thighs parted in the moonlight. The fur was pulled open, her dress torn up and sideways. Others pinned her arms. And the shadows multiplied the union in all the angles, violent, interlocking blackness.

None if any noticed Shiela, her mouth and eyes wide, and the tremor which spread through from her warmth, electrical at the nerve-ends, which suddenly, violently, splayed her feet. Shiela stifled a cry. But then while a few tried to preserve some detachment the majority were breathing in and shaking their heads at the spectacle, or making that perplexed clicking sound with their tongues. "Chhhhrist!" Garry let out hoarsely. He spoke for the majority. "They're animals, look at that."

The Cathcarts had addressed all the postcards and began licking the stamps.

Sasha had settled to the floor, her head in her arms, comforted by North. And Louisa with Borelli was crying, shaking her head.

But their own position was felt to be precarious, preventing intervention. Directly below were five armed with freedom of excitement and assorted flick-knives. At least up in the tree they were downwind.

She lay, an exhausted animal, the woman, a crippled furry thing, split and torn. She moved her foot as the last two fought over their turn. The tall white one fell on top of her.

Sudden darkness. The light was cut. They felt the bulk of the Ranger quickly swing around. "Who did that? Where are you?"

"We've seen enough," said Borelli.

The voices in the street rose and fell. Then there was quiet.

"This is not your country, boy. This is my business."

"You're wrong there."

"That's right," said North.

"It wasn't what we thought," Gerald explained.

"It wasn't what you thought? Oh you're rich." Fumbling around for the switch. "I'll find this and punch you in the face."

"This doesn't happen in our country."

"I'm going to punch you in the face."

Borelli's walking stick hit the window ledge. "The light can go in a minute. Then you can do what you like."

"Very well done. Splendid," said Kaddok, who had followed it through Gwen's whisper. "Well worth the trip. Thank you very much."

Gwen pulled him down. "We're not going just yet."

Muttering obscenities the Ranger shoved against one or two. Lunging forward he switched on the street lamp. It swam before them. They blinked. A white handkerchief fluttered on the ground, nothing more. They listened, and decided it was safe to go down. Hofmann and others quickly inspected the site before returning to the hotel.

PART FOUR

LUCKING OUT WITH A BAD PATCH OF ROAD

It was as if I had burst through the bottom of my plans and was falling through darkness. I would continue to fall: there was absolutely nothing to do until dawn. My feet hurt; I was tired, dirty, sweating; I had not eaten all day. This was not the time or the place to reflect on the futility of the trip, and yet Costa Rica had seemed to promise better than this dark end.

—*Paul Theroux*

NORMAN LEWIS

Born in London in 1903, Norman Lewis served in North Africa and Italy during World War II, and his Naples '44 *is considered by some to be one of the best books about the war. His travels in the early 1950s to Southeast Asia and Burma are narrated in* A Dragon Apparent *and* Golden Earth. *In later years he continued to travel all over the world, to Arabia, Africa, India, and especially to the Spanish-speaking countries of Central and South America. His many novels often include exotic settings abroad. A selection of his best journalism was recently collected in* A View of the World, *which includes what he considers his most influential work, the account of a 1968 journey to Brazil, when he reported at length on Indian genocide. His earlier travels to Asia were more disinterested. In the following excerpt, from his journey to Burma, he is traveling by lorry to Lashio.*

---

from GOLDEN EARTH

Through the brazen hours that followed high noon, we crept onward through a tunnel of glittering verdure. Then in the early afternoon came the official stop for breakfast. We were in a tiny hamlet, a few branch-and-leaf huts around a well. A single half-blind pariah dog slunk up to inspect us and was immediately chased away by a pair of lean, hairy swine that came rushing out of one of the huts. A cavern had been hollowed out of the wall of rock that formed the background to the village, and wisps of smoke trailed up through a sort of bamboo veranda that had been built over the mouth of it. This infernal place was the restaurant.

The moment had now come when all European prejudices about food had to be abandoned; all fears of typhoid or dysentery had to be banished resolutely from the mind. Even if I held back now and refused to enter this murky grotto, there was a long succession of others awaiting me, and ultimately sheer hunger would settle the matter. Remote journeyings had their advantages, the occasional sense of adventure, the novelties of experience. They also had their drawbacks, and this was one of them. And as there was no turning back from them, it was just as well to be bold.

In the dim interior—a model of most remote oriental eating houses—we were awaited by a cook who was naked to the waist. Tattooed dragons writhed among the cabalistic figures on his chest and arms. A snippet of intestine was clinging to a finger, which, shaken off, was caught in mid-air by an attendant cat. Tin Maung gave an order and in due course the headwaiter arrived, a rollicking Shan with shining bald head and Manchu moustaches, carrying a dish heaped with scrawny chickens' limbs, jaundiced with curry, a bowl of rice, and a couple of aluminum plates. When uncertain how to behave, watch what the others do. A few minutes later I was neatly stripping the tendons from those saffron bones; kneading the rice into a form in which it could be carried in the fingers to the mouth. But the *spécialité de la maison* was undoubtedly pickled cabbage, with garlic and chili pepper. This Shan delicacy was gravely recommended by Tin Maung as "full of vitamins." It had a sharp, sour flavour, for which a taste was easily acquired; I should certainly have missed this and many other similar experiences had I been able to follow the advice given in the *Burma Handbook*: ". . . there are no hotels, and the traveller, when he quits the line of railway or Irawadi steamer, must get leave from the deputy commissioner of the district to put up at government bungalows, and must take bedding, a cook, and a few cooking utensils."

Although Tin Maung had said that it was most unlikely that we should reach Lashio in one day, we found ourselves by the late afternoon within a few miles of the town. We had just crossed the Nam Mi river, where I had admired the spectacle of landslides of the brightest red earth plunging down the hillside into deep, green water, when we were stopped by a posse of soldiers. They told us that Chinese Nationalist bandits had temporarily cut the road, only four kilometres from Lashio, and had shot up and looted the truck in front of ours. As this had happened several hours before, it was not exactly a narrow escape. But there was a delay until an officer of the Shan police arrived to tell us we could carry on. As we came into the outskirts of Lashio, the sun set. Flocks of mynas and parakeets had appeared in the treetops, where they went through the noisy, twilight manoeuvres of starlings in a London square.

In accordance with the recommendations already quoted from the *Burma Handbook*, I asked the driver of the lorry to put me down at the Dak Bungalow, but there appeared to be some difficulty, and Tin Maung told me that it had been taken over by the army. He invited me to come to his house, where I could leave my luggage while making further inquiries. Lashio had been partly destroyed by bombing but, it seemed, rebuilt along the lines of the English hill-station it had once been, with detached bungalows, each with its own garden. We stopped at one of these. It was now nearly dark, and a young man clad only in shorts came running down the path, and opened the gate. Approaching us, he crossed his arms and bowed in a rather Japanese fashion, only partially straightening himself when he turned away. Tin Maung nodded toward the baggage, and uttered a word, and the still stooping figure snatched up both suitcases and hurried away to the house with them. He was not, as I imagined at the time, a servant, but a younger brother.

I was then invited to go and sit on the balcony of the house, where I was met by Tin Maung's father. U Thein Zan looked like a lean Burmese version of one of those rollicking Chinese gods of good fortune. Even when his mouth was relaxed his eyes were creased up as if in a spasm of mirth. He had learned, in fact, as I soon discovered, to express his emotions in terms of smiles: a gay smile (the most frequent), a tolerant smile (for the shortcomings of others), a roguish smile (when his own weaknesses were under discussion), a rueful smile (for his sharp losses, the state of Burma, and humanity in general).

In the background hovered the mother. In her case no formal presentation was made. The three of us, father, son, and myself, sat there on the balcony making occasional disjointed remarks about the political situation. From time to time the younger brother came out of the house, bowed, and went in. The mother appeared, curled herself up in a chair well removed from the important conclave of males, and lit up a cheroot. There was no sign of stir or excitement. Later I learned that this was the return of the eldest son after an absence of two years, during which time the brother next in age to him had been killed by insurgents. I could have imagined Chinese etiquette imposing these rigid standards of self-control, but it came as a great surprise that old-fashioned Burmese families should follow such a rule of conduct.

The matter of finding somewhere to sleep now came up, and the younger son was sent off to make inquiries about a bungalow belonging to the public works department. He was soon back to say that it was full of soldiers, although there might be a room free the next night. Upon this Tin Maung said that I would have to sleep in his father's house, and signalled for my baggage to be taken inside. I apologized to the old man for the trouble I was putting him to, whereupon he handsomely said, "Anyone my son brings home becomes my son," accompanying this speech with such a truly genial smile that it was impossible to feel any longer ill at ease.

But before there could be any question of retiring for the night, U Thein Zan said, there were formalities to be attended to. He thought that owing to the unsettled local conditions I ought to be on the safe side by reporting, without delay, to the deputy superintendent of police, and after dressing himself carefully, he took up a lantern and accompanied me to the functionary's house. The D.S.P. soon mastered his surprise at the visit, seemed relieved that I was under the control of such a pillar of local society as U Thein Zan, and found me several forms to fill in. In the morning, he said, I must report to the office of the special commissioner for the region, and to the commanding officer of the garrison. The latter obligation was one of which nothing had been said in Rangoon, and I decided to avoid it if possible. With Chinese bandits in the vicinity I could imagine this officer considering himself justified in putting me under some kind of restrictive military protection, or even sending me under escort back to Mandalay. When I brought up the matter of the attack on the truck, the D.S.P. firmly announced that it had been the work of local Shans.

We went back home and sat for a while chatting desultorily and listening to the radio. Two stations were coming in faintly well: La Voix d'Islam broadcast on a beam from Radio Toulouse, and a station which might have been Peking, because the announcements were in Chinese, and the music Western and evangelical in flavour, with the exception of one playing of a marching song of the Red Army. U Thein Zan was a fervent Buddhist and liked to talk about his religion whenever he could. He was delighted because the next day a famous abbot would be preaching several sermons at the local monastery and he was to play a prominent part in the welcoming ceremony.

Soon after this the family retired to bed. The house was a rather flimsy construction raised on piles about three feet from the ground. It consisted of two main rooms and a kitchen, had a palm-thatched roof and a floor of split bamboo. I was left to myself in one of the rooms, while the five members of the family—another brother had just turned up—were to sleep in the other. Clearly the old mother did not approve of this arrangement, which I gathered, from her gestures, probably went against her ideas on true hospitality. Perhaps she felt that I was not being treated as a member of the family. At all events she protested and was with difficulty overruled by Tin Maung, who probably told her that communal sleeping was not a European custom; and with a shrug of bewildered resignation she let the thing go as it was. Bars were put over the door and a shutter fitted to the window. The younger brother appeared carrying a camp bed, which he erected in a corner. By the side of this Tin Maung set a stool with a lamp, a glass of water, a saucer of nuts, and several giant cheroots. Before going into the other room he told me not to put the lamp out. I wondered why.

Taking off my clothes, I put on a cotton longyi which I had bought in Mandalay. It had been recommended as the coolest thing to sleep in. Turning the lamp low, I lay down on the camp bed, and was just dozing off when I heard a slight creaking, and through half-opened eyes saw Tin Maung, going slowly round the room, flashing an electric torch on the walls and ceiling. I asked him what he was looking for, and he said, "Sometimes there are moths." He then tip-toed quickly from the room. My eyelids came together and then opened, reluctantly, at a faint scuffling sound. The bungalow consisted of a framework of timber upon which sheets of some white-washed material had been nailed. It was like a very ramshackle example of a small black-and-white Essex cottage. On one wall, just above my feet, was a Buddha shrine, containing a rather unusual reclining Buddha and offerings of dried flowers in vases. From behind this there now appeared several rats, not large, but lively, which began to move in a series of hesitant rushes along the beam running round the room. There were soon seven of them in sight.

I watched this movement with dazed curiosity for a time, and then began to doze again. Then, suddenly, an extraordinary protective faculty came into use. Once during the recent war, I had noticed that whilst my sleep was not disturbed by our own howitzers firing in the same field, I was inevitably awakened when the dawn stillness was troubled by the thin whistle of enemy shells, passing high overhead. Now, on the verge of unconsciousness, I felt in the skull, rather than heard, a faint scratching of tiny scrambling limbs. Something, I half-dreamed and half-thought, was climbing up the leg of the camp bed. Turning my head I caught a brief, out-of-focus glimpse of a small black body on the pillow by my cheek. Then in a scamper it was gone. It was a scorpion, I thought, or a hairy spider of the tarantula kind. I linked its appearance with Tin Maung's mysterious inspection of the room with his torch. What was to be done? I got up, thinking that whatever this animal was, it would come back to achieve its purpose as soon as I fell asleep. I thought of sitting up in the chair and staying awake for the rest of the night, but when I picked up the lamp to turn up the wick, it felt light, and shaking it produced only a faint splashing of oil in the bottom of the container. In a short time then, the lamp would go out, and my scorpion or whatever it was, with others of its kind, would come boldly up through the interstices in the bamboo floor. The next impulse was to spend the night walking round Lashio, and I went to unfasten the door bar. Immediately the pariah dog that lived under the house, where it lay all night snuffling and whining, burst into snarling life, furiously echoed by all the dogs in the district. I thought of the trigger-happy police of Lashio, who would have Chinese bandits on their mind.

The best thing, I decided, was to use my mosquito net and hope that I could sleep without any part of my body coming into contact with the sides. Fixing it up as best I could, I crawled in and tucked the net well under me. For a while I watched the movement, blurred through the net, of the rats; then consciousness faded again. I was awakened by a not very sharp pain in the lip and putting up my hand found myself clutching a cockroach which had fastened there. This was the last disturbance; when I next woke it was to the mighty whirring of hornbills flying overhead, and the daylight was spreading through the shutters.

PATRICK MARNHAM

Patrick Marnham was born in Jerusalem in 1943 and educated at Oxford University in jurisprudence. His first book, Road to Katmandu, *describes his trip overland from Turkey to Nepal in 1968. His second book,* Fantastic Invasion: Dispatches from Contemporary Africa, *is a report for the Minority Rights Group on the nomads of Sahel. He has published a book on Lourdes and another,* So Far from God: A Journey to Central America, *about a journey to Central America in the mid 1980s, which won the Thomas Cook Award.*

···

from ROAD TO KATMANDU

The Indian trains were filthy, unreliable, stifling, and hopelessly overcrowded. And the third class had one other distinction. It was virtually free. Because of the great numbers traveling, it was quite impossible for any ticket collection to take place during the journey, and at the stations most of the mob just rushed the barrier.

Euphoric at the thought of a free ride as far as the Nepalese border, we took the wrong train and did not discover our mistake until we reached Patna on the south side of the Ganges. Not only was this too far south. It was too far east as well. The great trek to the southeast had to be completed by a final northwestern leg. At Patna we climbed wearily off the train and made inquiries for the Ganges ferry. In Delhi it had been reliably reported that the monsoon had reached Patna some weeks ago. The men in Delhi should not believe everything they read in the weather reports. Patna lay under an identical yellow pall, and the people waited sullenly for the rain.

We found the river with the aid of a bicycle rickshaw boy. There were no buses in town, and so we succumbed to his blandishments and loaded our packs and ourselves onto his carriage. He carved a path through the packed streets and the solid air, ringing his bell furiously—the sinews on his legs standing out like cords. Even on this short journey we both managed to sleep; free train rides are not restful. At the quay a great crowd was gathered waiting patiently for the boat. By the booking office window an old lady was sitting in a pool of her own water, a few feet away her grandchildren slept on the floor. Other children played by the river edge, jumping in and out of the brown flood and occasionally retrieving charred wooden trays that floated downstream. These they raced against one another: They were the cremated remains of the funeral rafts from Benares.

Eventually a tubby paddle steamer with a thin smokestack slipped its moorings and drew into the quay. There was a great rush to board the single gangplank. Somehow the press forced itself up, and after another pointless delay we set off. Out into the holy Ganges we paddled, while the glutinous tide rushed past the ship, its surface speckled with ashes and garlands. For the first time since the ferry over the Bosporus we had to cross more than a stream; it was an unnatural experience for islanders. Nobody could say when we would reach the far shore, or whether there would be a train there. Nothing was visible out on the water except the haze and the rushing ashes. Shortly after sailing we went aground.

The voyage dragged on during the afternoon, Perkins slept heavily sitting on a bench, and a curious crowd gathered silently around him to puzzle over the contrast between his ragged shoes and his expensive cameras. Smuts from the smokestack soon covered every passenger. They were less visible on us than on the white-clad Indians. Toward evening the mist cleared a little, and we could make out a mud bank on the horizon. Slowly, silently, we approached it—beyond, a rise in the ground revealed a railhead. As the boat drew in fifty men in black shorts and faded red vests, oblivious of the churning blades, leaped on with a wild shout. They were not dacoits but free-lance porters, and gangs of them fought for the privilege of carrying the richer-looking bags. We stumbled ashore and began the ascent to the train. Someone had said that it went to the border.

Even by Indian standards (we had heard of a train in Delhi which started twenty-four hours late), this train was remarkable. For a start it was the most crowded train we had yet seen. It was physically impossible to board it. People were already standing along its outer side, clinging to the window frames and climbing onto its roof. There was no question of us *and* our packs getting a ride. One or the other had to go. Nor were we the only disappointed travelers. Struggling up the hill behind us came a litter borne by two porters. A girl lay inside it, thin and pouring sweat. At every lurch she cried out in pain; she was followed by her family, her mother murmuring to her, the rest silent. There was apparently no room for her either.

The train was already an hour late, and there seemed every possibility that it would be lingering here for most of the night. In the event, and following the litter to the front, we found a better solution. There was a first-class truck which was virtually empty. The girl in the litter was lifted into one-half of this. We explored the other. Within were four major generals. And two empty seats. We climbed up. "One moment. This is a first-class compartment."

We knew. Did we have tickets? Of course. Could they see them? No, they were not ticket inspectors. So sorry; without our tickets being seen we would not be allowed to enter. The generals would see to that. And so reluctantly we departed to buy two first-class tickets from Manendru Ghat to Raxaul. And reluctantly the major generals allowed us to rejoin them. At least we had found out where we were and where we were going.

The generals next devoted themselves to interrogation. A toothy one began it. "Where are you going?" "Where have you come from?" "How?" "Are you from the Peace Corps?" "Are you students?" They could understand none of the answers. Why were we moving around India in this unkempt condition at this time of year? "What is the *aim* and *object* of all this movement?" Wearily we tried to explain, but the result was a failure. "Are you on a government grant?"

For the rest of the journey they stared at us, solemnly marking down each detail for some future identification. The train jolted slowly through the night from one crowded halt to the next. The electric fans did not work. The iron bars on the windows proved useful hand holds for the people outside. By the light of two dim bulbs I could make out the enormous cockroaches on the floor. It became a point of honor with me to kill any that moved. The generals were bemused by this— "Those creatures are *to*tally harmless."

Slowly the heat and the wagon melted us down; we began to resemble two half-consumed lollipops that had been dropped on a cinema floor. To boost morale, we applied a liberal sprinkling of baby powder. Then we curled up on the benches and slept. Powdered lollipops sleeping like babies in a nest of generals. Nobody who smelled like us could be really dirty. The generals sat erect in their starched British uniforms, cross-legged on their bench, brown-brogued and sockless, looking inscrutably on.

Once again the journey passed into a dream phase, only remembered through waves of tiredness and confusion. The train crawled along without the least sense of urgency. It paused on the half-hour for half an hour. At each halt, one could just make out the dim forms of a packed crowd lying on the platform. Nobody stirred. The engine, whenever one went forward to inspect it, was deserted. The signal room equally so. Suddenly without warning or reason we might jolt forward again through the night. It became possible to understand Indian Railways' enormous casualty figures. On the signal-box door, there was a prettily embroidered motto: "THERE IS NO ONE SO DESERVING OF PRAISE AS THE CAREFUL MAN. . . ."

In the deserted stationmaster's offices there would be a wood fire and a bank of gleaming brass levers. There were mugs of cocoa stamped with the company's monogram, and a jumble of Victorian telegraphic machinery. The whole place snugged and glowed like a northern Christmas. It was as though one had been transported to a small Welsh mountain branch line of fifty years ago. The machinery lay to hand, the domestic details were authentic, the stove had been cast in Derby. Only the will to operate the system was absent. But the relics of this impeccable plan remained—to render grotesque the chaos which had succeeded it. In the dark corner behind the broom cupboard one expected to see the ghost of Isambard Kingdom Brunel wringing his hands over these cunning and now misused devices. He would have felt at one with the legionnaires haunting Hadrian's Wall.

Somehow during the night, stumbling across stations with unreadable names, we managed two changes. At one of these we were told that we would have to wait a few hours for the train to Raxaul. The platform was too crowded to lie on. We dragged out two kitchen chairs from the stifling heat of the stationmaster's office and slept on these. We woke at dawn. It was freezing, it was misty, slowly the recollection returned that we had spent the night on a station platform. Farther down, groups were lighting fires and huddling close to them. Something was wrong with the day, something was different. Rain. The first since Teheran. Stiffly we made our way down to the waiting train. We were hopeful that the last day had begun.

MARK ABLEY

Mark Abley was born in England in 1955, grew up on the Canadian prairies, and graduated from the University of Saskatchewan. He then attended Oxford as a Rhodes scholar. He now lives and works as a critic and free-lance journalist in Montreal. In 1985, he returned to the prairies in an attempt to rediscover his place in their vastness. He drove south from Saskatoon, to the town of Forget (pronounced For-jay), and thence through Saskatchewan, Manitoba, and Alberta.

···

from BEYOND FORGET

Two days before my thirtieth birthday, I almost killed myself. I had warning: on the train ride from Churchill back to Thompson, I dozed into a dream that carried me along Clarence Avenue in the middle of Saskatoon. While my car moved from the riverbank toward 8th Street, gathering pace, I couldn't find its brake. In the dream I approached the clotted traffic of 8th Street expecting disaster, and the car threaded the free spaces like an engine-powered needle. I relaxed—but the car continued to speed down the tranquil suburban avenue. When it was out of control and racing across a sidewalk, I woke up sweating, the unpaved wilderness serenely all around.

In Thompson I had a long night's sleep and a fatty breakfast. It was the eve of Mother's Day, and I wanted to make good headway on the drive to Saskatoon. Unfortunately I had to wait for a bank to open. Churchill had emptied my wallet.

"Are you up here for business or pleasure?" the bank clerk inquired.

"It's sort of business."

She nodded sympathetically. "Nobody comes here for pleasure in May."

I drove then for three hours without stopping. The paucity of traffic and the day's cool brightness combined to make wildlife abundant: a swimming muskrat in a soaking ditch; a pair of mergansers; a spruce grouse immobile by the roadside, its black breast and barred belly vivid even at a glance. By the highway's side, the railway line to Soab Lake was unused. It stands on a high embankment from which, in three or four places, the gravel has crumbled away, leaving yards of track exposed crazily in midair. I thought of a long bone that had lost its flesh.

At Ponton I continued west, rather than following the main highway south toward Grand Rapids. More than a hundred miles of trees, boulders, and water awaited me, unbroken by a town or village: an asphalt tunnel through the green world. By the time I met another vehicle—a red station wagon heading my way, twenty-five miles out of Ponton—it seemed a hallucination, a trick of the coniferous light. The forest bowed and produced, for its next act, a sandhill crane above the road, turning as though lost, flapping slowly south to the Mitishto River. I pondered its direction, and the highway turned pink. From sandstone, not embarrassment, I assume.

When the road was grey again, I switched on the radio. The only signal that could penetrate the tunnel came from the mining town of Flin Flon far to the northwest. Out of the mouths of zinc and copper came the program "Meet the Legion." I listened to a song called "Mr. Sandman, Bring Me a Dream." Then I paused for a rest.

That lakeshore picnic site in the Grass River Provincial Park has lodged in my mind with absolute clarity: the clearing in the woods, the feeble pier, the white-throated sparrows with their treble yearnings, the stained brown table where I munched my raisins and sipped my northern water. The car sat quietly on its gravel sofa, ready for a few more thousand miles in the weeks to come. I had great plans for it in the newborn summer of the prairies and the western foothills. The farther I drove that day, the more I was recapturing spring: already the domain of needles and leafless branches had given way to a forest studded with green poplars. I looked up once from the leaves and the lake to find a flock of thirteen snow geese turning lazily against a high cloud. When the sun caught them, their feathers flashed a brilliant white. They turned again, and a serration of black wings appeared to cut the sky. I got back into the car and regained the straight, empty road.

It was early afternoon. The Flin Flon station was broadcasting a country-and-western lament. The male voice whined, the forest gleamed in the sun, and I looked down at the highway map to see how much longer this road would go on before I had to turn south to The Pas. I felt glazed by all the green. Or could I take a different route? I revolved the map, glanced up, and found that the car had left the asphalt and was hurtling over the gravel shoulder at more than sixty miles an hour.

I veered left to escape the ditch, slammed my foot on the brake, and lost control. The car swung onto the wrong side of the highway, lurched back toward the right shoulder, and pulled left again. The singer whined as the Dodge fought the road. Everything was happening so fast that I had no time to panic; my only emotion was a numb amazement that such chaos could emerge from nowhere. My sporadic fears of big-city pile-ups, slippery blacktop, treacherous backroads, misplaced wildlife, and drunken drivers had left no space in the imagination for me to abandon an excellent highway without another vehicle in sight. My body refused to believe the danger. I recovered concentration too late to scream or pray.

The only thing that flashed before my eyes was a green line of trees turning upside down as the car deserted the road. It flipped in midair and landed on its rear. An instant later, the front of the car joined the back in a grassy ditch, and the world fell silent. Maybe, for a second or two, I lost consciousness.

I found myself sitting in an upright wreck, stunned. If the first feeling was relief—*alive, can move, not in pain, not burning*—the second was shame. *What happened, why did it, how could I?*

My mind battled for order. After I had removed the keys from the ignition, I switched off the silent radio and pushed the gear lever from "drive" to "park." Then I unstrapped the seat belt, which had possibly saved my life, and tried to open the door. It was jammed. But the glass had shattered out from the side windows, allowing me to clamber across the passenger seat and jump to earth. I could hear nothing other than a small breeze playing through the forest.

The car was ruined. Its windshield lay in fragments, its roof was bent, and its hindquarters had the crumpled appearance of a shed skin. It looked like the surprised victim of some monstrous rite of spring. Or was it a rite of passage? The impact had forced open the trunk, and my belongings—everything from a hefty blue suitcase to a couple of fifty-dollar bills—lay scattered like old fillings in the jaw of the ditch. My first impulse was to gather up the money and the small objects that had rested, along with my wallet, on the passenger seat: an address book, a journal, a little camera, the map. I was still doing this when I noticed the distant throb of an engine.

It was approaching, I thought, from the west. I stepped into the highway and started to wave when the throbs became visible. A blue half-ton truck, empty except for the driver, a middle-aged man with short brown hair and a face of dismay, slowed and stopped.

"I've had an accident," I said through the window. "That was my car."

"Is there anyone inside?"

"No, I didn't have any passengers. I just drove off the road."

He looked relieved.

"How long ago did it happen?"

"Don't know. A couple of minutes?"

The man climbed out of his truck. "I'll take you into The Pas," he said. "Let's load up the back."

"But that's where you're coming from," I said.

He gazed at me and silently, gently, shook his head.

I had my directions completely askew. Only at that moment did I understand: after flipping over, the car had landed off the wrong side of the road, facing east. The half-ton had been following my path.

We lifted my possessions into the truck and sped away. I sat in the passenger seat of the cabin, my hair stuffed with shards of gravel, pressing a Kleenex against my only wound: a tiny cut on the left ear. Behind me, a sleeve of my plaid dressing gown protruded from the ripped suitcase and flapped for fifty miles until The Pas. In retrospect, I was beginning to feel afraid.

Apart from some loose change, there was only one item we had failed to discover, either in the car's shell or in the ditch: the golden pen I had been using to write my daily journal. I had passed the pen through Al Hochbaum's inukshuk to bring good luck. Perhaps it had accomplished its task.

COLIN THUBRON

A descendant of John Dryden, Colin Thubron was born in London in 1939. The account of his journey alone by car through western Russia was published in 1984 as Where Nights Are Longest *in the United States and as* Among the Russians *in Great Britain. His difficult but uncomplaining trip through China in the mid-eighties is recounted in* Behind the Wall, *which won the Thomas Cook Award. The author of several books on the Middle East, including* Journey into Cyprus *and* The Hills of Adonis, *he also makes documentary films about travel. Among his four novels are* A Cruel Madness *and* Fallen. *He is a Fellow of the Royal Society of Literature.*

··

from WHERE NIGHTS ARE LONGEST

For . . . four days I was followed everywhere. I came to recognize the techniques of the white Volgas (they were always white), sheltered by lorries a hundred yards behind me. Highly trained, they behaved in ways which were eventually so recognizable that by the fifth day I would pick them out at a glance. But by now I was riddled with nerves. I was afraid above all that my travel notes, compressed into the form of an illegible diary, would be discovered and taken away. Isolated, I began to partake in the condemnation of my silent spectators. I began to feel deeply, inherently guilty. A single friend might have saved me from this, but I didn't have one. I understood now the precious intensity of personal relationships among the dissidents. Because around me, as around them, the total, all-eclipsing Soviet world, which renders any other world powerless and far away, had become profoundly, morally hostile.

In the long, carpetless halls of the hotel, the walled-up faces of waiting men and the sunny voices of the Intourist girls became the scenario of nightmare. I began to behave guiltily. For a whole day I incarcerated myself in my room, illegibly writing up and disguising notes. I searched for a bugging device in vain; I did not dare even curse to myself. Then I wondered if I had implicated anybody else, and decided to destroy my list of Russian addresses and telephone numbers. The irony was that there was no person on it, dissident or other, who did not feel passionately for his country's good. But I could not decide how to destroy this paper. The problem became tortuous. If I shredded the list into my wastepaper basket, it might be reconstructed. If I went into the passage, the eyes of the concierges followed me; and all the public rooms were heavy with scrutiny. If I went out, I would be followed. So, like a cunning schoolboy, I burnt the list in my lavatory.

"Fire!" A fat laundry-maid burst in. "Fire! Where's all this smoke from? Fire!" She had a blotched, porcine face which sloped neckless into her body. I stared at her with pure hate.

A young concierge appeared behind. Her gaze hardened and flew round the room. "What's this?"

"I've been smoking."

"Only smoking?"

"Yes."

I felt angry, shaken by my own lie. The concierge marched back past her desk and descended the elevator. I imagined myself under inquisition, trying to clear myself. I never smoke. But in one corner of the stairway landing stood an ash bin where I found three cigarette stubs. As if participating in some third-rate thriller, I took them back to my room, lit them to foil forensic tests, and left them in the lavatory. Then I walked downstairs and out into the sun, refusing to look behind me. I was shaking.

It seems foolish, in retrospect, that Kiev should be so contaminated for me. I thought it a handsome city, but it remains discoloured in my mind. I remember staring into foodshops whose stock was wretchedly little and expensive: in one only a heap of decapitated chick-ens, in another some crates of aubergines. And this was the capital of the Ukraine, of the Black Earth! I began to feel terribly tired, as if some unnoticed strain from the past months were finally spilling over. In the hotel that afternoon I found a Soviet Greek, an engineer from Kazakh-stan with a delicate, mobile face. I befriended him with neurotic relief. His parents had come from Istanbul to Sukhumi after Ataturk's victories in 1922 and had died in old age without ever talking a word of Russian. But he himself never spoke Greek, although he understood it; and his children could barely even understand it. I prompted him anxiously about his people's history. The Greeks, founders of freedom! Had he read Sappho, Cavafy, Herodotus? Those books were hard to get, he said. But did he still feel Greek, I demanded? Absolutely, he said. Yet I could not tell in what the feeling lay. He knew the date of Lenin's birthday, but he could not remember who had built the Parthenon. In my present state this struck me as a parable of total corruption.

I had been given other addresses in the city: those of a priest, a journalist, and the wife of a poet who had recently been arrested. But all would have been compromised if I had met them. Although I did not know it at the time, the poet, a Ukrainian nationalist, was sentenced to ten years' hard labour on the day I arrived. I confined my trips to conventional tourist sites. I did not even see Babi Yar, where the Ger-mans massacred over a hundred thousand Kievan Jews and others. ("It's discouraged to go there," an Armenian had told me. "I suppose they're afraid of it becoming a Jewish shrine.")

The only people I had warned of my coming were a Georgian agronomist and his Russian fiancée, who appeared by taxi one evening to take me to their home for supper. They greeted me like old friends— he a man of mercurial darkness, she motherly, blond, and Slavic-calm. I warmed to them at once. In the taxi we talked at ease of mutual friends in England. But through its back window I glimpsed the number-plate of the white Volga following us. I felt sick. But I didn't tell them. The contrast between their blithe chatter and this paranoid shadow was somehow horrific. And I, in my knowledge, was condemned to the shadow. My guilty diary bulged in my coat pocket.

The Volga drifted to a halt beyond us when we stopped, and as we ascended in the flat-block elevator, I glimpsed a man in a leather jacket enter below. His face was enclosed, leaden, and I could hear the noise of his feet keeping pace with the rickety elevator as we rose, until he knew which apartment we entered.

But the moment the door closed, we were at peace. Mehrab and Vera had both left behind broken marriages, and were palpably in love. Theirs was a timeless attraction of opposites. Mehrab had the trim, agile physique of his people. In his swarthy face, with its high forehead and prominent but rather delicate bones, the eyes glittered with a febrile restlessness. He spoke to me about his work, but was distracted by the closeness of Vera, seated heavy-breasted beside him. His gestures incorporated a tender searching of her body with the elucidation of drainage around the Black Sea. Irrigation ditches somehow found their way across her thighs; harvest failures were offset by a consoling crop of squeezes; a bumper year collected her breasts.

And all the time, framed in page-boy hair, her blue eyes and broad lips gave out a happy and uncomplicated strength. The word "definitely" kept recurring in her talk. She was outspoken and often (said Mehrab) wrong. She had a puritan love of Siberia, where she had been born, and all of northern Russia. She preferred Leningrad to Kiev. "The people are more open-hearted there. Definitely. Here in Kiev they're enclosed, they live in their own circles."

When she went into the kitchen to prepare supper, Mehrab laughed affectionately: "She's biased. She was a child in Siberia, you see, and a student in Leningrad, living among students—but an adult only here. She looks back on those student days with nostalgia and on her childhood with love. So of course she sees the places in that order. But really, I think, the old gradations of north to south apply here too. Kiev, you know, is more casual and dirty than northern Russia, and the Ukrainians a bit more open. But Georgia is better still!"

Love, in many permutations and disguises, pervaded our evening. The flat was full of it: thumbed books, taped music, Black Sea driftwood which they had collected on holiday and lacquered in curious shapes. "A man should love his work," Mehrab said, "that's the secret, but I'm not sure if the young do that any longer." He spoke of "the young" as if they were another race; I supposed he was about thirty-five. "They're somehow more diffuse, perhaps more imaginative than we were at that age."

I said I hoped so. I was thinking of peace, the trust which needs imagination.

"If real peace comes, it'll come because people are selfish," Vera said. "Definitely. They'll have too much to lose."

"Yes," I said. That sounded like life.

A storm rumbled outside. I went to the window. The rain was lashing down on the road, the darkened trees, and the white car sheltered under them.

"The young have ten times as much as we had," Vera went on. "When I was five, I remember, I ached for a doll. I used to make wooden ones myself, but I longed for one with proper hair and a body made of something smooth, like skin, which I could dress and undress and wash." She laughed boisterously. "I got one when I was twenty! And I loved it just as much as if I was five! And now I see children with bicycles, radios, everything, and it hasn't improved them." She looked puzzled and fed up. "And you in the West, you have so much, but are you happier?"

I didn't know, I said (whatever we meant by happiness). *But we couldn't go back.*

....

When I returned to my hotel, I knew that something was wrong. The comfortable old concierge who had taken over duty on my floor, and who had previously shown a maternal benignity, now gaped at me with horror.

My room, in my absence, had been searched. It had been done near perfectly, everything repositioned almost precisely as it was. Only by the pinpoint siting of several objects before I left, and by the insertion in notebooks of tiny threads now dislodged, did I realize that everything I possessed—letters, clothes, wallet, books, documents—had been removed, scrutinized, and fastidiously replaced.

But my diary was in my pocket, and my address list ashes down the lavatory.

PAUL THEROUX

Paul Theroux's books of train travel include The Great Railway Bazaar, The Old Patagonian Express, The Kingdom by the Sea, *and* Riding the Iron Rooster, *an account of a year's travel in China. Among his numerous novels is the recent* My Secret History, *about a travel writer and based on some of its author's own experiences. Theroux believes you must travel alone. Of Costa Rica he writes: "I craved a little risk, some danger, an untoward event, a vivid discomfort, an experience of my own company, and in a modest way the romance of solitude. This I thought would be mine on that train to Limón." Unfortunately, scant experience of his own company has arisen, for he has been beset aboard by a garrulous Mr. Thornberry, from whom he now hopes to flee.*

·····································

from THE OLD PATAGONIAN
EXPRESS

Limón looked like a dreadful place. It had just rained, and the town stank. The station was on a muddy road near the harbor, and puddles reflected the decayed buildings and over-bright lights. The smell of dead barnacles and damp sand, flooded sewers, brine, oil, cockroaches, and tropical vegetation which, when soaked, gives off the hot moldy vapor you associate with compost heaps in summer, the stench of mulch and mildew. It was a noisy town as well: clanging music, shouts, car horns. That last sight of the palmy coast and the breakers had been misleading. And even Mr. Thornberry, who had been hopeful, was appalled. I could see his face; he was grimacing in disbelief. "God," he groaned. "It's a piss hole in the snow." We walked through the puddles, the other passengers splashing us as they hurried past. Mr. Thornberry said, "It blows my mind."

That does it, I thought. I said, "I'd better go look for a hotel."

"Why not stay at mine?"

Oh, look, it's raining. It blows my mind. Kind of a pipeline.

I said, "I'll just sniff around town. I'm like a rat in a maze when I get to a new place."

"We could have dinner. That might be fun. You never know— maybe the food's good here." He squinted up the street. "This place was recommended to me."

"It wasn't recommended to me," I said. "It looks pretty strange."

"Maybe I'll find that tour I was supposed to be on," he said. He no longer sounded hopeful.

"Where are you staying?"

He told me. It was the most expensive hotel in Limón. I used that as my reason for looking elsewhere. A small, feeble-minded man approached and asked sweetly if he could carry my suitcase. It dragged on the street when he held it in his hand. He put it on his head and marched bandy-legged, like a worker elf, to the market square. Here, Mr. Thornberry and I parted.

"I hope you find your tour," I said. He said he was glad we had met on the train: it had been kind of fun after all. And he walked away. I felt a boundless sense of relief, as if I had just been sprung from a long confinement. This was liberation. I tipped the elf and walked quickly in the opposite direction from Mr. Thornberry.

I walked to savor my freedom and stretch my legs. After three blocks, the town didn't look any better; and wasn't that a rat nibbling near the tipped-over barrel of scraps? *It's a white country*, a man had told me in San José. But this was a black town, a beachhead of steaming trees and sea stinks. I tried several hotels. They were wormy staircases with sweating people minding tables on the second-floor landings. No, they said, they had no rooms. And I was glad, because they looked so disgustingly dirty and the people were so rude; so I walked a few more blocks. I'd find a better hotel. But they were smaller and smellier, and they too were full. At one, as I stood panting—the staircase had left me breathless—a pair of cockroaches scuttled down the wall and hurried unimpeded across the floor. *Cockroaches*, I said. The man said, *What do you want here?* He too was full. I had been stopping at every second hotel. Now I stopped at each one. They were not hotels. They were nests of foul bedclothes, a few rooms, and a portion of verandah. I should have known they were full: I met harassed families making their way down the stairs, the women and children carrying suitcases, the fathers sucking their teeth in dismay and muttering, *We'll have to look somewhere else*. It was necessary for me to back down the narrow stairs to let these families pass.

In one place (I recognized it as a hotel by its tottering stairs, its unshaded bulbs, its moth-eaten furniture, its fusty smell), a woman in an apron said, "Them—they're doublin' up." She indicated a passage-way of people—grandmothers, young women, sighing men, glassy-eyed children, black, fatigued, pushing old valises into a cubicle and several changing their clothes as they stood there in the passageway.

I had no idea of the time. It seemed late; the people in Limón who were not room hunting were strolling the wet streets. They had that settled look of smugness that the stranger interprets as mockery or at least indifference. Saturday nights in strange cities can alienate the calmest of travelers.

Further on, a man said to me, "Don't waste your time looking. There are no hotel rooms in Limón. Try tomorrow."

"What do I do tonight?"

"There is only one thing you can do," he said. "See that bar over there?" It was a peeling storefront with a string of lights over the door; inside, shapes—human heads—and smoke; and broken-crockery syn-copations. "Go in and pick up a girl. Spend the night with her. That is your only hope."

I considered this. But I did not see any girls. At the door were a gang of boys, jeering at men who were entering. I tried another hotel. The black owner saw that his reply to my question distressed me. He said, "If you really get stuck and got no other place, come back here. You can set out here on that chair." It was a straight-backed chair on his verandah. There was a bar across the street: music, another mob of gawking boys. I slapped at the mosquitoes. Motorbikes went by; they sounded like outboard motors. This sound and the boys and the music made a scream. But I left my suitcase with this man and searched more streets. There were no hotels, no bars, no rooming houses; even the music was muffled. I decided to turn back, but I had gone too far: now I was lost.

I came to a precinct of Limón known as Jamaicatown—in this white Spanish-speaking country, a black English-speaking area; a slum. These were the worst streets I had seen in Costa Rica, and each street corner held a dozen people, talking, laughing; their speech had a cackle in it. I was watched, but not threatened; and yet I had never felt so lost. It was as if I had burst through the bottom of my plans and was falling through darkness. I would continue to fall: there was absolutely nothing to do until dawn. My feet hurt; I was tired, dirty, sweating; I had not eaten all day. This was not the time or the place to reflect on the futility of the trip, and yet Costa Rica had seemed to promise better than this dark dead end.

At one corner I asked some loitering men the way to the market. I asked in Spanish; they replied in English: they knew I was a stranger. Their directions were clear: they said I couldn't miss it.

I saw the row of hotels and rooming houses I had entered earlier in the evening. I had been disgusted by them then, but now they didn't seem so bad to me. I kept walking, and near the market square, skipping feebly across the street, one shoulder lower than the other because of the bag he carried, funny blue cap, bright green shirt, sailor pants, shuffling deck shoes: Thornberry.

"I've been looking all over for you."

I needed his company: I was glad—someone to talk to. I said, "I can't find a room anywhere. There aren't any in Limón. I'm screwed."

He took my arm and winced. "There are three beds in my room," he said. "You stay with me."

"You mean it?"

"Sure—come on."

My relief was inexpressible.

I got my suitcase from the hotel where the man had said that I could spend the night on his verandah chair. Mr. Thornberry called the place a piss hole (and over the next few days, whenever we passed it, he said, "There's your verandah!"). I went to his room and washed my face, then we had a beer and grumbled about Limón. In gratitude I took him out to eat; we had broiled fish and hearts of palm and a bottle of wine, and Mr. Thornberry told me sad stories about his life in New Hampshire, about his loneliness. Maybe he'd rent a house in Puntarenas for the winter. He couldn't take another cold winter. He had made a mess of his life, he said. It was the money—the IBM stock his sister had bequeathed to him. "The things I want, money can't buy. Money's just bullshit. If you have it. If you don't have it, it's important. I didn't always have it."

I said, "You saved my life."

"I couldn't let you walk around all night. It's dangerous. I hate this place." He shook his head. "I thought I was going to like it. It looked okay from the train—those palm trees. That travel agency was lying to me. They said there were parrots and monkeys here."

"Maybe you can get on a tour tomorrow."

"I'm sick of thinking about it." He looked at his watch. "Nine o'clock. I'm bushed. Shall we call it a day?"

I said, "I don't normally go to bed at nine o'clock."

Mr. Thornberry said, "I always do."

So we did. There was only one room key. We were like an elderly couple, fussing silently at bedtime, yawning, chastely putting on our pajamas. Mr. Thornberry pulled his covers up and sighed. I read for awhile, then switched off the light. It was still early, still noisy. Mr. Thornberry said, "Motorbike . . . Music . . . Listen to them yak-king . . . Car . . . Train whistle . . . Those must be waves." Then he was asleep.

MARY MORRIS

Mary Morris has published two collections of stories, Vanishing Animals *and* The Bus of Dreams, *and two novels,* Crossroads *and* The Waiting Room. *Early on in* Nothing to Declare: Memoirs of a Woman Traveling Alone *she confides that traveling alone often isn't easy, and is never easy for a woman. "Brace yourself for tremendous emptiness and great surprise. Anything can happen. The bad things that have occurred in my travels . . . have happened because I wasn't prepared. At times I wonder that I am still alive." In the following journey to Palenque, not even a traveling companion is enough to ensure immunity from surprise and emptiness. Morris lives with a young daughter in New York City.*

----

from NOTHING TO DECLARE

Nobody goes to Palenque in mid-August, and what we were doing there then remains a mystery to me. Perhaps it was just a case of bad planning. But there we were, and we experienced it in its full force. The minute we stepped outside in the morning the heat struck us, bowled us over like a blast furnace. Our jeans, which we'd washed out the night before, were stiff as boards, dry as clay in the morning sun. But my hair never felt dry the entire time I was in Palenque; it was always soaked with sweat. As we walked to the ruins, the people swung in their hammocks, expressionless, barely moving, dead-looking, brains boiled. The jungle of Palenque was not like that of the highlands. Here there were no hills, no vistas, no gentle rolling of the land. In Palenque you were at the bottom of a pit of the lowlands, enclosed in a jungle prison. No

180

breeze blew through this hollow. It felt ominous, treacherous, omnivorous, and indifferent, as if it would swallow you with a single gulp. If you stood still for just a moment, vines would engulf you, snakes would poison you, small crawling things would devour you, the air would be stolen from you. And you would be forgotten.

We entered the lost city of Palenque, a city of overgrown trails and crumbled ruins, a mysterious place about which little is known. Once a thriving city, Palenque was abandoned suddenly in the tenth century when all the great Mayan centers were abandoned for reasons unknown. I walked through its main causeways, among its temples and houses and courts where sports were played. I walked through these ruins with steam baths, public toilets with septic tanks, aqueducts, and drainage systems. I tried to imagine the city that had been.

Palenque, whose civilization was concurrent with that of the dawn of civilization in Greece and Egypt, is a place of questions, of things you must accept because no answers are forthcoming. Palenque isn't even its original name. After many years archaeologists have deciphered a date, which translates to 682 B.C.; they believe it is the completion date of the first pyramid. But no one can explain those pagoda-like temples reminiscent of those in China or at Angkor Wat in Cambodia. No one knows about Pakal, the prince entombed in an obsidian mask at the bottom of the great pyramid of the same name. He is believed to have been a captive, a prince of another tribe, yet the people of Palenque spent years building him the only pyramid in all of Mexico that is also a tomb.

Catherine and I climbed. We climbed each temple, every pyramid. We descended into the cool, wet depths of the tomb, then rose to see the astrological markings at the observation tower. We saw the entire valley from the observation tower, where the Mayan rulers observed the stars and charted their course and made their calendar—a calendar more accurate than ours. No one knows how they accomplished this, and no one knows why the Mayan people dispersed, leaving their cities and their religious centers centuries before the conquistadors arrived.

I left Catherine and climbed to the top of the Temple of the Sun;

I saw the Temple of the Foliated Cross and imagined in the distance people struggling up the hill. Mayans going to their places of worship, dragging boulders, building their temples, stone by stone, painting beautiful pictures on the walls. I saw them fighting back the jungle, futilely pushing it away. I could see them from where I stood, a great, passionate, religious people who had disappeared but for their ruins.

Then I walked into the jungle a little ways. A horde of soldier ants descended a tree. In my path were a red-bellied spider with skinny legs, reminding me of the black widow we thought we'd seen the night before, and butterflies of topaz, amber, turquoise, earth brown. Tigers, monarchs, delicate lace-leafed butterflies, little pearl and azul ones, big yellows and the giant blues—the cobalt-blues—all flew past me. I heard the sounds of strange animals as I made my way through the lush vegetation.

At dusk Catherine and I staggered back to the hotel with only one thought in our minds. We would strip, put on our suits, and take that swim. We walked in silence and I do not recall ever being quite so exhausted. As we approached the hotel, the pool appeared before us, turquoise. We kept walking, but the pool was not so shimmering as it had seemed the day before. As we drew nearer, I did not take my eyes from it. Catherine gaped as well. When we were only twenty feet away, I stopped. "Look," I said.

Catherine nodded. "It's not possible," she said.

We reached the edge of the completely empty swimming pool, the pool which had been full of water the afternoon before but did not have a drop in it now. We rushed to the man who sat in the office drinking a warm Coke, feet on his desk, and he told us that the pool was dirty so they had decided to drain it. We shook our heads in utter disbelief. We went to our room to shower and I felt someone was playing a cruel joke on us—there was no water. We rushed back to the man at the desk. He told us that they'd run out of water. For reasons we've never understood the hotel decided to drain the swimming pool on the same day they ran out of water. "When will you have more water?" Catherine asked.

The man shrugged. "Later," he said.

We went back to our room and lay on the bed, miserable, not speaking. Then we wiped ourselves off with half a dozen Wash 'n Dris each and went to the restaurant where we'd eaten the previous night. Petunia, who seemed to know me now, rolled over on her back to have her stomach rubbed throughout the meal, much to Catherine's annoyance. Eventually the owner came over and sat down. He asked if we liked Palenque and we said we did, but we were very hot and our hotel had no water. "Then you must go to Agua Azul," he said. "It is beautiful. Dozens of waterfalls. Yes, you must go there and swim."

We were lucky that morning. About a hundred people were waiting to push onto the local bus that would take us to Agua Azul, but the ticket taker took pity on Catherine and me. He was a young man of about seventeen with a kind and handsome dark face, warm brown eyes. And he wore pink. He wore a shiny pink shirt with some kind of animal— elephants, I think—all over it, and pink pants. One doesn't normally see a man dressed all in pink. That fact has stayed with me, and always will.

Since we were going all the way to Agua Azul, two hours up the mountain—not just to Egipto or Santa María, the mud and thatch villages along the way—and since we were the only blue-eyed gringas around, the ticket taker got us seats before the local people piled on. Then he opened a window for us and let everyone else board.

There seemed to be no limit to how many people the bus could hold. As many as showed up squeezed on. Mothers clutched screaming babies and pushed and dragged their chickens and goats. Men with machetes stood bleary-eyed in the heat. All had misery in their faces, the pain of drudgery.

The bus climbed and the breeze and the cooler air made everyone feel better. Slowly, as people got off, we felt the terrible heat letting up. The ticket taker in pink joked with us. He asked if Palenque had been hot enough for us. And he said Agua Azul was a beautiful place.

In two hours we reached Agua Azul, with its twenty or so main waterfalls and a series of lesser ones; small pools formed at the bases of some falls, and we could swim in these. Our driver said we'd stay for about two hours, then return. Catherine and I changed into our suits in a small wooden dressing room. A dead tarantula lay on the floor.

I headed for one of those little pools at the base of the falls while Catherine got a beer and started off on a walk. Our bus driver, a very gentle, elderly man with soft gray eyes, sat on the edge of a rock and pointed to a pool near him. He told me this was not a bad place to swim. I eased my way into the icy water and felt the cool go through me. I felt alive, tingly, happy to be in water. I began to swim. I swam out into the pool and back again, but about midway I could feel the current—strong, pulling at me.

Catherine came back. She said she'd seen a large wild boar, drowned, in one of the pools. "Be careful," she said. I looked at where I'd been swimming. The pool where I swam fed into a waterfall that fell about ten yards. It didn't look so treacherous and I wasn't very concerned. Catherine went to make us sandwiches with some vegetables, bread, and cheese we had brought from town. She said she'd be back with lunch.

I went into the water again. A boy had entered the pool and was swimming beside me. I swam out and back a few times, and each time I felt the current at that one place. Finally I decided it was dangerous and that I should not swim all the way across and back. But the boy, flailing about like a puppy, was not a very controlled swimmer, and he was making his way back and forth well beyond the place where I was stopping. I remember thinking to myself, I should tell him that the current is very strong. I should say something. But I did not. I didn't want to pry or bother him. He must know what he is doing, I told myself. Then Catherine called me for lunch.

I hoisted myself out of the water. As I walked toward her, my body felt cool for the first time in days and I smiled. I felt incredibly vigorous and content as Catherine held a sandwich out to me. Hungry and ready to eat, I reached for it, but our hands never connected. Her face changed from one of greeting to one of stunned horror. Her mouth opened, but all she could do was point to the place where I had been swimming.

From the corner of my eye I saw the boy who had been swimming next to me. He semeed to be riding one of those carnival watersled rides because he was practically sitting up and the current was just taking him along. I could see his face now and he looked familiar to me, like an old acquaintance you meet after many years but cannot quite place.

He was silent. That is what I remember most. The silence. He never screamed or shouted or cried for help. His face had the concentration of a good student taking an important exam. When he got to the falls, he twisted his body, trying to grab onto a branch, and then he was gone without a sound. Suddenly we were both screaming and pointing at nothing, at nothing at all except the rush of water.

The Mexicans did not believe us. They said no boy was missing. No one was missing anyone, but we were hysterical. "Someone went over that fall," we told them. At the same time I could not help thinking how I had done nothing. How that boy had been swimming near me and I had thought to say something and had said nothing. And then I thought how close it had come to being me. If I had gone out just a little farther, it would have been me.

Then our bus driver came toward us slowly, eyes glassy. He clasped in his hands the pink shirt and pink pants of the ticket taker, who had given us our seats. He said nothing. He simply held out the boy's clothes.

It took a while, but a search party was organized. About a dozen young Mexican men stripped down to their shorts and with sticks went to the base of the falls, where they formed a line. We sat on the bank over the falls, watching. Catherine seemed nervous and soon began pacing. But I sat, transfixed, never taking my eyes off the search party. I watched the bodies of young men, bodies so perfect and beautiful that I wanted to touch them as they bent over the water and put their faces in, like divers after mother-of-pearl. They walked and probed as I sat and waited, but no body was found.

A Mexican who seemed to be in charge came over to us. "He is at the bottom of the falls. It has happened here before. The body will be trapped there forever." The bus driver was in tears now. He knew the boy and his family well. The Mexican shrugged. "We'll keep looking," he said. They searched for two hours while we waited on the bank.

Finally the driver patted me on the shoulder. "Let's go," he said.

"I should have done something," I said to Catherine as we got on the bus. "When we were swimming, I should have said something."

"Be grateful it wasn't you," she said.

"I am, but I should have done something."

Catherine opened up a copy of *Tropic of Cancer* and read all the way back to Palenque. I tried to talk to her, but she would not discuss the incident with me. She just said, "It wasn't your fault. It was an accident, so forget it."

RONALD WRIGHT

Born in England in 1948, Ronald Wright read archaeology and anthropology at Cambridge, where he received his M.A. in 1973. His books include Cut Stones and Crossroads: A Journey in the Two Worlds of Peru, On Fiji Islands, *and* Time Among the Maya: Travels in Belize, Guatemala, and Mexico. *He has traveled widely in the Americas, Africa, and the South Pacific, and now makes his home near Toronto, as a free-lance journalist and broadcaster. He is a Fellow of the Royal Geographical Society.*

························

from CUT STONES AND
CROSSROADS

My copy of the *South American Handbook* is out-of-date. I was planning to take the Santa railway to Huallanca at the north end of the Callejón de Huaylas. But I learned at breakfast that the line was another victim of the earthquake. It seems that the tracks have been taken up and the railbed is now being used as a road. Moreover, my informant (a cook with a filthy vest and a forearm so covered in scales that it looked like a large fish) suggested this "road" is dangerous. Peruvians seldom remark on the hazards of roads. . . . Still, a detour will be tedious and probably no safer.

I wait all morning at a service station on the edge of Chimbote for a vehicle going my way. Gasoline architecture varies little around the world: this place has two greasing bays, four pumps, and an office full of oil tins and girlie pinups. Blondes, of course. Latin Americans' ideal of beauty has nothing at all to do with racial fact. Advertising, pornography, and images of Christ all share a taste for pallid Aryans. They like the girls a little heavier than the current gringo vogue: skinniness is too suggestive of poverty.

A salient concrete roof shades the pumps. The only clues to my whereabouts are the sign for PETROPERU and the fact that urine defeats diesel in the contest of smells.

The sun chases me and the shadows beneath the roof. Outside, greasy asphalt shimmers and stinks, soft as toffee, a mosaic of embedded bottle caps.

After siesta a three-ton Ford arrives. A sticker on its windshield says: VIRGINITY CAUSES CANCER—GET YOUR VACCINATION HERE. The driver is a young, intelligent man with a shock of black hair and supple movements. He offers me a place on top of the load, says the road is perfectly safe, and makes me promise one thing: "Lie absolutely flat when we come to the tunnels or you'll lose your head. There isn't clearance for a fart in most of them."

"How many are there?"

"Sixteen."

For a long time we wind through a former sugar hacienda, now a co-op; we stop often to pick up small loads and people wanting short rides. The usual yellow haze veils the sky, intensifying the heat, robbing the landscape of contrast. Wherever is water, is color—greenery and flowers: frangipani, bougainvillea—infrequent and insecure, like patches of paint left on a peeling fresco. Dust coats everything near the road; even the trees and gaudy houses seem camouflaged for desert warfare.

There is harvesting in the fields, which have been burned to remove the dense, rasping leaves from the cane. Workers wearing only briefs slash rhythmically at the charred stems with machetes. Their bodies run with sugar, soot, and sweat; the air reeks of molasses.

Have things improved for these workers since the reforms? The answer, as far as I can tell, is a much-qualified yes. At first the rhetoric of worker control alarmed the supervisors and technicians on these estates. They threatened to resign en masse, and were placated only by the gift of disproportionate power in co-op affairs. This alienated the laborers, who went out on strike after calls from their APRA union bosses. Then there came an uneasy truce presided over by "military coordinators," resented by both sides. The situation was more complex than the architects of the land reform had realized—many of the cane cutters were seasonal workers, and the co-ops' fulltime members were reluctant to share their new wealth with these outsiders as the army insisted they must. Now the army has backed off and the co-op members have become a proletarian élite; but recent drops in world sugar prices will no doubt threaten their prosperity.

At last we leave the desert plain and enter the lower Santa canyon, so rocky that one sees no life here, even beside the river. I long for the sierra. Already Chimbote is a memory of only three colors: khaki land, houses, and sky, and rock islands white with guano standing in a black sea.

The old railbed soon leaves the valley floor, which becomes too wild, and clings to the canyon wall on a ledge blasted from the rock. It is seldom more than six inches wider than the truck on either side: the former railway was narrow-gauge. Abandoned mine workings pock the cliffs like rodent burrows; long tongues of debris depend from their small black mouths. The tunnels are indeed low, unlined and jagged inside. According to the other passengers, more than one traveler has had his head "smashed like a melon."

In twilight we reach one of those tiny hanging pampas that one finds so unexpectedly in the Andes. "Pampa" in Peru has a less specific meaning than in English: it is the Runasimi adjective for "flat," and a noun for any flat space, no matter how small. There are a few huts here, some chickens, children, and dark green-orange trees. Though we are a thousand feet above the river, its water is brought from upstream by a long channel cut into the valley wall.

The driver stops and shouts up: "Flat tire. Good thing it happened here!" Yes, very. I climb down and walk to the edge of the gorge. The sky has cleared with the height we have gained and is navy blue with approaching night. All around are folded masses of rock torn by shadow. At the bottom of its dark, dry vee, the river's violence makes it conspicuously white.

The spare is flat (of course), and the puncture is on the inner dual, requiring removal of both wheels. It takes half an hour of hammering and cursing to break the bead from the rim; but it's not until the tube has been patched and replaced that the real work begins. The problem is the pump, one of those tiny plunger jobs suitable for bicycles. It needs lots of spittle inside before yielding any air. The driver, his helper, and one of the more vigorous passengers take turns at a hundred strokes each. I remember an earlier flat tire, on the Huancayo road in 1975, the driver shouting exhortations to his helper—a dull-witted and potentially rebellious teenager—exhortations satirizing government propaganda: "Pump for Peru! I'll tell Velasco how valiant you are. Work hard so the country can afford to buy him a wooden leg."

It is now quite dark. An hour's pumping has failed to inflate the tire to within a quarter of its working pressure. Lights can be seen in the distance coming down the mountain. The driver says, "That's strange. The road is one-way going up today." As with several roads in the Andes, traffic is supposed to switch directions on odd and even days. One of the pumpers hopes for a new Dodge truck with compressed air, but the wish is unfulfilled. Ten minutes later another violator of the traffic code arrives (or is it we who are wrong?) and he does have air.

I return to the *canasta*, the extension of the truck box that overhangs the cab, and get comfortable on my back among some sugar sacks. The stars seem very close, blotted from time to time when tunnels sweep overhead.

Much'aykusqayki Pacha Ruwaq,	Blessed Maker of the World
Qhawarillaway	Watch us
Sumaq qoyllur ñawiykiwan.	With your eyes, the glorious stars.

I must have slept. Around midnight, very cold, the driver shakes me awake: "This is Yuraqmarka. We can eat here, and there's lodging." He leads me through the darkness to a restaurant. An old woman is shuffling about, half asleep. It takes her ten minutes to bring a candle. I ask how much I owe for the ride. Nothing, the driver says, but he wants the miniature flashlight I lent him while the tire was being repaired. I have to refuse, and feel mean. I need it for camping and there are none available in Peru.

The woman serves an execrable cold dish that was once hot: *seco de cordero*, an old foe of mine, but I am hungry enough to eat it. Seco is usually made from sheep neckbones braised in a gravy flavored with cilantro, coriander leaves. It sounds harmless enough, but so much cilantro is used that the result is cloying and sickly, like rotten parsley. The flavor is utterly different from coriander seed, a main ingredient of curry powder.

"Lodging" turns out to be a tin shack behind the restaurant. Two of the four beds are already occupied by bulky forms, from which come snores and gusts of alcoholic breath.

My first sight of the day is the avalanche of refuse that begins at the back door of the kitchen and drops away into the ravine: plastic, tins, corncobs, offal, and rags. Three very hairy black pigs are scuffling for the edible items. Yuraqmarka means White Town; I had imagined a pleasant sierra village, but daylight reveals a collection of metal huts that is little more than a truck stop. I go inside the kitchen, looking for water, and do not immediately realize that what appears to be an old coat hanging from the ceiling is in fact a sheep's haunch, invisible beneath a regiment of flies. The insects settle on me as I wash. Their feet are cold and moist.

The old railbed joins a true road at Yuraqmarka; the truck carrying advice to virgins has left for the north. After the vision of the kitchen I am content with a cup of tea for breakfast. The only other customers are two men conversing intently through the forest of empty beer bottles on their table. One is tall, thirtyish, European-looking, but obviously, from his neat polyester shirt and slacks, a well-to-do Peruvian; the other, a sallow mestizo with Asiatic eyes and blighted four-day stubble. He wears—or, rather, appears to live in—a wrinkled suit and a shirt with no collar.

The tall one (also the soberer of the two) speaks: "Gringo! Where are you going?"

"Huallanca, and Huarás."

"So are we. Come and have a drink with us." I take my tea over to their table.

"Carlos García Cárdenas *a sus órdenes!*" the tall one says, "and my fellow traveler Policarpo Ruíz Huillca." I give my name, we shake hands. Their touch is soft and clammy and reminds me of the flies. (Handshaking in Latin countries is always frequently and lightly done, with the loose grip that Anglo-Saxons believe shows lack of "moral fiber.")

"I am from Lima," García says, in the voice of the Peruvian *Herrenvolk*; "my . . . friend here lives in Carás, in the Callejón." Ruíz looks up, belches, swallows quickly, says nothing. "He's a justice of the peace."

At this Ruíz comes to life, nods at the Limeño as if he were far away, and leans toward me conspiratorially: "He's a PIP. You understan'?" The voice drops to a whisper. "Policía de Investigaciones del Perú!"

The PIP is the élite plainclothes police force. It has political functions (not always those of the government), a reputation for corruption, and a taste for power. Its members are supposed to operate undercover, but are usually too swaggering to be inconspicuous. The acronym is pronounced, appropriately, as *peep*.

"Peep," the judge continues, "you'll see. When a truck comes we'll get a ride. No problem. Nothing to pay. Peep!" He flashes his hand as if he held a badge. García looks embarrassed. Ruíz calls for more beer. I decline.

"From what country?" García asks.

"England originally—I live in Canada."

"You're my friend!" Ruíz interrupts, seizing my hand and continuing to hold it in a flabby grasp. "This gentleman is a PIP! If anything comes by . . . he'll stop it for us. . . ."

"So, what do you think of us two 'bad functionaries' of the government?" (García must be making ironic reference to the newspaper campaigns of Velasco's day calling on people to denounce corrupt officials.)

"That's not for me to say."

"Have a beer. I'd feel much better if you'd join us."

"No, really I'd rather not."

"Yes! Waiter, three beers!"

"No, please. I'll have a soft drink instead."

"You don't drink?"

"Never before lunch."

" 'Never before lunch'—you gringos have such rules, such discipline. We Peruvians . . ."

"There are plenty of gringos who drink."

"But not you, Ronald?" The "peep" persists.

"Not when I'm traveling. I seem to lose the taste for it."

"You don't smoke marihuana, do you?"

"Of course not." I don't like this line of questioning.

Ruíz revives again and leans across: "What country you from?"

"He's from England . . . and Canada."

"Ah," Ruíz sighs, "England. England is the mother country of Canada and the United States. That so? Just as Spain is the mother country of Peru!"

I reply without thinking: "It's not really the same. Spain isn't the mother country of Peru in the same sense. In North America most of the people have originally come from Europe, but Peruvians are mostly native, descended from the Incas. . . ." The look on Ruíz's face tells me how he has taken my effort to instill national pride. He knocks over his chair and shoots to his feet with impossible speed.

"There are no Indians in Peru! *No Indians in Peru!*"

Huillca, his Runasimi matronymic, must be a terrible shame to him.

·············

At eleven, a truck comes at last. Ruíz is now at the incapable stage. García and I hoist him up the tailgate and the passengers inside haul him over the top. He props himself in a corner, crimped at the middle like a furled rug.

A woman sitting on the floor nearby has a large basket holding about a hundred eggs; when the driver puts the motor in gear the truck lurches and the judge's foot goes in. "*Ay, señor!*" the woman wails, pushing him away. He has smashed at least a dozen—equivalent in value to a laborer's daily wage, or two bottles of the beer that has brought him to this state. But the woman does not dare ask compensation and none is offered.

Later there is poetic justice: Ruíz tries to climb out of the moving vehicle and his fedora blows away in the wind.

....

Judge and "peep" decide to stop at Carás, where the Callejón proper begins. It is already early afternoon; I continue to Huarás by colectivo.

There has been plenty of rain here. From Carás south the valley is a study in greens and reds: silver-green maguey and eucalyptus saplings, emerald stands of young maize, bottle-green alfalfa; the adobe walls and houses are russet, and so are the wounds of paths and erosion channels on the land.

"Callejón" (Spanish for "alley" or "corridor") is an apt name for this long valley running between the two cordilleras. The Cordillera Negra is a sad range. Its eighteeen-thousand-foot heights are too low to capture eternal snows; too low, even, to receive much of the scanty moisture that remains in the winds sweeping up from the sea. For that reason it is black, and the ranchers of sheep and llamas on its slopes are forced into conflict with the farmers of the valley whenever drought sears their pastures. But the White Cordillera, which forms a great wall to the east, is magnificent. Clouds are hiding the twenty-two-thousand-foot summits of Huascarán and Huandoy, but as I watch, the vapors swirl and part to reveal a kaleidoscopic world of illusion, dazzling against the blue-black sky. I cannot tell what is cloud, what ice, what blowing snow; and when the sun catches the glaciers their refulgence stabs my eyes.

Climbers look on these mountains the way some men regard beautiful women: as objects to be wooed, conquered, and then left. Only a new ascent, like a new sexual practice with an old lover, will tempt the mountaineer to a longer dalliance.

In the case of mountains I am the "pedestal" type, content to worship them from afar. The Runa call the mountains *Apu*, "Lord," the same title that was applied to the Lord Inca and the four Apus who ruled over each quarter of the Tawantinsuyu. To Runa the mountain is an ancestor, a protective deity, as well as a kind of underworld in which life and flesh are held in reserve. All life is cycled through the mountains that preside over an ayllu, just as water is recycled by the process of condensing on the peaks and running down through the streams and irrigation channels of the ayllu lands. Apus are "fed" with offerings of coca, alcohol, and food. Only if an Apu is given the proper respect will he provide for his community's needs. When José María Arguedas was doing anthropological reserach in Puquio, he was given this description of the Apu concept by the head of a Runa ayllu (in that region, the Apu as a spiritual entity is more often called *Wamani*):

> The Wamani is really our second God. The Wamani exists in all the mountains; all high places have the Wamani. He provides the pasture for our animals, and to us he gives his veins, the watercourses.

The mountains can also be dangerous, not only to foolhardy climbers, but to anyone living in the shadow of their influence. The 1970 earthquake dislodged a great mass of partly frozen mud and rock from the upper slopes of Huascarán. The *aluvión* hurtled down the mountainside, reaching a speed of more than sixty miles per hour. At one place in its path a sudden rise in the topography was sufficient to launch the whole slide into the air. It is said that it flew over a small Runa settlement, inflicting no physical harm, though several people were deranged by the sight and sound of it passing overhead.

A large town near the valley bottom was not so lucky: the mass dropped on Yungay like an Old Testament judgment. All the buildings and twenty thousand people were buried. When the first relief helicopters arrived they saw an unbelievable sight: sticking up from the middle of the waste of boulders, ice, and clay were the tops of four palm trees, still in place, marking the corners of the central plaza.

Until now, the road has been straight, but at Yungay it must snake its way between colossal boulders. The driver and other passengers cross themselves repeatedly. I see only a raw landscape like the bed of a dry river, in which some hardy shrubs are starting to grow.

The valley rises gently from Carás at seventy-five hundred feet to Huarás at ten thousand. The slope is barely perceptible, except perhaps by the drowsiness brought on by gradual rarification of the air. People are more numerous as we draw near the city. Everywhere Runa are returning home, the men dressed dowdily in shabby Western clothes, the women bright and traditional in flowing skirts of crimson, blue, or black. Both sexes wear battered felt hats that look like Humphrey Bogart hand-me-downs. The rest of the female costume has changed little in its essentials since the Indian writer and illustrator Felipe Waman Puma captured it in his great work, *El Primer Nueva Corónica y Buen Gobierno*, which he wrote between 1585 and 1615. Now, as then, the women wear the handwoven *lliqlla*, a shawl and carrying cloth, fastened in front with a large pin or brooch still called *tupu*. Beneath the *lliqlla* and skirt are frilly blouses and petticoats elaborately stitched in a style that must have been introduced during the eighteenth century. Those with fields to guard carry the slings that were once an Inca war weapon but are nowadays used for killing birds; those with livestock wear home-spun lariats around their waists.

Munankichu willanayta	Do you want me to tell you
Maymantachus kanichayta?	Where I'm from?
Haqay urqu qhepanmanta,	I'm from behind that hill,
Clavelinas chawpinmanta,	Amid the carnations,
Azucenas chawpinmanta.	Among the lilies.
Castillamantam warak'ay,	My sling is of Castilian fabric,
Merinomantam seqolloy:	And my lasso of merino wool:
Enteramente durable,	Very long-lasting,
Enteramente aguante.	Very strong.

Night has fallen when we reach Huarás. Unshaded lightbulbs shine dimly from the doors of one-room shops and bars. Some people are dancing to *waynos* played on scratchy phonographs. No matter how gay the tune, Andean music always wrenches me: there is a desperation to the gaiety that evokes the tragedy of Peru.

CHARLES NICHOLL

Charles Nicholl was born in London in 1950 and now lives in Herefordshire. His journalism has appeared in Granta, Rolling Stone, The Sunday Times, *and* The New Statesman. *He has published a book on Elizabethan alchemy and a biography of the pamphleteer Tom Nashe. Nicholl's interest in the storytelling techniques of fiction are evident in both his travel books, the recent* Borderlines: A Journey in Thailand and Burma *and* The Fruit Palace, *an adventurous investigation into the cocaine underworld of Colombia.*

··

from THE FRUIT PALACE

The San Felipe slaughterhouse lay behind a supermarket in the nebulous northern outskirts of Bogotá, where the city laps around the old outlying villages of Suba and Nissa, depositing its flotsam of shopping malls and housing projects on the high green savannah. I presented myself at the gates and said I wished to see Señor Santander Gomez Cuartas, Junior Vice-Superintendent of the slaughterhouse.

Getting this far had indeed been easy enough. A visit to the offices of the Colombian Meat Producers' Federation had secured, along with reams of information and statistics about the meat trade, the name of Señor Gomez. As Jefe de Relaciones Públicas at the slaughterhouse, he was the official unfortunate delegated to deal with occasional visiting nuisances like myself. I flourished my business card at the security man. This describes me as a "consultant researcher," with a Mickey-Mouse–company address and telex number underneath, a useful tool in the nose-poking trade. Judging from the security man's blank gaze it might just as well have described me as an Egyptian rope-dancer, but the general effect was enough. He telephoned through to Gomez and told him he had a visitor at the front gate.

Presently Gomez appeared, a small, worried man with a goatee beard. He wore a white coat with splashes of blood on it, and carried another over his arm. Oozing plausibility, I explained my mission. I was compiling a "business opportunities" report on Colombia, was very interested in the meat business, had your name from Señor So-and-so at the Federación, and would be most grateful—esteemed *señor*—to be shown around this major meat-processing plant of yours. He said he would show me round with pleasure. He gave me the white coat to put on, and I was in. If Rikki was right, this was where the Snow White pipeline disgorged 100 kilos of cocaine a week. I didn't quite know what I was looking for, but surely something must show. I noted the trucks parked at one end of the abattoir, dusty flat-bed trucks and larger covered lorries that brought the cattle up from the lowland grazing plains of the east. There must have been thirty or forty trucks there. How to spot a few sacks of coke?

The job in hand, however, was my guided tour of the slaughter-house. I wasn't looking forward to this. We watched the cattle being herded into the corrals behind the abattoir. Most of them were *cebú* oxen—big, placid, humped, white beasts, South American versions of the Brahmin ox, though unfortunately for them not sharing their Hindu cousins' immunity from slaughter. Gomez rubbed his hands and said that a stout, well-covered *cebú* bullock was worth upward of 30,000 pesos. Each of these big fellows would weigh about 500 kilos and yield over half that weight in meat and assorted offals. Meat is measured in the traditional unit of *arrobas*—12.5 kilos—and a good animal is always said to yield *una arroba mas*, one *arroba* more than half its body weight.

As we walked round the block of the corrals, Gomez stopped. Gesturing me to follow him, he walked over to a group of three men standing round a station wagon. A fourth was sitting in the opened back, pulling on a pair of rubber boots. Gomez introduced me to a tall, lugubrious man, the *matadero*'s senior vice-superintendent, and to the young, bearded manager of the Cafam supermarket next to the abattoir. Small talk was exchanged. Sixty million kilos of beef left the slaughterhouse every year, I learned.

The small, elderly man in the back of the station wagon was discussing something with a white-coated official—instructing him, it seemed, for now the official said, "Yes, señor, right away," and hurried off, checking his watch like the White Rabbit. Gomez promptly launched into obsequious greetings. "What a pleasure it is to see you, Don Rafael," he cried, ducking and bobbing like a courtier. He plucked fussily at my sleeve. "May I present to you Señor Rafael Vallejo Aragon? He is one of our most distinguished and successful figures in the meat business."

The small man took this heralding as no more than his due. He wore a smart tweedy suit, check shirt, heathery woollen tie. His rubber boots were brand new: blue with bright yellow soles. The whole gave a careful effect of well-breeched country gent. He stood to shake hands. The palm was hard and calloused, the figure beneath the squire's tweeds stocky and powerful. He hadn't been born distinguished, I guessed.

I fired in a couple of polite questions about his meat interests. His answers were vague and grand. He soon turned to the others to discuss beef matters. Gomez hung in for a bit, larded Vallejo with more compliments, then said, "We must leave you, Don Rafael, you are a busy man." Vallejo said to me, with mechanical largesse, "You must come to my stud-farm in Cundinamarca one day, señor. I will tell you *everything* about the meat business in Colombia." He laughed a gravelly laugh. "The meat business is very good. We are a nation of carnivores!" He made a grimace, gnashed his teeth comically. The others laughed fulsomely. Gomez cried, "It is true, Don Rafael, it is true!" Vallejo frowned for a moment. "In England you have these"—he searched for the word, and spoke it with distaste—"*vegetarianos*. Not in Colombia. It is not natural. For rabbits, maybe." There was a sudden bullying note in his voice. He covered it with a loud, false laugh, echoed once more by the entourage. Gomez writhed with delight, but I saw his eyes flick over to me to see how I was taking this slur on my homeland. I thought of making some smart-ass riposte, but the odds were against me. For a moment, though, I found myself staring straight into the little man's hard grey eyes.

"He's an important man, then?" I said to Gomez as we walked on.

"*Millonario!*" whispered Gomez, pouting with pleasure at the thought.

···············

From a raised walkway we could view the entire corral. In the corner was a pen with a few steers lying awkwardly, some moving and struggling. These animals, immobilized by sickness or injury, would be dispatched *in situ*. All the other animals were progressing, hour by hour, pen by pen, towards the *corriente*, the narrow black-railed ramp that led up into the abattoir proper. There a man in white overalls and a safety helmet prodded them up, in single file, with an electric goad wired up to a live overhead cable. The ramp led to an opening, with steel half-doors, like saloon doors in a Western. The patient oxen plodded up. The leading one glimpsed the scene inside, beyond the steel doors. If there is a bovine notion of hell, this was surely it. It skidded back, but the animals behind blocked its retreat, and the prod goaded it on.

Without really meaning to, I said, "He doesn't want to go in."

Gomez laughed, as if I had made some polite little joke. "It is sad, isn't it?" he said, unconvincingly. We walked on into the *matadero*, the killing place.

Just inside those swing doors, the steer came into a square well, about twenty feet long. A man stood high above it, wielding a long steel pole with a sharp spike at the end, like an elongated ski-stick. As the animal was released into the well, he held the *pica* vertical above him, two-handed, and brought it down in a swift, hard jab into the steer's neck, just behind the horns. The animal fell, stunned and helpless, eyes lolling, legs cavorting crazily. Another worker now nipped down into the well and slipped a heavy chain loop around its left hindleg. This was a deft operation, with half a ton of flesh and bones thrashing about on the floor. A third man, up on a level with the *picador*, pressed a button. The hoist clanked into action, winching the beast up, upside down. It hung swaying from the overhead rail. This rail ran on circuitously, like a ghost train, through the various departments of the slaughterhouse. With a brisk, practised slash the man next to the *picador* cut the upended animal's throat. Blood poured out like water from a pail, thick crimson blood, splashing and steaming on the wet concrete floor. The next man sliced off the head and feet, a surprisingly easy operation with those big, scoured knives. The whole process, from living creature to headless carcass, took no more than half a minute. At the San Felipe slaughterhouse eight hundred to one thousand cattle are dispatched every day. When the darkness comes they switch on flood-lights over the corrals, and the sacrifice continues.

The carcass continued along the overhead rail till it came to the skinners. Skinning is done with a kind of modified chainsaw. This sliced up the belly, and a hook was then passed through the skin at the back, and the chain-winch pulled upwards, bringing the whole hide with it. The skin was stretchy and pink on the inside, peeling off like a long pale glove. The guts piled out: strange coils and tubes, white, red and blue. The skins were carted off in one direction, the guts in another. In another room they were sorting great vats of the stuff— *viscera roja*, the offal; *viscera blanca*, the intestines, paunch, etc. Nothing will be wasted. The carcass now looked like a recognizable piece of butcher's meat, and off it went along the rail to the other half of the *matadero*, to be packed whole into cold-store trucks, or chopped and packaged ready for the butchers, restaurants, roadhouses and kitchens of this nation of carnivores.

Gomez was at my shoulder throughout, explaining it all, casual and precise, like Mephistopheles giving a guided tour of the inferno. When he judged I had seen enough, he took me to his office, up a few steps behind the gut room. When he closed the door I realized what a huge din had filled the slaughterhouse. The whole gory business had made such an impact on my eyes that I had hardly noticed the noise. I felt sick and tired. I saw my knuckles whiten as I leant on the metal desk. There was a pile of S-shaped hooks and a wooden-handled knife sharpener in the in tray.

Looking out of the barred window on to a small, enclosed yard outside, I saw two men talking. One was the little meat baron, Rafael Vallejo. He had his back to me, but the tweed jacket and the white hair were unmistakable. The other was the white-coated minion he had been talking to when I first saw him. I watched with idle curiosity. Gomez was hunting out some statistics for me, tetchily complaining of the lack of a secretary to keep his papers in order. I heard a door opening into the yard. Vallejo turned. Another white-coated figure came into view, from some room next to Gomez's office. There was something vaguely troubling about his back view. The broad, slightly hunched shoulders, the square head of spiky black hair. I had seen it before. With a jolt, I realized. I had seen it walking out of The Place a couple of nights earlier, clad in sky-blue. It was Oddjob.

Rikki was right, Snow White was real, and I was right slap in the middle of it. Under no circumstances must Oddjob see me here. He did not look like a man who had much time for funny coincidences. I shrank back, grateful for the grimy film over the window.

Gomez had found the figures, the annual tonnages and percentage breakdowns so vital for my study of the meat business. He brought a few folders over to the desk and began to drone out the data. I mechanically wrote as he spoke, but all the while I was keeping an eye on the trio out in the yard. Vallejo was talking, with jabbed gestures of emphasis. Oddjob was listening, head still, occasional sulky monosyllables of agreement. The more I watched, the cosier it looked. Could it be possible? Had I stumbled right up the ladder all at once? Vallejo was no small-time spiv. If that was cocaine talk going on in that yard, then the distinguished millionaire and carnivore Don Rafael was something pretty big. The sun glinted on his white hair. Was he the *capo*? Was he Snow White himself?

In a pause between statistics, trying to sound casual, I said, "Look, there's Señor Vallejo again. He does a lot of business here, does he?"

"Oh yes. He has many cattle ranches in the *llanos*. We handle all his stock."

"And the meat itself? He has distribution networks, that sort of thing?"

"Of course. Transcarne. One of the biggest meat transportation companies in Colombia."

It was all falling into place. Out in the yard there was just Vallejo and Oddjob now. The third man had left. Oddjob's sleazy, slant-eyed, tom-cat's face was half-turned toward me. He was talking, with choppy, robotic gestures from his big paws. It was the first time I'd seen him utter a word. "Who's that Vallejo's talking to?" I asked.

Gomez had his glasses off for reading the figures and now had to fumble them out of his white coat. "That? Oh, that's one of our packing managers."

Somewhere a siren shrilled. Gomez looked at his watch, closed his folders. "Midday," he announced. "The end of the morning shift. You would like a beer?"

As in all the comedies, the booze was in the first-aid cabinet. He took out two bottles and two glasses. Vallejo and Oddjob were still conferring, but with a hasty, last-minute air now. Gomez was washing the glasses in a hand-basin. No: the glasses were on the desk—Gomez was washing two *more* glasses. He was walking to the door that led out into the yard. It opened with a squawk of metal on the stone floor. The two men outside wheeled around. Gomez bobbed in the doorway. "Don Rafael! Rodolfo! You will take a beer with us?" A curt wave from Vallejo. "How kind, Señor Gomez." A nod of assent from Oddjob, a.k.a. Rodolfo. Gomez fussed happily back into the room, polishing a glass on his coattail. "We will have a party," he chirped.

Fear is blank. Brain dazzled, body frozen, a rabbit caught in the headlights. I heard the fizz of beer, the thin clatter of bottle tops on the metal desk. You bloody idiot, I thought. You've really done it this time. Vallejo was walking slowly towards us, still talking. Oddjob glided resentfully beside him. In a few seconds he would be here. He would recognize me, he would start asking questions, he would go on asking till he didn't need any more answers. Then he would probably hook me up on the overhead rail and loosen my guts with one of those skinning saws.

There was only one way out: back into the slaughterhouse. I hunched up, hand to my mouth, and blurted, "*Estoy enfermo! Voy a vomitar!*" Vallejo had just stepped in through the door as I rushed out of the office. The last thing I saw was Gomez's startled face, and the beer spilling past the glass as he looked up from pouring.

I sprinted down the steps, back into the mayhem of the killing-floor, through the gut-room, slowing to a trot, trying not to attract attention. I kept my hand over my mouth, so everyone would think the gringo *maricón* couldn't handle all the blood and death. I heard Gomez's voice behind me. "Señor Nee-col, this way! Not there, señor!" I dodged down a corridor, passed through an empty room with a long line of severed calves' feet dangling from chains, crossed a yard, and came into what was evidently the pig section of the *matadero*. There were squeals without, but in this room all was quiet. A man in a rubber apron was thoughtfully prodding a few dead porkers in a vat of hot water. Another, wearing a cap with a cloth down the back of his head like a legionnaire's képi, was scraping the hairs off a strung carcass. I slowed to a walk. White coat on, notebook in hand, just an official on his way from this door to that.

I came out into another yard. Pigs milling in slatted stalls, but no one around that I could see. I tried to get some bearings. There was a sort of fenced runway through which the pigs were herded into the stalls. Beyond it I saw trucks and cars parked: the back of the *matadero*, I reckoned, the opposite side from the one I'd come in at. If I could just get myself out through some back gate. I edged along the side of the stalls and was just about to break cover when I heard footsteps and voices. I shrank back, but I was still in full view if they came into the yard. The stall nearest me was empty. I clambered over the side and dropped silently into a rich mulch of straw and pig shit. A few inches from my face, in the neighboring stall, a dozen fear-crazed pigs bumped and snuffled against the slats. I crouched shivering while the voices passed.

Skulking at the edge of the truck park I saw that there was indeed a rear gate. A few yards away a man was closing up the back of an old flat-bed truck. He wore blue overalls and a battered straw hat: a pig-man, I supposed. He climbed into the cab and started the engine. He'll do, I thought. I stripped off my dung-smeared white coat, dumped it in a corner and trotted briskly up to the truck. "Excuse me, señor. Are you going? Can you give me a lift?"

The pig-man surveyed me, chewing on a toothpick. I was breathing heavily: fear at high altitude. There was muck on my hands, my tie, my notebook. He ran a hand over his grey stubble, amiable and puzzled. I tensed with impatience. Then he nodded slowly, and said something in a rich *campesino* brogue. It sounded like "I'm going to Zoggo."

"That'll do nicely," I said, and climbed up into the cab. He smiled a broad, toothless smile, fished out a crumpled pack of Pielroja, and offered me a cigarette. I fumbled for matches, trying to speed everything up. Any moment now Gomez and Oddjob were going to come round the corner and start the hue and cry. "My car won't start," I said. "I'm terribly late." He shook his head philosophically and said something else I couldn't understand. Lateness was not a concept that meant much to him. At last, clamping the cigarette in his mouth, he eased the pickup into gear. The truck chugged off lazily down along the red-brick back of the *matadero*. My eyes darted around, looking for the familiar little-and-large figures. The truck seemed to be firing on about half a cylinder. Optimum speed was reached at five miles an hour. The pig-man slumped comfortably in his seat, elbow resting on the window. Jesus, I thought, jiggling futilely, I've picked a real winner here.

I regretted my move even more when we reached the roadway, and instead of turning toward the rear gate he swung the truck right, heading for the front of the *matadero*. This brought us right into the central thoroughfare: offices, canteen, lunch-hour crowds of white coats, slaughterers, truckers. Almost immediately I spotted Gomez, talking to a security-looking man in a peaked cap. He was tugging at his little beard, puzzling away at the mystery of the vanishing journalist. Then, off to one side, I saw Oddjob, silently watching, his fat brown face ranging slowly round like a radar dish. From where he stood he could see both exits from the *matadero*. He was waiting for me to break cover. He was bound to see me as we passed.

We chugged serenely to my doom. I squeezed my hands in mute supplication. In doing so I felt the box of matches still cradled in my sweating palm. With a swift, purposeful movement I spilt the contents on to the rusty floor at my feet. "*Maldita sea*," I cursed, "how clumsy," and bent myself double to retrieve them. In this position, I fervently hoped, I was just out of view below the line of the window. "It's all right, señor, I have matches," said the pig-man. "No, no," I called up from my jackknife position, "I'll get them." He shrugged. The truck hiccoughed on towards the gate. I scrabbled in the dust for the little waxy white matches. With this meagre camouflage I passed beneath and beyond the gaze of Oddjob.

When the truck stopped I straightened up, thinking we were at the gates. But we were still a good twenty yards short of them. The pig-man had stopped to talk to someone, another *campesino*, another crumpled hat. It was going to be one of those slow, mulled conversations full of pauses.

Craning around, I saw Gomez and the peaked-cap fellow walking purposefully up the roadway toward us. Clearly they were coming up to the gate. They were going to warn the security guard: a mad Englishman on the loose. The pig-man was talking about the price of pork, warming to his theme. I heard again the butcher's phrase Gomez had used, *"una arroba mas."*

Oh yes, we're all after that little bit extra, that one *arroba* over the top. Only sometimes it costs us more than we can pay.

It was now or never. "Thanks for the ride," I said, and jumped out of the cab. The truck shielded me from Gomez. Those twenty yards to the gate were a fast walk through eternity. I waited for the shout behind me but none came. As I passed through the gate the security man waved. I saw him jot something down on a clipboard. One consultant researcher, business done, leaves the slaughterhouse. He must be a busy man. Look how he's running . . . .

JONATHAN RABAN

Jonathan Raban was born in England in 1942, and has written about London in Soft City. *His travel books include* Hunting Mister Heartbreak, Arabia Through the Looking Glass, Coasting, *and* Old Glory, *which won the Thomas Cook Award. He has published a novel,* Foreign Land, *and collected his journalism in* For Love & Money: A Writing Life, 1969–1989. *He is a Fellow of the Royal Society of Literature, and now lives in Seattle. The following excerpt includes the final pages of Raban's account of a three-month voyage alone in a sixteen-foot boat down the Mississippi in 1979.*

---

from OLD GLORY

In the morning the air was so still that I could feel the ripples of turbulence I caused by passing through it. A fine salt mist had put the water towers out of focus. They had lost their supporting pillars and looked like silver dirigibles adrift in the sky.

The earth felt like powdered glass underfoot. It was a mixture of black dirt and the shells of millions of tiny white mollusks. With every step, it crunched and snapped. There were mangled stalks of sugar cane on the road and on the bayou, and isolated stands of uncut cane as high as houses in the fields.

I eased the boat out onto the bayou. A faint tidal drift made the water hyacinths and the cane stalks wander sluggishly away from the direction of the sea. Following their lead, I ran up to the end of Lockport and turned left into Lake Fields: miles and miles of open water with the same veined, soapstony sheen. On the southern bank, someone had raised an improvised levee of crushed automobiles. The salt in the air had rusted them together so that they looked like an earthwork, oddly posted about with spots and scraps of their old, gaudy Ford and General Motors livery.

A muffled fisherman in a pirogue raised his hand in a salute as I went past. It was the kind of morning and the kind of place where it was important to acknowledge the existence of other people. The sheer, motionless space of sky and water tempted one into the hallucination that one had been given the world entirely to oneself. The intermittent reminders of human tenancy were unfailingly odd. There was a crumbling jetty sticking out of the mud. No road or track led to it. There wasn't a house in sight. Yet on the jetty there was a waterlogged sofa, its stuffing leaking from its sides. It was a queer foreign exile; it looked as if it were badly in need of the company of a coffee table, a television set, and a standing lamp. A mile farther on, a line of willows ran out across the water on a neck of land as narrow as a sidewalk. At the foot of the trees, three frame houses had been joined together and mounted on the hull of a barge. I rode up to the front door of one of them. The whole place was a ruin. The glass had gone from the windows; part of the roof had fallen in. I tied the boat to the porch and walked through the gutted rooms. Nothing had been left behind except for a few rags and some bits of old newspaper. The *New Orleans Times-Picayune*. June 1968. It had been preserved under a curling sheet of brown linoleum. I wondered what had driven the people from this ingenious and once beautiful house. The lonely vacancy of the view from its windows? Yet the hull of the barge alone must have been worth a fortune in scrap.

I made a long southwesterly loop and rejoined the Intracoastal Waterway, where towboats were busy stirring up the water and the morning. I was glad to see them. They were difficult companions to live with, but their general boisterousness came as a relief after the weird, evacuated stillness of the reach of swamp at my back.

At Houma, I turned up the arched Venetian canal of the Bayou Terrebonne and went to look for a bar. The one I found had the air of a place that scorned the daytime and had created its own perpetual night; it had a pool table and enough bare, dusty space to run several brawls in at once.

"Have you got anything to eat?" I asked the bartender.

"I can do you a shit on a shingle," she said.

It sounded interesting and disgusting in equal parts. My curiosity narrowly beat my feelings of incipient revulsion.

"Okay, I'll have a shit on a shingle," I said, trying to sound as if I'd been shitting on shingles for years.

Waiting for this object to appear, I played pool with a man who'd arrived in Houma five days before. He had come down to Louisiana from Connecticut and was looking for a job as a roustabout on a Gulf oil rig. Houma had scared him half out of his wits.

"Ain't this country something else, though? You should've been here last night. There was a guy came in the bar waving a three-five-seven Magnum and yelling that he wanted to shoot some niggers. I'm telling you, man: if there'd have been a black sitting here he would have been a dead man. That guy wasn't joking. I've only been here five days. It's crazy. What I need most in this town is a gun. If you're in Houma, you need a gun."

"That's pretty easy in Louisiana, isn't it? You only have to show your driver's license."

"Yeah. That's my problem. I don't have a driver's license."

My shit on its shingle was put out for me on the bar. It was only corned-beef hash on toast, but its revolting name had somehow worked its way into the flavor of the thing; it tasted foul.

I was trying to rid my mouth of the memory of it by smoking a pipeful of tobacco when I found Houma in person standing behind me. He was short and skinny, in his twenties; but his face had the creased and yellowed look of someone well past fifty. He had the shakes.

"What you think you tryin' to put over on me, man?"

"Me? Nothing."

"Why you come in here?"

I shrugged. "A drink . . . a game of pool . . . something to eat."

"What the fuck is *that*?"

He was pointing to the loose cellophane pouch in which my tobacco was wrapped.

"That's my tobacco."

"Tobacco—shit!"

My pool partner came over. "Hey, what's the trouble?"

"And you keep *your* shit out of this, I'm warning you," Houma said. Connecticut backed off. His alarmed eyes were telegraphing *What did I tell you?* at me.

Houma's face was six inches away from mine. The top of his head came up to my nose. "I'm just asking you, polite, now, to get your fucking shit out of this bar."

"Would you mind telling me why?"

"I don't have to spell nothing out to you—Fed!"

"I'm not a Fed," I said.

"You don't fool nobody. You're a fucking Fed narc. You and your shit *bait*."

"Look—" I said, and started to reach inside my pocket to find my passport. I could hardly be an accredited Englishman and a Fed narc. My hand had been stopped and gripped almost before it had begun to move. I could feel the fierce trembling in Houma's wrist. He had a knife in his other hand.

"You pull your fuckin' gun on me, man, I'll cut you—"

"Look, please—" I said. The whole episode was so insane and sudden that I hadn't yet had time to be frightened by it. "I haven't got a gun. I was trying to show you my passport. I'm British. I'm not a policeman. I'm not an American. I'm not a Fed. I'm not a narc. Now, please . . . look inside my pocket. You'll find my passport with my wallet." I could see Connecticut at the far end of the bar. He had seen the knife and was watching shamefaced. I thought: If I were in his position, all I'd do would be watch too.

Houma's knife came up and flipped the lapel of my jacket aside. He saw at least that I wasn't armed. His fingers twitched at the contents of my pocket, and they scattered in front of me on the bar floor: checkbook, wallet, passport, pen and, as I saw with real alarm, the business card of Clarence Carter, superintendent of the Shelby County Penal Farm in Memphis. I had visited his jail. At this moment, he was the last person in the world with whom I wanted any visible connection.

"You see my passport there? Now, look at it."

"*You* get it," Houma said. "I'm watching you, man."

I picked it up and showed it to him.

"What is this shit?"

"It proves that I'm an English citizen. I'm a foreigner. I'm a visitor to this country."

"It don't prove fucking nothing—" The madness had gone out of his voice, though. Connecticut, feeling the tension slacken, came over to us again.

"He's just a goddamn tourist, man—"

Houma took my packet of tobacco from the bar and sniffed at it. "Shit. Why you keeping it in this fucking stuff, man? You want to get yourself killed?" His voice had turned to a feeble whine. He was just a little runt with a knife in his belt and an addict's jitters. "Okay . . . so I made a mistake. I was wrong, okay? Will you shake my hand now?"

Absurdly, ceremonially, we shook hands.

"You're my friend now, okay, man?" He tried to put his arm around my shoulder, but it didn't quite reach. "You want another beer?"

"No, thanks."

"Come on—you and me, we'll shoot some pool, huh?"

"Okay."

His cue trembled in his hands; my cue trembled in mine. The balls on the table went everywhere except into the pockets. When Houma shambled jerkily off to the men's room, I fled the bar, and didn't stop running until I reached my boat.

A single-engined seaplane was coming in to touch down on the Waterway, and I had to pull over to the dock where a fleet of little planes rocked on their pontoons. A pilot came across to talk: he had spotted the Wisconsin registration on my boat and wanted to know what it was doing so far from home.

"God, that's something I'd like to do sometime. That's just the kind of thing I'm into myself."

He was a stranger here too. He had gone broke in the Florida Keys, flying a one-man passenger service. The day before, he had signed on as a pilot here, ferrying crewmen and supplies out to the drilling platforms offshore. He and his wife were living in a camper down the street. They had lost their house in Florida: Louisiana was their chance for a new start.

"So where are you going now?" he asked.

"I'm not sure. Morgan City, I think."

"Morgan City? I heard that place is a *real* dump."

"So did I."

I pushed on up the waterway as it cut from bayou to bayou: Bayou Cocodrie . . . Bayou Chene . . . Bayou Boeuf. Ahead of the boat, the water was like jade; behind, it was roiling cocoa. Wherever there was a bump of high ground in the swamp, someone had built himself a shack with a muddy yard full of chickens, a dock, a tethered boat. One could live like Crusoe here. The income-tax man would have to paddle out in a canoe to collect his revenue in crawfish, alligator skins, and the pelts of nutria rats; there'd be no mail, no telephone calls—just pelicans and vultures in the garden and the slow tidal swill of the water around one's house. Louis Beauregard's story of the froomids did correspond to something real: somewhere up the Bayou Capasaw or the Bayou Penchant there must be secret places where men have been living in hiding for years. I had heard rumors of a clandestine colony of Chinese shrimp fishermen who occupied a stilt city in the swamp and shot anyone curious enough to stumble on their hideout; the rumors weren't wholly unbelievable, and the pilots of the seaplanes must often have noticed things that were best left uninvestigated.

The Bayou Boeuf opened into the estuary of the Atchafalaya River, and Morgan City was a ramshackle patchwork of low roofs squatting on the junction. I cruised along its beach looking for a place to land. On the edge of the estuary there was a fisherman's jetty with two jonboats moored to its few remaining piles. I grounded on soft mud, and was met by an old man trailing a line of catfish hooks.

"What you want?"

"I wondered if I could tie up here for the night."

"You could lose your boat. Nothing's safe in this town."

"Why's that?"

"*Lot* of drifters about."

He took in my scuffed cases with a glance of scornful recognition.

"Oh. Why do *they* come here?"

"Looking for work." He looked at me again and gave an amused snort. "They don't get none, though. It'll cost you a dollar—"

"Fine."

"In advance."

Across the street there was a grocery with a pay phone. It took half an hour to raise a cab which was circling the town picking up passengers as it went along. The driver, a huge morose youth, introduced himself as Tiny; the elderly woman in the front seat was Miss Leonie.

"You new in town?" asked Miss Leonie.

"Yes, I've just arrived."

"You come to the armpit of the world," she said, making every vowel of the phrase last as long as it possibly could, like a particularly toothsome sweet.

We came to a scruffy little housing project, with piles of old clothes flapping in yards of unplanted sand. Tiny hooted, and a black teenager came out dressed in a sharp dude suit and wearing pink-framed glasses. He sat beside me. "Know what I'm going to do?" he said. "I'm gonna buy me a machine gun."

"Why's that?" Miss Leonie said. "What you want with a machine gun?"

"Climb to the top of the highest building in Morgan City . . ." He swiveled in his seat, holding an imaginary carbine and spraying us all with bullets. "Rat-a-tat-a-rat-a-tat-a-rat-a-tat-a-rat-a-tat-a . . ." He rolled back and laughed, holding his knees.

I had asked to be set down at the best motel in Morgan City. This had driven Miss Leonie into a cigaretty coughing fit.

"*Best* motel in Morgan City? You ain't asking much, are you, mister?"

"Rat-a-tat-a-tat-a-tat-a . . ."

In the event, I was set down by a cluster of peeling cabins grouped around a courtyard with a dead banana plant in the middle. I was given a key to a room with a bare concrete floor. The sheets on the bed looked slept in; the single blanket was riddled with burns and stains. The floral shower curtain was cracked on every fold. I went back to the motel office to talk to two identically fat girls in tight stretch pants and Hawaiian blouses.

"Haven't you got a better room than that? One with a bath?"

"They don't none of them have *baths*."

"It's about the worst motel room I've ever seen."

"Oh, it ain't *good*. Ain't no worse than none of the others, though."

"Is there another motel in town where I could find a better room?"

"Nope. The rest of them, they're *worse*."

"Jesus." I was deeply impressed by Morgan City's pride in its own scabbiness. "What do people *do* in Morgan City?" I asked.

"Fight. Get drunk. Pick up women."

"You can get rolled around here," said the other girl tentatively, picking at a speck on her scarlet-panted buttock.

I wasn't sure whether "rolled" meant mugged or laid.

"I don't think I much want to get rolled."

"Okay," she said.

I went for a long walk around the town. It had a certain repetitious charm, since it consisted of acre after acre of exactly the same house. Half a dozen rough brick platforms, eigtheen inches high, supported a shack with a corrugated-iron roof, a veranda draped in torn screening, a single, gray Grecian column made of wood, a broken rocker and a faded blue statue of the Virgin on the doorstep. There were many more cats than people on the streets, and the cats had the same glandular fattiness as the girls at the motel. They grazed on the little heaps of garbage that stood in front of almost every house, spilling appetizingly from leaky bags.

Three miles later I was back to where I'd started, on Brashear Avenue, which was as near as Morgan City seemed to come to possessing a Main Street. In the middle of the road there was one of the most arresting exercises in civic statuary that I had ever seen. It was called *The Spirit of Morgan City* and had been molded in some kind of lividly colored fiberglass. A life-size shrimp boat was in collision with something that at first I took to be the Eiffel Tower, but later decided was meant to be an offshore oil rig. The hideous glory of this marvel had been a little softened for Christmas: it had been wrapped up in tinsel ropes, stars and bangles, as if Morgan City were thinking of mailing it to someone as a surprise gift.

One building in Morgan City didn't fit at all. On the far side of the street beyond a high wall and a row of trees, a colonnaded mansion with a texas-deck front looked out over the Atchafalaya River. The rest of the town barely came up to the windows of its ground floor. This sugar planter's castle had once been all there was of Morgan City; now it was loftily marooned in a cheerful slum, so grand and tall that its owner might never have noticed the steady encroachment of the shanty-town around his feet. From his bedroom, he could probably see clear across to Texas and halfway down to Mexico; with luck, he might not even yet have set his eyes on Morgan City. Perhaps he took its tin roofs for a widening of the river and was wondering whether, granted this addition of a paddy field to his plantation, he might change from sugar cane to rice.

The bars on Front Street looked like places where I was certain to be ringed as a federal narcotics agent. I walked away up Brashear Avenue, searching for somewhere a little more salubrious, and ended up in a lounge crowded with other, bewildered strangers musing on their exile in Morgan City.

"What's *happening* here? I don't get it. I come from Chicago. In Illinois, or Missouri, you never see a dead dog on the highway. Here in Louisiana, Christ, you see more dead dogs than you can shake a stick at. What's happening? People here, they go out of their way to run a dog down. It's a goddamn sport!"

"Yeah, I'm from Tennessee. You don't see none of that there neither."

"Hell, when we was kids, we used to break off a car's antenna, make a zip gun out of it. But now it's *senseless*. Here, they take your antenna, no reason. Shoot! That's thirty-nine bucks!"

"But them dogs on the highway . . . Who are these people? People who'll kill a guy's dog just for fun . . . I never seen anything so crazy, not till I came down to Louisiana."

"Me neither."

Me neither.

<hr />

The morning was a wide-open door, the sky empty except for a single violet-edged cloud in the far north. I took the boat across Bayou Boeuf and into the seaward neck of Bayou Shaffer, sliding past gleaming mud flats and reedbeds where the tide sucked and whispered in the grasses. Ahead, the color of the water ran from streaky green into an even blue.

It was rich water. Dark with peat, thickened with salt, it was like warm soup. When the first things crawled out of the water, they must have come from a swamp like this one, gingerly testing the mud with their new legs. I trailed my hand over the gunwale and licked my wet forefinger. It tasted of sea.

If the man at Lockport was right, there should be alligators still awake out on these salt flats. If there were, they weren't showing themselves. I made a slow circle around an inlet, watching for something to move on the bank. I took an oar and prodded at a bank of mud. It was as soft and greasy as black butter, and the oar went in as far as my hand. There was no alligator there.

Ain't nothing.

I had crossed, or thought I'd crossed, the line from green to blue.

I turned the motor off and let the boat drift out on the tide for a while, then pointed the bow back, in the same dumb, urban direction that the armadillos set their noses.

TED CONOVER

Ted Conover was born in Japan in 1958. He graduated from Amherst College in 1981 and studied as a Marshall Scholar at Cambridge University. His adventures riding freight trains with hoboes all over the United States is narrated in Rolling Nowhere. *The more recent* Coyotes *tells of his travels with Mexican illegals on the underground railway into and throughout the southern United States. His risky travels remind us of Robert Louis Stevenson's anxiousness "to see the worst of emigrant life," and of George Orwell's going down and out. Conover lives in Denver.*

·····································

from ROLLING NOWHERE

We almost kept going when we reached Spokane. Often I have wondered what might have turned out differently if we had.

The idea of stopping in Spokane to work a day or two had been discussed since Fargo. The St. Vincent de Paul charity store there employed transients, paying them partly in cash and partly in the necessities of life: food, clothing, showers. Sleeping bags, in particular, were the currency Pete and BB hoped to receive, for though they each slept in two, one inserted inside the other, often wearing all their clothes, the bags were too old and thin for the autumn nights ahead.

But just a few steps off the train, BB stopped. "Wait a minute," he said. "It's Friday night. Tomorrow's the weekend, and St. Vinnie's ain't open on the weekend. We'd have to wait till Monday."

"Forget it, then," said Pete. "Let's keep going."

They had already turned around when I spoke up. It was Thursday night, I asserted, and tried to prove it to them by counting back the days since the last weekend. But both of them refused to listen. Just then, however, a brakeman swung out from between two cars, not far from us, and I posed the question to him.

" 'Course it's Thursday," he said, laughing. BB and Pete were humorless. Silently they changed directions again, and we arrived at a weedpatch not far from where they had jungled up just a few weeks before. The tramps had been traveling so much that they were the victims of their own kind of if-it's-Tuesday-this-must-be-Belgium syndrome.

I was up at dawn. Arrive at St. Vinnie's much later than that, BB said, and they might already have all the guys they needed. Because of his ever-worsening wound, Pete would not work; instead, I would donate the bedroll I earned to him, since I already had the best bedroll of the three, and BB would keep the one he earned. We were, after all, partners, and among partners, as Pete had said, it was "all for one and one for all."

But BB, strangely, lingered over his coffee, and then spent a lot of time helping Pete wrap his hand in a clean bandage "borrowed" from the first-aid kit of a caboose. "You better get goin'," he said. "I'll finish this and be right over."

The work involved a lot of loading trucks and moving furniture. I was somewhat annoyed as the day progressed and BB failed to show, but other things kept my mind off it. One was the arrival of a police car and paramedics at the loading dock of a plant across the street. "Old Willy's been hurt," I heard one of the workers tell another. It seemed that Willy, a well-known personage around the yards, often slept under the dock. Apparently, the night before an eight-by-eight-inch wooden beam had fallen on him while he slept, pinning him and fracturing his ankle. It was midday now, and he had just been discovered. After learning Willy was still alive, though, nobody seemed worried: "He's got it good, now. Two or three weeks in the hospital, with clean sheets, a real roof over his head, new clothes, free food, nurses . . . I want to go there, too! Only there's no wine. Poor Willy!"

My salary, at day's end, was a small pouch of Bull Durham tobacco, rolling papers, two dollars, and the bedroll for Pete, consisting of a green blanket, comforter, and a length of twine.

Back at the jungle, BB and Pete were packed and ready to continue west, this time to Wenatchee, in central Washington. Pete grunted his thanks for the bedroll and then sat silently. After rekindling the fire, I reached for my knapsack to get out a can of chili I knew I had there. But . . . one of two straps on the knapsack had been left undone, and not by me. Odd. Maybe Pete or BB had needed some little cooking item, I thought, and had taken a quick look to see if I had it. It was a violation of etiquette—you *never* went in another tramp's pack without permission—but probably not serious.

Yet the chili was not where I had put it. And where were the old cotton gloves I used as hot pads when cooking? And my knit hat—that was gone, too. Suddenly I became alarmed. I looked over toward the campfire—BB was sitting there, chewing on a match and staring into the flames and Pete was gone. My railroad maps—the maps I had not told them about, which had been so hard for me to find, had been hidden at the bottom of the pack. Now they were gone, too. Apprehension grew in my stomach. To mention this or not to . . .

"Hey, uh, BB," I said, deciding. "Were both you and Pete around all day?"

"Well, yeah, I believe we were," said BB, closing the only route of escape from the impending conflict.

"That's funny. Stuff is missing from my pack."

"Oh, yeah? Like what?"

I recited the list, including the train maps.

"I didn't know you had no train maps."

"Well, I did."

BB chewed silently on the match, not looking at me. "So, you want to search my pack, right?"

"No, I don't want to, but I don't know any other way to go about this." The offer had caught me off guard.

"Well, there it is. Go ahead. I got nothin' to hide." He gestured toward his small carry bag. I looked at his bedroll, too, to which he had tied Brandy Lee. If he had offered to let me search his little bag, the stuff was probably in his bedroll.

"Okay if I look at your bedroll after that?"

"Sure."

I approached his pack, on the ground next to BB, my anger

growing. I knew I had to ask this of them—if I didn't press it, what would be taken next? How far behind the loss of respect for my property would be the loss of respect for my person? Yet, as I reached into BB's bag, I was scared. BB, clench-fisted, hovered above.

"Careful—my knife's in there," said BB. It was an oblique threat.

My missing gear was not in the bag. I stood up. BB straightened, too, raising himself to his full height, a head above me. I gestured toward the bedroll.

"What should I do with Brandy Lee?" I asked.

"You'll leave her right fuckin' where she is, you son of a bitch!" snarled BB.

I stepped back. "You said I could look in your bedroll."

"Sure, you can look in it," he said, "but if you don't find your map I'm gonna bash your motherfuckin' head in."

It was just like with Roger. Everything fine one second, and then the next—bam. Complete changeover. But I was not drunk, and I had a dispute to resolve with BB.

BB advanced. I took another couple of steps backwards, out of the range of his fists, and put my hand in my pocket, on the canister of Mace. "I don't want no trouble, BB—just my stuff back."

He wasn't even listening. BB, prison-trained, was sizing up the fight. He stopped walking toward me.

"I see you got your piece," he said, eyes on my pocket. "Well, I got mine, too."

He thought I had a gun, a mistake that would work in my favor. He claimed to have a gun, but I was almost certain he did not: few tramps did, because of a gun's high pawn value. Also, BB almost certainly would have told me about it before, in his own menacing way, if he did have it. But things were moving too fast. All I knew was that BB had stopped moving toward me. And his knife, in the pack, was closer to me than to him.

"Look, man, all I want is for us to be fair and square with each other. You don't want your ass whipped by me, and I don't want mine whipped by you. So play it straight with me."

"I tell you what, if I didn't have no faith in the sumbitches I was travelin' with, I wouldn't be travelin' with the motherfuckers," said BB, drawling at triple speed. "And if I lost somethin', I wouldn't go lookin' through your shit, I'd say, 'Yeah, I take your word for it, man,' and all that. And then I'd just go lookin' for the shit."

"If I didn't find it," I returned, "I'd owe you an apology, and I'd give it."

"I don't accept fuckin' apologies, I sure as fuck don't," said BB heatedly. "They ain't worth the fuckin' paper it's wrote on."

Pete, I noticed, had quietly returned to pick up his gear, and was starting to leave. BB, still hollering, started to do the same. Along with his own bedroll, he picked up the one I'd gotten for Pete. I moved suddenly toward him as he did, my only offensive move of the night.

"You'll leave that," I said.

He drew back from the blankets, cursing me. He and Pete, with Brandy Lee trailing, began crossing the yard toward the tracks.

Pete's neutrality infuriated me. "Hey, Pete," I cried after him. "What ever happened to 'all for one and one for all'? Here we are, friends one minute and the next you split without a word. What happened, did you lose your voice?"

"You shut the fuck up, man," said BB, turning around and shaking a fist at me. "You ain't been straight with us."

"What the hell do you mean by that?" I said. But they disappeared into the strings of trains. I stood alone in the field, desolated and stunned. More than two weeks of round-the-clock companionship had just unraveled in about three minutes.

Gradually my heart slowed, and replacing the anger and adrenaline was fear. The field seemed suffused with BB's malice. I was afraid that he might circle around, trying to catch me unawares while I slept. I couldn't bring myself to eat anything at all. I repacked my gear and walked away, disposing of Pete's bedroll in a ditch as I headed toward the main road. I didn't want any tramp to have it.

To my disgust, two tramps walking in the opposite direction approached me to ask about the jungle conditions. I answered curtly, but they kept talking, filling me in on life at the Spokane rescue mission, though I hadn't asked. Slowly, I began to listen; it sounded like a good destination. Then, to my surprise, I told them why I was leaving the jungle. They seemed genuinely sympathetic. "Town's about five miles from here," said one. "You oughta take the bus. Got change?"

I did not.

"Here," he said, and handed me a quarter, dime, and nickel. "That's handicapped fare, so just make sure you look it. And if that mission's full, you just come back and jungle up with us, okay?"

"Okay," I said. The moment I turned, my eyes flooded with tears. I waved them good-bye without looking.

PART FIVE

WRITERS AND THE EFFECTS OF WAR

Standing in the aftermath of violent death is a numbing experience: the air about one feels torn, ripped and stretched.
                                        —*Dirk Bogarde*

IRVING LAYTON

Author of many volumes of poetry, including The Improved
Binoculars, The Collected Poems of Irving Layton, *and*
Lovers and Lesser Men, *Irving Layton established his rep-
utation in Montreal in the forties and fifties, winning the
Governor General's Award for poetry in 1959. He has been
prominent in the evolution of poetic sensibility in Canada,
where he remains outspoken and prolific. A wide traveler,
Layton was born in Romania and came to Canada at the
age of one, in 1913. In 1982, he was nominated for the
Nobel Prize.*

POSTCARD

For Aviva

In Venice
when it stormed
(ah, where have the years fled?)
you clasped me to you
in terror and love

Each thunderclap
was a fresh embrace
under the sheets;
we were never so close
as when the elements
seemed bent to destroy us

Tonight
as if another
War of Liberation
were in progress
thunderclashes
rock Budapest
and flares
light up the city
to direct fiery
salvos of rain
against roofs and bridges

Marauders
are hammering
on the windowpanes
and I cower
under my blanket
—but where are you, my love?

DIRK BOGARDE

Born in England in 1921, Dirk Bogarde was commissioned in the British army in 1941 and later served in Europe and the Far East. The following account describes his impressions of Normandy in August 1944, where he found himself an "air photographic interpreter attached to 39 Wing of the Royal Canadian Air Force," and where he also painted as an Unofficial War Artist and kept a diary. Bogarde, who began his film career in 1947—appearing in over sixty films—is more recently the author of several volumes of autobiography, including A Postillion Struck by Lightning *and* An Orderly Man, *as well as three novels. For the last twenty years he has lived in Provence.*

----

from BACKCLOTH

The sky was always blue, that strange intense blue of northern France, sea-washed, wind-cleansed, limitless, criss-crossed with lazy scrawls of vapour trails like the idle scribbles of a child in a crayoning-book.

In the orchards the shade lay heavy beneath the trees, spiked here and there with emerald blades of grass and clumps of campion.

But everywhere the land was still. There was no birdsong.

Sometimes a bee would drone up and away, or a grasshopper scissor in the crushed weeds of the chalky soil, and then fall silent as if the effort had been too much, in the still heat, or as if, perhaps, reproved that there was no response in the ominous quiet.

No rabbits scuttled in the hedgerows, the corn stood high, ripe, heavy in the ear, unharvested, and in the meadows cows lay on their sides, stiff-legged, like milking stools, bellies bloated with gas.

Sometimes one of them would explode with a sound like a heavy sigh, dispersing memories of a lost childhood in the sickly stench of decay.

Death was monarch of that summer landscape: only the bee and the grasshopper gave a signal of life, or suggested that it existed. The familiar had become unfamiliar and frightening. A world had stopped and one waited uneasily to see if it would start again: a clock to be rewound in an empty room.

But that comforting tick-tock of normality, of the life pulse, had been provisionally arrested. In some cases it had been stopped for good, for a little farther back, toward the beaches, they were burying those who would remain forever in silence.

There was plenty of noise back there: of gears grinding, engines roaring, tracks rattling, metal groaning.

At the edge of an elm-fringed meadow, I stood against a tree watching, curiously unmoved, the extraordinary ballet between machines and corpses, which proved conclusively that the human body was nothing but a fragile, useless container without the life force.

For some reason it had never fully occurred to me before: I had seen a good number of dead men and had, as a normal reaction, felt a stab of pity, a creep of fear that perhaps it could be me next time, but I had become accustomed to them and got on with my own living.

But that afternoon in the shade of the elms I stood watching the bulldozers (a new toy to us then) shovelling up the piles of dead very much as spoiled fruit is swept into heaps after a market-day, and with as little care. Shuddering, wrenching, jerking, stinking of hot oil in the high sun, they swivelled slowly about with open jaws ripping at the earth to form deep pits, and then, nudging and grabbing at the shreds and pieces, rotting, bloody, unidentifiable, which heavy trucks had let slither from raised tailboards in tumbled heaps of arms and legs, they tossed them into the pits.

Back and forth they droned and crunched, swinging about with casual ease, manoeuvred by cheerful young men, masked against the stench and flies, arms burned black by the August sun.

"Tidying up," said someone with me. "One day they will turn this meadow into a war cemetery. Rows and rows of crosses and neat little walks; perhaps they'll erect a fine granite monument, a flagstaff will carry a proud flag to be lowered at the Last Post, they'll plant those bloody yew trees, and relatives will walk in silence through the toy-town precision and order, looking for their dead."

I remember what he said, because I wrote it all down later, but I can't remember who he was.

Fairly typical of me, I fear.

The words stayed with me for the simple reason that they moved me more than the things which I was observing. The dead lying there in putrid heaps among the sorrel and buttercups didn't move me at all: they were no more than torn, tattered, bloody bundles. The soul had sped; there could only be regret for those who had loved the individual bodies in this seeping mass: for everyone there had once belonged to someone. That was the sadness.

The absolute anonymity of mass death had dulled grief.

The silence didn't last long—silence in war never does. One gets to discover that very early on.

The ominous stillness which had reproved both grasshopper and bee simply preceded a gigantic storm: Caen fell, the Germans began their terrible retreat to the east. The battle for Normandy was over.

I use the word "terrible" advisedly, for the retreat, estimated at that time to be composed of at least 300,000 men plus vehicles and arms, crammed the dusty high-hedged roads and lanes, even the cart tracks through fields and orchards, in a desperate attempt to reach the ferries across the river Seine: the Allied armies surrounded them on three sides. We knew that all the main bridges had been blown, so it appeared evident to us that we contained the entire German fighting force in one enormous killing ground. Tanks and trucks, horse-drawn limbers, staff cars, private cars, farm carts and all kinds of tracked vehicles, anything in fact which could move, inched along the jammed lanes and roads in slow convoys of death.

Unable to turn back, to turn left or right, they had no alternative but to go ahead to the river, providing undefended, easy targets for Allied aircraft which homed down on them as they crawled along and blasted them to destruction: ravening wolves with cornered prey.

By 21 August it was over.

Across the shattered farms, the smouldering cornfields, the smoking ruins in the twisting lanes, smoke drifted lazily in the heat and once again the frightening silence came down over a landscape of shattering carnage.

Those of us in the middle of things really thought that a colossal victory had been achieved. The Germans had been destroyed along with their weapons. There could be nothing left of them to fight, the Russians were about to invade their homeland, surely now victory was ours and war would finish before the end of the summer?

We were wrong. The people who are in the middle are nearly always wrong. The canvas of war is far too great to comprehend as one single picture. We only knew a very limited part—and even that part was not as it seemed. Gradually we began to realize that the war was not over, that it was going to go on, that the Germans were still fighting, still highly armed, stubborn and tougher than they had been before. Slowly "a colossal victory" faded from our minds and we accepted the fact that something must have gone a little bit wrong in our jubilant assessment of an early peace.

It had indeed gone wrong. But it was only some years later, when the generals who had squabbled, quarrelled, and bickered all the way through the campaign began to write their autobiographies, that one learned that, far from a victory, the retreat had been a catastrophe.

By that time it was far too late for thousands of men to worry.

They were laid out in neat rows under white crosses.

What had happened, quite simply, is that the Allied generals, by disagreeing among themselves, had left the back door open to the killing ground permitting thousands of Germans, and their arms, to escape and live to fight another day.

But we didn't know it, fortunately, at the time.

Standing in the aftermath of violent death is a numbing experience: the air about one feels torn, ripped and stretched. The cries of panic and pain, of rending metal, though long since dispersed into the atmosphere, still seem to echo in the stillness which drums in one's ears.

On the main road from Falaise to Trun, one of the main escape routes which we *did* manage to block, among the charred and twisted remains of exploded steel, dead horses indescribably chunked by flying shrapnel, eyes wide in terror, yellow teeth bared in frozen fear, still-smouldering tanks, the torn, bullet-ripped cars and the charred corpses huddled in the burned grass, it was perfectly clear that all that I had been taught in the past about hell and damnation had been absolutely wrong.

Hell and damnation were not some hellfire alive with dancing horned devils armed with toasting forks. Nothing which Sister Veronica or Sister Marie Joseph has told me was true. Clearly they had got it all wrong in those early, happy Twickenham days. Hell and damnation were here, on this once peaceful country road, and I was right in the middle of it all.

My boots were loud on the gravel, oily smoke meandered slowly from smouldering tyres. Blackened bodies, caught when the petrol tanks of the trucks and cars had exploded, grinned up at me from crisped faces with startling white teeth, fists clenched in charcoaled agony.

Down the road in a haze of smoke stood a small boy of about seven; in his hand a tin can with a twisted wire handle.

I walked toward him and he turned quickly, then scrambled up the bank where a woman was bending over a body in the black grass, a hammer and chisel in her hand.

The boy tugged at her skirts, she stood upright, stared at me, shading her eyes with the flat of her hand, then she shrugged, cuffed the boy gently, and bent again to her task.

Hammering gold teeth from the grinning dead.

The boy raised the tin for me to see. It was almost a third full of bloody nuggets and bits of bridge-work.

Waste not, want not.

In the ditch below us a staff car lay tilted on its side, the bodywork riddled with bullet holes in a precise line as if a riveter had been at work rather than a machine gun from a low flying plane.

A woman was slumped in the back seat, a silver fox fur at her feet, her silk dress blood-soaked, a flowered turban drunkenly squint on her red head. A faceless man in the uniform of the SS lay across her thighs.

I kicked one of her shoes lying in the road, a wedge-heeled cork-soled scrap of coloured cloth.

The woman with the hammer shouted down, "Sale Boche! Eh?

Collaboratrice . . . c'est plein des femmes comme ça! Sale Boche!"

I walked back to my jeep. My driver was sitting in his seat smoking.

"Where do they all come from?"

"Who?"

"Those blokes . . . wandering about having a good old loot. They just go through the pockets, get the wallets, pinch the bits of jewellery. There's a squad of women civilians in all this lot. Gives you a bit of a turn seeing dead women in this sort of set-up."

Here and there, pulling at the blackened corpses, wrenching open the doors of the bullet-riddled cars, a few elderly peasants clambered about the wreckage collecting anything of value. God knew where they had come from—every building nearby was destroyed, but like the woman on the bank with the boy, they had come to scavenge what they could.

As we drove away the first bulldozers began to arrive to clear the road. I didn't speak: the sight of the dead girl with the red hair had distressed me profoundly.

I was prepared for people to be dead in uniform, but my simple mind would not come to terms with the sight of a dead woman in a silk dress on a battlefield. That didn't seem to be right. They hadn't warned us about *that* on the assault course in Kent.

We had to pull aside to let a bulldozer grind past; I looked back and saw an old man dancing a little jig. In a fox fur cape.

JAMES FENTON

All the Wrong Places: Adrift in the Politics of the Pacific Rim *includes the author's eyewitness accounts of the fall of Saigon, and of Ferdinand Marcos's overthrow in the Philippines. Fenton has reported from various countries, including Korea. He has also traveled in Borneo with Redmond O'Hanlon, where he almost drowned. (Asked by his fellow English author to accompany him on a second arduous journey, this time to the Amazon, Fenton is reported to have replied, "I would not come with you to High Wycombe.") His collections of poems include* Children in Exile *and* Manilla Envelope. *He is a foreign correspondent for the* Independent *newspaper.*

from ALL THE WRONG PLACES

My first experience of Vietnam was quite different. I was impressed, overawed, by the scale and age of the subject: a war that had been going on for longer than I had been alive; a people about whose history and traditions I knew so little. I had read some books in preparation, but the effect of doing so was only to make the country recede further. So much had been written about Vietnam. I hadn't even had the application to finish *The Fire in the Lake*. The purpose of the book seemed to be to warn you off the subject.

De Quincey's "barrier of utter abhorrence, and want of sympathy" was up. I could well have believed that somebody was trying to tell me something when I came out of my room on the first morning in Saigon and stepped over the decapitated corpse of a rat. I was staying, as most

British journalists did, in the Hotel Royale, but even there I felt myself to be something of an intruder. I had to find work, I had to sell some stories, but I was afraid of trespassing on somebody else's patch. There was an epidemic of infectious neurosis at the time: As soon as one journalist had shaken it off, another would succumb. It would attack without warning—in the middle of an otherwise amiable meal, in the bars, in your room. And it could be recurrent, like malaria.

The reason for this neurosis was not far to seek, indeed it sought you out, and pursued you throughout the day: Saigon was an addicted city, and we—the foreigners—were the drug. The corruption of children, the mutilation of young men, the prostitution of women, the humiliation of the old, the division of the family, the division of the country—it had all been done in our name. People looked back to the French Saigon with a sentimental warmth, as if the problem had begun with the Americans. But the French city, the "Saigon of the piastre" as Lucien Bodard called it, had represented the opium stage of the addiction. With the Americans had begun the heroin phase, and what I was seeing now were the first symptoms of withdrawal. There was a desperate edge to life. It was impossible to relax for a moment. Saigon was a vast service industry clamoring for the attention of a dwindling number of customers: "Hey you! American! Change money, buy *Time* magazine, give me back *Time* magazine I sell you yesterday, buy *Stars and Stripes*, give me back *Stars and Stripes*, you number one, you number ten, you number-ten-thousand Yankee, you want number-one fuck, you want *Quiet American*, you want *Ugly American*, you give me money I shine shoes, number one, no sweat. . . ." On and on, the passionate pursuit of money.

The bar at the Royale was half open to the street. The coffee at breakfast tasted of diarrhea. You washed it down with Bireley's orangeade ("Refreshing . . . and no carbonation!"). Through the windows peered the shoeshine boys—"Hey! you!"—it was starting up again. One morning I was ignoring a particularly revolting specimen when he picked up a handful of sand which he pretended to eat: "You! You no give me money, you want I eat shit!" His expression, as he brought the dirt to his mouth, was most horrible. It was impossible to imagine how a boy of that age had acquired such features: He was about ten years old, but his face contained at least thirty years of degeneration and misery. A few days later I did give him my boots to clean. He sat down in the corner of the bar and set to work, first with a matchstick and a little water, meticulously removing all the mud and dust from the welt, then with the polish. The whole process took about half an hour, and the barman and I watched him throughout, in fascination. He was determined to show his superiority to all other contestants in the trade. I was amused, and gave him a large sum. He was furious, it wasn't nearly enough. We haggled for a while, but I finally gave in. I gave him about a pound. The next day, at the same time, he came into the bar; his eyes were rolling back in their sockets and he staggered helplessly around the tables and chairs; I do not know what drug he had taken, but I know how he had bought it.

Of all the ingenious and desperate forms of raising money, the practice of drugging your baby and laying the thing on the pavement in front of the visitor seemed to me the most repulsive. It did not take long to see that none of these children was ever awake during the day, or to notice from the way they slept that something was amiss. Among the foreigners, stories circulated about the same baby being seen in the arms of five different mothers in one week, but the beggar who regularly sat outside the Royale always had the same child, a girl of eighteen months or so. I never gave any money either to the girl and her "mother," or to any other such teams.

One day, however, I was returning from a good lunch when I saw that a crowd had formed around the old woman, who was wailing and gesticulating. The child was more than usually grey, and there were traces of vomit around her face. People were turning her over, slapping her, trying to force her eyes open. At one point she and the old woman were bundled into a taxi. Then they were taken out again and the slapping was repeated. I went into the hotel and told the girl at reception to call a doctor. "No," she replied. "But the child is sick." "If baby go to hospital or doctor"—and here she imitated an injection—"then baby die." "No," I replied, "if baby *don't* go to hospital maybe baby die." "No."

I took the girl out into the street, where the scene had taken on the most grotesque appearance. All the beggars I had ever seen in Saigon seemed to have gathered, and from their filthy garments they were producing pins and sticking them under the child's toenails. "You see," I said to the girl, "no good, number ten. Baby need number-one hospital." "No, my grandmother had same thing. She need this—number one." And the receptionist produced a small phial of eucalyptus oil. "That's not number one," I said, "that's number ten. Number ten thousand," I added for emphasis. But it was no good insisting or appealing to other members of the crowd. Everybody was adamant that if the child was taken to the hospital, the doctor would kill it with an injection. While I correspondingly became convinced that a moment's delay would cost the child's life.

Finally, after a long eucalyptus massage and repeated pricking of the fingers and toes had produced no visible results, I seemed to win. If I would pay for taxi and hospital, the woman would come. I pushed my way through the crowd and dragged her toward the taxi—a battered old Renault tied together with string. The baby was wrapped in a tarpaulin and her face covered with a red handkerchief. Every time I tried to remove the handkerchief, from which came the most ominous dry gaspings, the woman replaced it. I directed the taxi driver to take us to number-one hospital and we set off. But from the start everything went wrong. Within a hundred yards we had to stop for gas. Then a van stalled in front of us, trapping the taxi. Next, to my amazement, we came to what must have been, I thought, the only level crossing in Saigon, where as it happened a train was expected in the near future. And around here we were hit by the side effects of Typhoon Sarah, which at the time was causing havoc in the northern provinces. We also split a tire, though this was not noticed till later. Driving on through the cloudburst, the taxi driver seemed strangely unwilling to hurry. So I sat in the back seat keeping one hand on the horn and the other attempting to alleviate the restrictions around the baby's breathing apparatus. I also recall producing a third arm with which to comfort the old woman from time to time and I remember that her shoulder, when my hand rested on it, was very small and very hard. Everything, I said, was going to be number one, okay: number-one hospital, number-one doctor, babysan okay. We were traveling through Cholon, the Chinese quarter, on an errand of Western mercy.

All things considered, it took a long time for it to dawn on me that we were not going to a hospital at all. We even passed a first-aid post without the driver giving it a glance. In my mind there was an image of the sort of thing required: a large cool building dating from French times, recently refurbished by American aid and charity, with some of the best equipment in the East. I could even imagine the sententious plaques on the walls. Perhaps there would be a ward named after the former U.S. ambassador. It would be called the Bunker Ward.

It was when the old woman began giving directions that I saw I had been duped. We were now threading our way through some modern slums, which looked like the Chinese equivalent of the Isle of Dogs. "Where is the hospital? This is no hospital," I said. Yes, yes, the taxi driver replied, we were going to hospital, number-one doctor. We stopped by a row of shops and the driver got out. I jumped from the car and seized him by the arm, shouting: "I said number-one hospital. You lie. You cheap charlie. You number-ten-thousand Saigon." We were surrounded by children, in the pouring rain, the taxi man tugging himself free, and me gripping him by the arm. It was left to the woman, carrying the little bundle of tarpaulin, to find out exactly where the doctor lived. Finally I gave in, and followed her up some steps, then along an open corridor lined with tailors and merchants. At least, I thought, when the baby dies I can't be blamed. And once I had thought that, the thought turned into a wish: A little cough would have done it, a pathetic gurgle, then a silence, and my point about Western medicine would have been proved to my own satisfaction. I should have behaved very well; of course I should have paid for, and gone to, the funeral.

In retrospect it was easy to see how the establishment would command confidence: the dark main room with its traditional furnishings, the walls lined with photographs of ancestors in traditional Vietnamese robes, a framed jigsaw of the Italian lakes. And in the back room (it would, of course, have to be a back room) a plump, middle-aged lady was massaging the back of another plump, middle-aged lady. They paid hardly any attention when we came in. There was not the slightest element of drama. Indeed, I began to see that I was now the only person who was panicking. When she had finished the massage, the doctor turned her attention to the baby. First she took some ointment from a dirty bowl at her elbow, and rubbed it all over the little grey body. Then from another bowl she produced some pink substance resembling Euthymol toothpaste, with which she proceeded to line the mouth. In a matter of minutes, the child was slightly sick, began to cry, and recovered. I had never been more furious in my life. To complete my humiliation, the doctor refused any payment. She provided the old woman with a prescription wrapped in newspaper, and we left. We drove to the miserable shelter in which the old woman lived. "Sit down," she said, indicating the wooden bed which was the only feature of her home apart from the roof (there were no walls). In any other mood I might have been moved by the fact that the only English she knew beyond the terrible pidgin currency of the beggars was a phrase of hospitality. But I so deeply hated her at that moment that I could only give her a couple of pounds, plus some useless advice about keeping the baby warm and off the pavements, and go.

I left the taxi driver at a garage not from the Royale, where I also gave him some money toward repairing the split tire. "You number one, Saigon," he said, with a slight note of terror in his voice. The weather had cleared up, and I strolled along past the market stalls. You could buy U.S. Army foot-powder in bulk, K-rations, lurp rations (for Long-Range Reconnaissance Patrols), souvenir Zippo lighters (engraved "Yea though I walk through the valley of the shadow of death I shall fear no evil, for I am the evilest sonofabitch in the valley"), khaki toothbrushes and flannels, and model helicopters constructed out of used hypodermics. You could also buy jackets brightly embroidered with the words "When I die I shall go to heaven, for I have spent my time in hell—Saigon," and a collection of GI cartoons and jokes called *Sorry 'bout that, Vietnam*. As I approached the hotel, people began asking how the baby was, and smiling when I replied "Okay."

And I began to think, supposing they were all in it together? Suppose the old woman, the taxi driver, the man whose van stalled, the engine driver—suppose they were all now dividing out the proceeds and having a good laugh at my expense, congratulating the child on the way it had played its role? That evening I would be telling the story to some old Saigon hand when a strange pitying smile would come

over his face. "You went to Cholon, did you? Describe the doctor . . . uh huh . . . Was there a jigsaw puzzle of the Italian lakes?
Well, well, well. So they even used the toothpaste trick. Funny how
the oldest gags are still the best. . . ."

Indeed I did have rather that conversation a few days later, with
an American girl, a weaver. It began "You realize, of course, first of
all that the taxi driver was the husband of the old woman. . . . But I
do not think it was a conspiracy." Worse, I should rather conclude that
the principals involved were quite right not to trust the hospital doctors
with a beggar's child. It was for this reason that the hotel receptionist
had countermanded my orders to the taxi man, I learned afterward,
and many people agreed with her.

When the old woman came back on the streets, I hardly recognized either her or the child, who for the first time looked conscious
and well. "Babysan okay now, no sick," she said, gazing at me with an
awful adoring expression, though the hand was not stretched out for
money. And when I didn't reply she turned to the child and told it
something in the same unctuous tones. This performance went on for
the rest of my stay: Whenever I was around, the child would be made
to look at the kind foreigner who had saved its life. I had indeed wanted
to save the child's life, but not in *that* way, not on the old woman's
terms.

I was disgusted, not just at what I saw around me, but at what I
saw in myself. I saw how perilously thin was the line between the
charitable and the murderous impulse, how strong the force of righteous
indignation. I could well imagine that most of those who came to
Vietnam to fight were not the evilest sons-of-bitches in the valley. It
was just that, beyond the bright circle illuminated by their intelligence,
in which everything was under their control and every person a com-
pliant object, they came across a second person—a being or a nation
with a will of its own, with its own medicine, whether Fishing Pills or
pink toothpaste, and its own ideas for the future. And in the ensuing
encounter everything had turned to justifiable ashes. It was impossible
in Saigon to be the passive observer. Saigon cast you, inevitably, into
the role of the American.

GAVIN YOUNG

As foreign correspondent for the Observer *Gavin Young covered at least fifteen wars and revolutions around the world. Many of his experiences are recounted in* Worlds Apart: Travels in War and Peace *(1987), from which the following extract is taken. He has written about living with the Marsh Arabs of southern Iraq in* Return to the Marshes *and of his journey through Mesopotamia in* Iraq: Land of Two Rivers. *The story of his improvisational voyage around the world in whatever would float is told in* Slow Boats to China *and* Slow Boats Home.

·······································

THE MURDER OF HUÉ

Hué, 3 March 1968

It is hideously unreal, yet you can feel real rubble underfoot; put a handkerchief to your nose and you can still smell the corpses. I visited Hué first in 1965, and came to know and love it. Now, between them, in the name of the people's salvation, General Giap and the U.S. High Command have killed the flower of Vietnamese cities. Today Hué is no more the city I knew than a friend lying in a street, charred and ripped by a bomb, is the human being one talked or made love to. You can disguise it in whatever military terms you like but in Hué murder has been arranged.

Along the airport road to Hué, which I used to travel in a minibus full of cheerfully chattering Vietnamese, I was made to feel like one of General Patton's soldiers storming across occupied France in 1944. I came, of necessity, in a convoy of fifteen vehicles, huge petrol tankers, trucks full of GIs, lewd or comic slogans painted on the camouflaged covers of their helmets, crouching with Lucky Strikes clamped in dusty and unshaven jaws, guns at the ready for ambushes, tanks spewing up the dust, their drivers' feet stepping hard on the gas.

Fear of the enemy and the enemy's persistent power is everywhere evident. By little bridges, blown and hastily repaired, Americans crouch in sandbagged strong points. Jets and helicopters scream overhead without cessation, airstrikes and artillery barrages send napalm and bombs down on the surrounding green countryside. Impassive Vietnamese villagers line the road in the dust and stare at the pandemonium, the clanking machinery, the big-nosed foreign soldiers. Are these the saviours?

Coming into Hué is like a dream in which you turn a corner expecting to see a familiar scene and find that it has undergone a sudden and hideous change. You twist and turn through deep mud roads between blighted gardens and skeleton houses and shops, looking for the makeshift pontoon bridge the Americans have thrown across the canals. Bewildered Vietnamese carrying bundles of possessions press into the roadside to avoid being crushed by the trucks. There are soldiers everywhere, Americans in helmets and bulky in flak jackets, tense Vietnamese fingering sub-machine gun triggers. Huge armoured personnel carriers are waiting down side alleys like gangsters in ambush. There is no transport; you walk, and that is better because you can escape with the Vietnamese from a military machine that is more and more irritable now that its omnipotence has turned to myth.

Always in the past I had stayed with a rather poor Vietnamese family who live in an old-fashioned, rambling building on the north bank of the Perfumed River between the river bank and the Citadel, where the North Vietnamese and Vietcong held American mobility and firepower at bay for three weeks. From the south bank it seemed as if they could not possibly have survived. The north bank area looked like the worst parts of London after the Blitz. Formerly, I had always hired a bicycle in Hué and ridden across the great-girdered bridge over the river. Now the central span plunges into the water, dynamited by the Vietcong who held it for a time. I had to push my way through a horde of Vietnamese struggling desperately across the one narrow gangway. When too many people force themselves on it you wade calf-deep. Machine guns and mortars cracked and thumped in the river bank trees not far away, where the Vietnamese used to take me on picnics. The Citadel has fallen, but the Americans are still fighting in Hué. The family's street is a blackened shambles of gutted houses. The market and teashops across the road on the river bank have ceased to exist. Miraculously, my Vietnamese friends were there, standing outside their door, running through the rubble to meet me. Their house is one of the very few that has not been razed.

They led me in excitedly. One or two were crying. They began to explain that they had gathered as usual in the house for the Tet (New Year) holiday, ten of them, uncle, aunts, cousins, sons, and daughters, with two small babies, and Mimi, the old dog with stubby legs. Since then they had had three weeks of unimaginable nightmare. The upstairs rooms no longer exist. They were torn apart by American fire during the Buddhist "struggle group" demonstrations against the Ky Government. In 1966 I stayed in the front upper room and we watched the angry torchlight processions parading through the street shouting: "Peace." Now there are four walls and no roof. The floor is littered with broken tiles and burned beams. The American mortar bombs had thrown the family's little Buddhist shrine into a mass of coloured tatters in the dust; a piece of shrapnel had embedded itself in a French translation of *The Grapes of Wrath*; the braided, ceremonial uniform cap of the eldest son, who was shot in action last year, lay on the wreckage of the balcony.

We sat downstairs in a room pocked with bullet holes and a floor littered with tiles from the roof. There was a small mortar crater in the cement floor. Madame Dinh, a tiny, frail and very wise woman of about forty-five, who runs the house, explained: "When the first fusillades began we were all asleep. The Vietcong were firing across the river at U.S. headquarters. We thought it was like any other bombardment, and would stop. But then we all got up and came downstairs and saw the Vietcong in the street outside. There were about twenty of them, then sixty. They made for the bridge. The first ones to come wore shorts and khaki shirts and no caps. They were very young—seventeen or eighteen. They didn't come into the houses here because everyone had barred their shutters. I knew then that in the end the government would drive them out. But I didn't know when, and I knew we would suffer.

Madame Dinh has lost a husband and her eldest son in war. Tam, the eldest surviving son, who studies Government administration in Saigon, said: "One Vietnamese soldier lay wounded and bleeding outside our door all the morning. Nobody dared come out and help him. Then one of a Vietcong patrol walked up and just shot him. He was harmless, but he just shot him."

What about the bombing?

"That happened after the Vietcong had left—at least in this street. When the Americans shelled us the Vietcong had retreated toward the Citadel," said Tam. "Can you imagine, shelling twenty-four hours for fourteen days?"

For all that time this family huddled together with no link to the outside world except the radio. They listened avidly to the BBC or Saigon Radio. At U.S. headquarters in Hué an American colonel, phlegmatically contemplating his artillery shelling a suburb, said next day: "You know what BBC stands for? British Communist Broadcasting Corporation." Only hawks are really welcome in the North now among the military.

Behind Madame Dinh's house, outside the colonel's field of vision, the teeming residential and commercial areas resemble something out of Goya. Whole streets are laid waste. Rubble chokes the sidewalks. There are craters in the streets and blackened shells of cars. A truck is embedded in a wall. At two points I saw crowds who scrabbled and clawed at the grilles of stores where rice was being sold. The lucky ones—paying four times the normal price—quickly loaded the sacks onto bicycles and scurried away. They looked, if one approached too close, as if they would turn and defend the rice like famished dogs with a bone. The Americans had dropped huge bombs—750 and 500 pounders—on what they imagined were the Citadel walls. Where they fell is one of the more fearful parts of a fearfully shattered city. It was a residential area packed with families like Madame Dinh's gathering for Tet. Now, like the Vietnamese, you walk there with a handkerchief to your nose.

A wispy Vietnamese teacher of French came up. He was trembling, and looked as though he might cry. What did he think of all that had passed?

"We don't think any more, *monsieur*. We are like dogs. We live by instinct. Instincts are all that are left to us." He pointed to a monstrous pile of rubble. "The man who lived in there was shot by the Vietcong. Now his house has been destroyed by the Americans. Curious, eh?" He stopped in front of another. There were plenty to choose from. "There are thirty people under this one." Vietnamese were digging in another mound of bricks and mortar. "They are still bringing the bodies out of there. Two families, about twenty people, eight survivors."

Here the stench of the dead was overpowering. In an open space between the houses mutilated corpses were being wrapped in sheets. Three men in nose masks dug graves. Women and children stood around keening, and shaking with sobs. A woman flung herself on a new mound of earth, hammering on it with her fist, and rolling on it in a paroxysm of grief.

We stepped through fragments of glass, pathetic muddied wrappings of Tet holiday gifts, filth and dead rats, to where a crowd of Vietnamese were passing under the great ornamental gate to the Citadel stormed by the U.S. Marines. They shuffled through quickly, holding their noses because here three rotting bodies of Vietcong soldiers lie as yet unburied. The Citadel's solid walls are punctured by shells, and the gate itself riddled by everything from bullets to rockets. Inside the Citadel there seems to be no shop nor house that is not wholly or partially destroyed. The Americans used tanks here, after the airstrikes. The Vietcong and North Vietnamese used rockets from the camouflaged foxholes you see everywhere.

In a dazed way the people are friendly. There is no doubt they are glad the Communists were driven out—a number of civil servants live in the Citadel. In another quarter of Hué inhabited largely by army officers and civil servants they are still digging up the bodies of relatives, men, women, and children, who had their hands tied behind their backs and then were shot by the Vietcong. There are still many families missing. Mothers stand about weeping as the diggers work, and rush forward to try to recognize relatives as the bodies are taken out of the earth. This is in a secondary school garden used by the invaders as a command post. Thirty bodies have been recovered so far. But scores more may be there.

There are thought to be three hundred to six hundred government employees buried in two mass graves somewhere in the city, but no one has been able to find them yet. In any event, Government here is like the city itself—in ruins. Officials have disappeared for the most part, kidnapped or killed. Official records were destroyed by the invading Vietcong and North Vietnamese when they occupied the municipal buildings, which are themselves in ruins.

No one knows how many civilians were killed. Perhaps they never will. Some were killed deliberately by certain Vietcong, others by American bombing and mortaring. Two French priests were shot by a Vietcong patrol at eleven o'clock one morning in a crowded street, and their grave now stands in the grounds of their house near the Collège de la Providence in West Hué. Yet other priests were not molested, the Father Superior told me. "The North Vietnamese—they were from Tonkin—occupied the college. I would describe them as very well disciplined and ferocious."

In the Citadel an old Vietnamese with a wispy beard said: "They came into the house but didn't harm us. They said they were winning the war and we should support them. They were forty percent Tonkinese, the rest Vietcong from this region." So they behaved well in some areas, badly in others.

In Madame Dinh's house one evening, a family came in which had had to put up with Vietcong units in their house for eighty days. "They blew down part of our walls and fired out through them, and they knocked down walls into neighbouring houses all down the street, linking them all up," said one.

A student called Minh said: "They tried to organize young people like me to study their doctrines, carry arms for them. They sat about singing communist songs." He sang one to illustrate the point. The Dinh family rocked with laughter, out of sheer relief that the worst is temporarily over.

The song was the souvenir of a monstrous experience. Did many young Vietnamese respond to Vietcong propaganda? "Only a few spivs and the very poor—some trishaw drivers, people like that."

What did students like Minh think?

"Well, the Vietcong told us they were fighting for the independence of Vietnam from the Americans. I don't like the Americans, but I don't like the Vietcong either. I am sure some students went with the Vietcong, but, believe me, not many."

These student attitudes are extremely significant. All the student friends I have made in Hué were militant "struggle group" members in the days when Hué and Da Nang rebelled against the Government of General Thieu and Air Vice-Marshal Ky. Minh and Tam both took carbines down to Da Nang and manned the barricades against Ky's troops. They wanted then—and they want now—an end to the Thieu-Ky Government and really free elections, which can throw up, they think, a representative government with which the National Liberal Front would bargain. They say they are true nationalists. They feel the Vietnamese nationality is being swamped by a massive American presence, which rules Vietnam against its better interests through unrepresentative people like the generals. They did not even like the Buddhist monk, Thich Tri Quang, who played a leading part in the struggle movement. They suspect he might be playing along with the Vietcong. They did like the dynamic General Nguyeu Chanh Thi, who commanded the Vietnamese armies in Hué, where he was born, and was opposed to Thieu and Ky, and who is now living in Washington where the government exiled him. All this Minh and Tam and other students have explained to me in Madame Dinh's house many times. They did not want the Vietcong. They wanted honest government. They did not want American domination. Yet few American officials in Saigon have ever been convinced that the struggle movement *en masse* was not pro-Vietcong. They thus approved Ky's dispatch of troops to Hué and Da Nang, and the bloodshed that followed.

But now the battle for Hué has highlighted something of considerable political significance. The Vietcong occupation of Hué provided the ultimate test of the students' real feelings. Since Tet they have had every opportunity to go with the Vietcong. Apart from an extreme leftwing minority, they did not, even when it was much safer for them to go than to stay and risk a bullet from angry Vietcong soldiers. Perhaps now the Americans will realize their grave political misjudgement over the struggle groups. In any event the Vietcong, too, must have had a sharp surprise.

Another student in the Dinhs' house that night lives in a suburban area where the Vietcong tried to organize a temporary administration. "A tailor down the road was appointed chairman for youth. Only a few peasants were enthusiastic," he said. And several friends were obliged to carry Vietcong wounded up into the hills during the fighting. "We were sixty—four of us to each wounded man. We marched at night because the Vietcong officers said we must get past the villages and U.S. flares and helicopters before dawn. We must have gone fifty kilometres, with no food and no water. They seemed to have no medicine. They did not seem to know the way very well either. At certain crossroads we had to stop and wait for other soldiers to come and show us which track to take. We didn't wait long, there were lots of Vietcong soldiers coming and going. When we got to a rough shelter on a hill we were made to sign a paper saying that we had delivered so many wounded for the soldiers of the National Liberation Front—they got very angry if anyone referred to them as Viet Minh or Vietcong. In my village they shot one man for saying 'Viet Minh.' Then they asked each of us to stay with them, saying they had already won in Hué and everywhere else, and that now was the time to make a choice. But we said we would go home. And we went all alone back through the dark."

Not every Vietnamese in Hué was so lucky. "Before they left our village they took a lot of young men with them," I was told. And Madame Dinh's chief concern is to get her sons and nephews out of Hué in case the Vietcong return and take them off. In one quarter of Hué hundreds were led off with bandaged eyes and hands tied.

"They seemed to think that because we were Buddhist students and were in the struggle movement we would welcome them here."

I asked my student what his attitude and that of his friends was now.

"I think you know what we have always told you. That has not changed. We think—I mean the educated people, more or less, from university and secondary school, like us—that the Vietcong is no good; that the Americans are not good for us, because they destroy our houses and our souls; that the present government is no good because it doesn't represent anyone much, and its Army destroys whole streets because of four snipers."

Once I said to them in Madame Dinh's shattered living room,

while she and some women friends were playing cards: "What a catastrophe for you."

Tam leaned forward intently: "Not a catastrophe," he answered. "It's normal, it's war, and this is normal. . . . Well then," he cried, with a rising note of great anguish unusual for a Vietnamese. "Well, we must have peace, mustn't we? Oh yes, yes, yes!" At that moment a violent explosion rocked the already weakened building and a shower of loose tiles fell into the room. I discovered later that it was a U.S. ammunition ship blowing up after two direct hits from a Vietcong mortar. It was about six hundred yards away.

Because things like that can happen, and are likely to continue to happen for some time, Hué is almost totally isolated from the outside world. The Vietcong are strong on both sides of the river that is Hué's main lifeline. The airport is open only to military aircraft. The road south is hopelessly insecure. With an almost non-existent local government, the refugees, about 30,000 of them officially, are likely to get only the bare necessities for the time being, and their numbers are likely to increase. This week I watched thousands more scrambling to safety from a thickly populated suburb in which there were said to be Vietcong snipers and which the Americans and Vietnamese preferred to mortar rather than invade. Shops are still largely closed. Prices are up and there is a black market. Many families have suffered from the looting, of which there are unending complaints. The Vietnamese Army units undoubtedly took what they could, wherever they found it. Nor are the U.S. troops above suspicion. A local French resident says he found his house denuded after U.S. troops had occupied it. The safes were blown open, he claims, and everything that could not be taken was destroyed, including his desk.

So far American aid to the chief of the Vietnamese province is stymied because of a lack of men who know the region's problems. Perhaps twenty to thirty Americans were killed in Hué—nobody will say—and certainly several were taken off by the Vietcong. The local U.S. administrator, a man of long Vietnam experience, is now, it seems, suffering from nervous exhaustion and can hardly be much good on his own. Most American civilians in the northern sector work in a cloud of foreboding. It is obvious that pacification and development programmes are in ruins. Today there are large American, Vietnamese, and North Vietnamese, and Vietcong forces in the neighbourhood of Hué. Military casualties arc heavy and still rising. I watched U.S. jets striking with napalm and rockets a few hundred yards away from Hué's stadium. American dead were being brought in there, wrapped in green plastic shrouds and loaded into helicopters. Cartloads of captured Vietcong weapons, many as good as anything the Americans have, were being stacked. There was a growing pile of uniforms of American dead, their water bottles, rifles, pathetic letters ending, "With love, and try and write soon, Mom."

And what has the battle of Hué meant? Tragically, it has symbolized the entire war. The people have been raped by two forces which they have come to distrust and fear. The Americans have regained Hué at the cost of destroying it. They will be blamed for that. General Giap's men thought they could win over people they wrongly considered ripe for conversion, simply because they have opposed the Saigon government. In the main they, too, have had to learn that there are three political forces in South Vietnam, not two, and that the third one, the one that rejects the big-stick images of Hanoi and Saigon, is both large and, when opportunity arrives, courageous. Militarily, the holocaust that enveloped this beautiful city and its thousands of Madame Dinhs, Vinhs, and Tams has ended in stalemate after the initiative with the North Vietnamese and Vietcong. Neither side has won any appreciable number of Vietnamese hearts and minds.

And standing in the stench of Hué's streets, contemplating the ruins of the university and schools—there will be no education in Hué for upwards of a year from now—and foreseeing the inevitable exodus from this cultural centre and former imperial capital of central Vietnam when travel from it is again possible, one can see only one thing very clearly: that a criminal act has been committed here since Tet. One is tempted to refer to other ruined cities: Warsaw or Budapest. But there is only one Hué, victim of cynical ideologists who talk with unctuous arrogance of nationalism and democracy from their loudspeaker vans and who between them have destroyed perhaps the most purely nationalist city in either North or South Vietnam.

Madame Dinh said one evening: "You know, during the bombardment I sat thinking, 'Suppose President Ho Chi Minh and President Johnson visited Hué at the same time and saw all this, and they said to each other: 'Why are we doing this?' and shook hands.' " She added shyly: "You think that's very stupid. Of course, I am not serious. It was only my dream."

JOHN RYLE

John Ryle's Warriors of the White Nile *is a popular eth-
nography of the Dinka of eastern Bahr-el-Ghazal, and his*
An Unfinished Country *is a book on Brazil. In late 1988
he and two other relief workers drove to the southern Sudan,
a week's journey from Khartoum, to report for a relief agency
on its operations there among Dinkas displaced by famine
and the five-year civil war between the Sudan People's Liberation Army and the government's National Army. The
following excerpt is from an article about this journey that
first appeared in* Granta. *Ryle lives in London.*

···

from "THE ROAD TO ABYEI"

SUPPING WITH THE DEVIL IN EL MUGLAD

The next day we drove to El Muglad, the heart of Humr Misseriya
territory. Here the road to Abyei meets the road to El Meiram. It was
the last place where there was any semblance of civil, as opposed to
military, administration. As in Babanusa there was a large camp of
displaced Dinkas by the railway. In Babanusa we had been forbidden
to speak to them; in El Muglad we were not even allowed to visit the
camp.

There was one relief agency in El Muglad. We arrived there at
an awkward moment. The agency had arranged a supper party for local
dignitaries, but that morning an order had come from Khartoum ex-
pelling all foreign relief workers from Southern Kordofan. It looked as
though their soirée might turn out to be an envoi—for us too. But their

field officer, a genial Irishman, was unphazed, and, by lunchtime, the expulsion order had been revoked.

The field officer had a certain fame. At a time when no one was able to enter Abyei, he had succeeded in getting five hundred sacks of dura into the town—in the rainy season, on donkeys, having hired local militiamen to ride shotgun. He made no bones about it: nothing moved between El Muglad and Abyei without their say so. The priest in Abyei had sent him a message: dozens of Dinkas were dying every day. The only way to help them was to employ the same militias who had driven them from their homes. It was a heightened version of the dilemma facing all the relief organizations. The field officer knew where he stood.

"They're killers, aren't they, the militias?" I asked.

"Of course," he said, stroking his beard. "So are the SPLA."* And then he added: "I'd sup with the devil to get food to Abyei."

At dusk the guests arrived for the field officer's party.

In the yard of the house, under the mango trees, a long table was laid with food and flowers, and easy chairs made of bright nylon cord were arranged in a square.

On one side of the square sat the Misseriya elders in snow-white *jallabias*, with fine cotton scarves thrown over their shoulders and turbans perched on their heads like whipped cream. They clutched heavy walking sticks and murmured to their neighbours while waiting to eat. On the other side sat the agency staff. Government officials in western dress were on the third side—the chiefs of police from Babanusa and Abyei, the army commander and the head of military security in El Muglad. Next to the head of military security, and engaged in intimate conversation, was a small man in a pale-coloured safari suit. He was also clutching a walking stick. The field officer pointed him out to me. "That is the head of the Misseriya militia," he said. "Al Capone. Mr. Big. If he says 'Kill,' they kill."

Between Mr. Big and the head of military security was an Arab trader with a gold tooth and an ingratiating smile. This was Mr. Fixit, the go-between with the militiamen. Majak recognized him. Gold-tooth had grown up in Abyei. "He was just a truck driver then," said

*Sudan People's Liberation Army

Majak. But it seemed he had grown rich on famine. It was he who had arranged the agency donkey train to Abyei. He owned many houses in El Muglad, including the one we were sitting in. We were, in a sense, his guests. Mark mentioned to him that we were planning to go to Abyei the next day, and soon Gold-tooth was arranging an escort for us. There was a whispered conversation and a nod from Mr. Big.

"We'll protect you against the SPLA," he said warmly. But we knew the SPLA was not the problem on the road to Abyei—it was not from them we needed protection: it was from the militiamen themselves. Nevertheless, Gold-tooth was very persuasive, and by the end of the conversation Mark and I found we had arranged to meet him for breakfast the next day to pick up an escort.

A nervous young northerner was circulating among the guests, a journalist on a Khartoum paper, *Senabil*, the voice of the fundamentalist Islamic Front. He wandered about with a Nikon camera round his neck, but never used it. He was a Misseri from Tibbun, where the slave market was supposed to be, and since he was a journalist, I felt it was reasonable to ask him about the market. He moved aside so that no one could hear.

"What is going on is *bad*," he said. "But you have to remember we are tribal people. All of us—Arab, Dinka—everyone. Even I—I am a Muslim, but I am also a Misseri. I practice *rituals* that are not Muslim at all. There is a tradition to everything we do, a *subtext*, a tribal subtext."

"Really?" I said, startled by the salon language, but aware that he had not answered my question.

"Yes," said the journalist, "my people are Arabs. But they are Africans also. It is their way. They come out of the forest on horses. They think everyone is their slave. When they take cattle it is not just for them, it is for the good of the tribe. They are not thieves, they are— what is the phrase?"

"Social bandits?" I said.

"Yes, yes," said the journalist. "Sociable bandits."

At that moment the only other expatriate in El Muglad arrived, a British employee of Chevron, the oil company that has the lion's share of the concessions in the southern Sudan. He was wearing a white

T-shirt with a red inscription. In the twilight I could not quite make it out. One of the Misseriya elders gave it an uncomprehending glance.

The journalist studied it intently. "What does that say?" he asked.

I looked again. On the chest of the man from Chevron were the words "Fuck the World with Yuppie Condoms."

I said something about it being a tribal subtext, but I wasn't sure if the journalist got the joke. I wasn't sure if I got it myself. In the circumstances literary theory and the delinquent language of T-shirts both seemed obscene. Words had come unhinged from events; people took refuge in subtexts and incomprehensible slogans. I thought about our car with its bloody handprints, about the Misseriya elders with their beautiful white clothes, about slaves and social bandits, yuppie condoms, gold teeth. Bloodstains. The milk of birds. I felt stoned. I thought about what was happening in the South, just south of here, behind this screen of lies. Burning, looting, pillage, killing, torture, rape, starvation. I thought about the massacre in Ed Da'ein the year before. Such things could happen again. I tried to remember why I had come, why I had imagined there was anything I could usefully do or say about these terrible things.

THE ROAD TO ABYEI

In the morning Mark and I woke with the same feeling. We had gone too far: we felt ashamed in front of Majak; arriving in Abyei under the protection of the militia was not the right way to begin. We drove to breakfast discussing how we could get out of the arrangement, but in the event the trader was all smiles and shrugs. On our heads be it. It was clear he reckoned that any transport operation we set up would require his services in the end. He wrote a letter of recommendation for us to a fellow-trader in Abyei. As we talked, a police sergeant stepped into his shop, looked around and exchanged a word with him. The policeman left with a fifty-pound note. Gold-tooth winked and sighed. "Their salaries are so low," he said. As we got up to leave we saw the leader of the militia, the sociable bandit, crossing the street; we moved away rapidly and drove out of town.

We followed the railway south of Abyei past pools of lotus flowers. To cross the watercourses, still deep with mud, we had to straddle the tracks and bump along the cross-ties. After a few miles, we branched west, hoping we had chosen the right road. There were no other vehicles. An Arab rode ahead of us on a donkey, a huge rusty spear under his arm. He looked like Don Quixote, an anachronism from the age before automatic weapons changed the rules of the game.

The road worsened and our progress was slow. There were Dinka boys herding cattle and goats. One was malnourished and needed a stick to walk. He was about six years old. We stopped to speak to him. His mother, he said, had given him to an Arab because she had no food. We drove on. Two boys in rags froze when they saw our car. We stopped and Majak got out and spoke to them in Dinka. They told him they were brothers; the elder was nine, the younger five; they were running away from their Arab master and trying to rejoin their mother in El Muglad. They did not know what had become of their father. We gave them food and money, but their chances of making it without being recaptured were not too good.

Farther ahead, we saw another group of men under some trees. They also were on donkeys, but instead of spears they carried GM3 rifles, a type used by the army. They were not in uniform.

They motioned us to stop and we did so. I stowed my camera. Mark kept his foot poised over the accelerator. They asked where we had come from but they did not ask about the boys we had just spoken to. They peered in the back of the car and stared at the bloody handprints on the body-work. Then they waved us on.

We were entering what had once been Dinka territory. There were deserted villages with rusting water tanks and unused pumps; there were charred huts, and fields reclaimed by the bush. The vegetation was lusher and the woods thicker but many trees had been burned in forest fires. The evening sky grew dark, and we entered Abyei. The town looked eerie, swathed in smoke from cooking fires, with a faint glow on the trees as though the undergrowth was alight.

Just as we passed the first buildings, a soldier in camouflage ran from the shadows. *"Sebit!"* he shouted, "Halt!" He crouched down in the road with his rifle pointing at the windscreen. Mark doused the headlights and switched on the cabin light. The sentry demanded a password that we did not have. He asked where we had come from. There was only one place we could have come from. And there was only one place he could take us to. We drove on with him to the police post.

In Kordofan you are not supposed to arrive anywhere after dark. In Abyei it was rare for anyone to arrive at all. We did not know if the authorities had been advised of our departure from El Muglad, but it would not have been unusual if the message had not got through. In the event the police were perfectly civil. They took us to a nearby compound where the medical team were staying. Most of the team were asleep outside. Their mosquito nets shone in the moonlight like sails in harbour. The policemen, off-duty in their long white *jallabias*, glided like pleasure craft among them. For the moment we were glad to anchor there.

THE HARVEST OF SKULLS

In the morning Mark and I registered formally with the chief of police. To our surprise, he gave us permission to move around the town. A soldier accompanied us.

The army had burned the huts to the south of the town to discourage infiltration by the SPLA, and we were not allowed to go there. We could see a bare mound under a tree, the grave of a former Paramount Chief of the Ngok. Close to the airstrip there was the army compound, and beyond the airstrip were the ruins of the Harvard Project, an ill-fated scheme that was supposed to have made Abyei into a model of integrated rural development for the Sudan.

Abyei is a small town in normal times: a market place, a street of shops, three schools, the airstrip and a sprawl of grass huts. It has a dry season population of about five thousand. That five thousand is composed of Dinka villagers, government administrators, and Arab traders. It is the administrative centre for the Ngok—in normal times. It is also a market town for other Dinka tribes from the South. It was these tribes who now formed the majority of the displaced population of the town. The dry season is the busy time in a place like Abyei: the harvest is over and people move between the surrounding villages and the cattle camps near the rivers; the rivers are low and travelling is easier. People come and go from October until April when the rains come again and planting begins.

But 1988, of course, had not been a normal year. Plenty of people left their villages to come to Abyei, but few went back. The seasonal movement had become one-way. The buildings of the town had diminished—the army having burned whole sections to the ground—but the population itself had tripled or quadrupled. It had been even larger in the months before we arrived, but malnutrition and disease had taken their toll. The rains had been plentiful, but the harvest had been pitiful—no one dared risk attacks from the militia. The only good thing was that the rains had brought fish. The dry season is the fishing season, and, in Abyei, fish had very likely saved more lives than relief agencies.

We walked through the centre of the town. There was a scattering of brick and cement buildings—schools commandeered by the army. The *suq*, the food market, was virtually empty; there were a few traders. In the crowded huts behind the *suq* lived the famine victims. Not everyone looked hungry: the worst cases were hidden. In many of the huts were sick children and old people, their skin in folds. One struggled to rise to her feet to greet us but she failed. They could not get to the hospital; the medical workers were forbidden to go to them.

In the hospital we found the medical team. It was administering the MUAC test—measuring children's middle and upper arm circumference—to discover the incidence of malnutrition. The children were given coloured wristbands to identify them as participants in the supplementary feeding programme. They got a mixture of dried skimmed milk, sugar and cereal called Unimix, brewed up in oil drums over charcoal fires in the hospital grounds. The hospital had no water supply. That also came in drums from the pump near the airstrip.

All over the town were children with pencil legs and balloon bellies wearing those tiny wristbands. They wore them like jewellery.

Some had nothing else to wear. Some of them were too weak to walk and had to be carried by their siblings a mile or more from their huts to the hospital. Many had perpetual diarrhoea. Weak children are wiped out very quickly by diarrhoea. In the hospital they were given rehydration fluid, with one measure of salt to half-a-dozen of sugar; the measuring spoon bore this inscription: DO NOT USE IF MORE SALTY THAN TEARS.

There were few men under the age of forty in Abyei. Among the Dinkas there were only women and children and old men to be seen. The young men had been killed by soldiers or by militiamen, or they had stayed deep in the bush with the remaining cattle, or they had joined the SPLA. But as we walked among the huts near the *suq* we were startled by half-a-dozen tall youths, bare-chested, sleek and healthy, with red berets and guns, who strode past us looking straight ahead. The youths did not acknowledge us or return our greeting—until we spoke to them in Nuer, the language of a Nilotic tribe to the east of Ngok. They were, we established, members of another government-backed militia, Anyanya II. Most of Anyanya II had abandoned the government side and gone over to the SPLA, but not these ones. They had been driven out by the SPLA and had fallen back on Abyei. The Nuer and their families had safe passes from the government. In one section of the town they had even set up a machine gun emplacement. It was pointing directly into the market place. The Nuer boys had exploited their position to loot the displaced Dinka. They had stolen all the fishing nets. In the whole town only the Nuer and a few Arab traders had cattle. It was a complicated war.

We were forbidden from visiting the church in Abyei, but in the open space in front of the barracks we met a Catholic father, the Italian priest who had alerted the relief people in El Muglad to the situation in Abyei earlier that year. At the height of the famine, he told us, he had fed seven thousand people in one day. "Beats Jesus," I murmured. Then I felt ashamed, because the priest was old and ill. Luckily he was also very deaf. He told us that the local church representative on the food distribution committee in Abyei had been arrested and the church, which arranged the relief supplies, was now prevented from distributing them.

We spent the night with the medical team again, and in the morning accompanied members of the Red Crescent on a burial detail. On the northeast side of the town there was a field of skulls. Corpses had been thrown there in the last months of the rains when the grass was tall. Now the grass was pale and dry. It had died down to reveal the shame of people too weary and ill to bury their dead. Vultures and hyenas had spread the remains far and wide. The Red Crescent volunteers, northerners, collecting the scattered bones to bury them in a single grave, made much of this. "We even gave them money to bury their dead," said the team leader, a doctor, "but they took the money and left the corpses in the grass."

"What would you have done?" I asked, "if you got money when you were starving? Wouldn't you feed the living first?"

The Red Crescent doctor turned back to the bones. The volunteers had dug a very shallow pit. The bones would soon be gnawed out of their graves again.

I walked across the plain with Majak counting skulls and noting the size of the skeletons. Adults and children seemed to be represented in equal numbers; on one skull the tribal marks of the Dinka tribe to the south were faintly visible—four lines across the forehead in a broad V-shape, gouged to the bone in early adolescence. Tiny zig-zag cracks flickered across the cranium like streambeds on an extinct volcano. Everywhere there were bones. In the distance women came out of the woods with bundles of grass and firewood on their heads. It was a glimpse of normality in the charnel house. Famine or no famine, in Africa it is women who do the work.

A glimpse was all we got of the situation in Abyei. Someone had been talking to the chief of police and overnight he became distinctly sour. "Why are you here?" he kept asking us. "We do not know why you are here." In the end he turned to me. "You will have to leave on the next plane," he said. Majak, born and bred in Abyei, might have asked the chief of police the same question—why was he there?—but he did not. He had come back to find his hometown half-burned to the ground and under military occupation.

He told me he was trying to think of Abyei as another place altogether, a place where he had not been before.

"Why are you here?" As for me I couldn't really answer the question in a way that would have satisfied the police chief. I was there to assess the effectiveness of the relief programme. But the authorities in Abyei did not seem to think that it was a relief agency's job to assess its own programme, or, for that matter, even to administer it. In particular they did not think it was an agency's job to know anything about the people it was trying to help—especially if those people were Southerners, causing the government so much grief and dying in such embarrassing numbers.

More and more in the Sudan the most valuable function of relief agencies has come to be to protect people from their own government. The government does not take kindly to this.

CAROLYN FORCHÉ

In the foreword to Carolyn Forché's first book, Gathering
the Tribes, *Stanley Kunitz wrote: "In her search for poetry,
in her effort to understand it, she has bent over the potter's
wheel, climbed mountain ranges, ventured into the Mojave
Desert." In her second book,* The Country Between Us
(1981), *Forché has traveled out of her own country into El
Salvador, as may be observed in the following poem. Born
in 1950, she was raised in Michigan and now teaches at
George Mason University in Virginia. She has traveled
widely and lived in Paris, Beirut, El Salvador, and South
Africa. She is currently at work on a collection of essays, a
novel, and a third book of poetry,* The Angel of History.

···

RETURN

for Josephine Crum

Upon my return to America, Josephine:
the iced drinks and paper umbrellas, clean
toilets and Los Angeles palm trees moving
like lean women, I was afraid more than
I had been, even of motels so much so
that for months every tire blow-out
was final, every strange car near the house
kept watch and I strained even to remember
things impossible to forget. You took
my stories apart for hours, sitting
on your sofa with your legs under you

and fifty years in your face.
                              So you know
now, you said, what kind of money
is involved and that *campesinos* knife
one another and you know you should
not trust anyone and so you find a few
people you will trust. You know the mix
of machetes with whiskey, the slip of the tongue
that costs hundreds of deaths.
You've seen the pits where men and women
are kept the few days it takes without
food and water. You've heard the cocktail
conversation on which their release depends.
So you've come to understand why
men and women of good will read
torture reports with fascination.
Such things as water pumps
and co-op farms are of little importance
and take years.
It is not Che Guevara, this struggle.
Camillo Torres is dead. Victor Jara
was rounded up with the others, and José
Martí is a landing strip for planes
from Miami to Cuba. Go try on
Americans your long, dull story
of corruption, but better to give
them what they want: Lil Milagro Ramirez,
who after years of confinement did not
know what year it was, how she walked
with help and was forced to shit in public.
Tell them about the razor, the live wire,
dry ice and concrete, grey rats and above all
who fucked her, how many times and when.
Tell them about retaliation: José lying
on the flat bed truck, waving his stumps
in your face, his hands cut off by his

captors and thrown to the many acres
of cotton, lost, still, and holding
the last few lumps of leeched earth.
Tell them of José in his last few hours
and later how, many months later,
a labor leader was cut to pieces and buried.
Tell them how his friends found
the soldiers and made them dig him up
and ask forgiveness of the corpse, once
it was assembled again on the ground
like a man. As for the cars, of course
they watch you and for this don't flatter
yourself. We are all watched. We are
all assembled.

                Josephine, I tell you
I have not rested, not since I drove
those streets with a gun in my lap,
not since all manner of speaking has
failed and the remnant of my life
continues onward. I go mad, for example,
in the Safeway, at the many heads
of lettuce, papayas and sugar, pineapples
and coffee, especially the coffee.
And when I speak with American men,
there is some absence of recognition:
their constant Scotch and fine white
hands, many hours of business, penises
hardened by motor inns and a faint
resemblance to their wives. I cannot
keep going. I remember the American
attaché in that country: his tanks
of fish, his clicking pen, his rapt
devotion to reports. His wife wrote
his reports. She said as much as she
gathered him each day from the embassy
compound, that she was tired of covering

up, sick of his drinking and the loss
of his last promotion. She was a woman
who flew her own plane, stalling out
after four martinis to taxi on an empty
field in the *campo* and to those men
and women announce she was there to help.
She flew where she pleased in that country
with her drunken kindness, while Marines
in white gloves were assigned to protect
her husband. It was difficult work, what
with the suspicion on the rise in smaller
countries that gringos die like other men.
I cannot, Josephine, talk to them.

And so, you say, you've learned a little
about starvation: a child like a supper scrap
filling with worms, many children strung
together, as if they were cut from paper
and all in a delicate chain. And that people
who rescue physicists, lawyers and poets
lie in their beds at night with reports
of mice introduced into women, of men
whose testicles are crushed like eggs.
That they cup their own parts
with their bedsheets and move themselves
slowly, imagining bracelets affixing
their wrists to a wall where the naked
are pinned, where the naked are tied open
and left to the hands of those who erase
what they touch. We are all erased
by them, and no longer resemble decent
men. We no longer have the hearts,
the strength, the lives of women.
Your problem is not your life as it is
in America, not that your hands, as you
tell me, are tied to do something. It is

that you were born to an island of greed
and grace where you have this sense
of yourself as apart from others. It is
not your right to feel powerless. Better
people than you were powerless.
You have not returned to your country,
but to a life you never left.

1980

PEREGRINE HODSON

Peregrine Hodson read Oriental Studies at Oxford. In 1984
he left his career as a barrister to travel to Afghanistan as a
free lance for The Sunday Times. *With the* mujahedin, *he*
walked into Afghanistan with arms and ammunition for the
rebels, and his narrow escapes from drowning and ambushes
are recounted in Under a Sickle Moon. *In the following*
excerpt he has just eluded Russian commandos and is hoping
to make his way back to Pakistan with two other free-lance
journalists. (Within a week of his return to London he was
hospitalized with hepatitis.) Hodson is now at work on a
book about Japan, where he lived for five years employed as
an investment banker. He is a Fellow of the Royal Asiatic
Society.

---

from UNDER A SICKLE MOON

Nuristan

The cave was our home for the next few days. There were two or three
families in the vicinity and the men used to visit us. Yaqub, the man
who had given us handfuls of nuts and berries when we first arrived,
visited us every day and once his elderly father accompanied him. There
was also a lapis trader on his way to Pakistan and a middle-aged man
who, it was said, had two beautiful wives in a cave on the other side
of the river and a Kalashnikov to protect them.

The days were bright and clear but autumn was already in the
air and the leaves of a nearby spinney of beech trees were turning gold.
From eight or nine o'clock in the morning till six o'clock in the evening

the jets attacked in waves; the sound of bombs exploding reverberated up the valley and every few hours spotter planes flew over.

"Bombing and spotter planes getting a bit oppressive," I wrote in my diary. "Cold days being in cave, but dangerous to be outside. Makes men feel like mice under the unpredictable eye of savage birds of prey. Washing socks and hearing the sounds of jets sweeping through the roar of the water and the wind through the booming rocks. The scene like a Shell calendar but everything somehow discoloured."

The syntax reflects my state of mind when I wrote the passage: time was fractured and suspended in a vacuum, events were isolated and had no connection with one another. It required a considerable mental effort to think beyond our immediate situation and we were struggling to ignore an undermining sense of fatalism. I wrote my diary. Julian listened to Bob Marley tapes. In desperation we took turns reading my pocket Bible.

Peter was very quiet. He spent most of the time in his sleeping bag at the back of the cave and I noticed that the whites of his eyes had a yellowish tinge, suggesting hepatitis. Every evening we tuned in to the World Service but there was no mention of any new offensive in the Panjshir valley.

It was disturbingly unreal to be caught in the middle of a forgotten war. At times it was like being in the grip of a massive hallucination. living on nuts and berries in a cave, being bombed by Soviet jets. The outside world acquired another meaning.

Early in the morning, when the mountains were still dark against the dawn, I used to go to the torrent, splash its icy water on my face, then watch the sunlight gradually cover the peaks high above the cave. But before the chill of the night had faded from the rocks, the bombing began once more and I returned to the gloom of the cave.

The uncertainty was weighing on our minds and our tempers began to fray: Julian complained bitterly when I lit a cigarette in the cave; I accused him of wasting the batteries of my Walkman; Peter sulked in his sleeping bag. There were long silences between one conversation and the next. To stop our morale deteriorating further, we tried once more to find a guide, but most of the men we asked were ignorant of the way or unwilling to go with us. Once it seemed as if we had succeeded when Yaqub reluctantly agreed to take us; but he qualified his promise with *"Insha'allah"* in a wilting tone of voice and I realised we would not be able to rely on him.

We also needed food for the journey into Nuristan, and spent hours negotiating with two shepherds to buy a sheep. One of them was a slow-witted youth of seventeen with a sun-darkened face and clumsy movements, wrapped in the folds of a torn petou. His companion was the owner of the sheep, a small, wizened man with a shrewd eye for business. Unfortunately, a speech impediment rendered him virtually dumb and the bargain was pursued through a bewildering sequence of gestures, sharp inarticulate moans and shaking of heads, while the simpleton made dismal attempts to mediate. In the end, several days and numerous meetings later, the deal fell through.

Without food, we could not rely on the kindness of our neighbours indefinitely. Entries in my diary got shorter and I could not conceal my misgivings about our future: "Our situation in a nutshell: we only have one escape route, we don't have much time or strength—and we don't have a reliable guide. We have to get the trip right. If not we will be too weak to do it a third time."

I decided to go down the valley once more to find a guide. On the way down I made enquiries of groups of villagers camped under rock overhangs or in the shelter of sheepfolds, but none of them knew of a guide to take us over the pass. I arrived at the *kargah* at twilight; there was heavy fighting in the village and there were only a few *mujahedin* present. I wrote another letter to Commander Kohzad outlining our probable route into Nuristan and gave it to one of the *mujahedin*. He was against our departure.

"Wait another few days. The Shuravi will go and then it will be easy. We will find your horses and equipment and there will be no problem." But his optimism seemed misplaced and did nothing to reassure me. Once he realised we were determined to go his manner changed.

"If you go now, you go without the permission of Commander Kohzad. Your safety is no longer his responsibility. If you meet with bad men that is your affair." He warned me of the unreliable character of the Nuristanis. "Some say they are not true Muslims, but *kafir*. They are a stupid and lazy people: the women work in the fields and the men do nothing but drink chai. If they want something they steal it from travellers. Only a fool travels in Nuristan without a gun."

He went on to describe notorious acts of brigandage, each more bloodthirsty than the last, until he was in a more cheerful mood. "But if you must go it is God's will, *Mosafer aziz khodast*—the traveller is beloved of God. I will give you some food for your journey; you'll be lucky if you can buy an egg in Nuristan." We tied bundles of sugar, tea, bread and meat into my petou and said good-bye to one another. It was now dark and I still had no guide.

I descended a path and came to a shadowy collection of buildings; closer to them I saw that most of the houses lacked roofs and tarpaulins had been stretched across the walls. Here and there the gleam of a lamp shone in the darkness. I went from one to the next in search of a guide. Once again I was unsuccessful, but several times the name "Mustapha Khan" was mentioned as a man who might help me. A group of men invited me to join them for a glass of chai and one of them set off in search of the elusive Mustapha Khan.

It was almost like a homecoming to be alone once more among Afghans and for the first time in several days my spirits lifted. But the conversation was solemn. "Tell your people what is happening here. Tell them what you have seen with your own eyes," were the constant refrains. "If your people believe the Shuravi we are lost."

Half an hour later Mustapha Khan stepped into the circle. He was older than I had expected, a man of sixty or so with a slight stoop.

"Who is seeking Mustapha Khan the hunter?" he called out. "I know every pathway, every stream and every cave in this valley. I can guide a man anywhere, for a price."

We shook hands and studied each other's faces in the lamplight. His eyes were quick and knowing and when he smiled I saw his two lower front teeth were missing. He looked a rogue, but I liked his confident lack of modesty and we quickly agreed a price.

We set off back to the cave with Mustapha Khan leading the way, staff in hand. He moved over the rough stones at a good steady pace, and only an occasional rattle of loose pebbles marked his passing. The moon rose, bathing the rocks and trees in still, shining light. We climbed without a rest until we came to an icy spring hidden in the shadow of the cliffs.

As we moved through the crystalline night air the subdued roar of water tumbling in the darkness beneath us, the war was unimaginably distant. Mustapha Khan beckoned to me to leave the path and I followed him down to the torrent's edge. He knelt down and removed a small tin box from underneath a boulder and poured its contents on to a flat rock. From a waistcoat pocket he produced another packet of powder and carefully measured out some of it on to the rock beside the first mound. He mixed the mounds together in a practised rhythm, several times dipping his hand into the stream and shaking sparkling drops of water over the darkened surface. Then he chose a smooth pebble from the water's edge and ground the mixture in a swift circular motion until it was spread in a thin layer. Up till then he had said nothing, but after patting the substance and sprinkling it with a few more drops of water from the river he turned to me. "Take some, Abdul," he said, "it will do you no harm." By now I had guessed that the mysterious substance was naswar and I put a pinch under my tongue. A satisfying heat radiated under my tongue, my pulse quickened and the heaviness vanished from my legs.

We had just begun to cross the river when there was the sharp whistling sound of a mortar to our right and we glimpsed a bright light disintegrate with a bang a few hundred feet below us. Mustapha Khan muttered something and launched himself across a makeshift bridge of branches paved with stones. Halfway across he stumbled, dislodging two large rocks which slipped into the hissing water with a heavy splash, and he only just managed to scramble to the other side. The branches were still in place and I teetered across them towards the staff which Mustapha Khan held out towards me. There were no more mortars and we continued on in silence. But the spell of the moonlight was broken.

When we reached the cave it was in darkness and Peter and Julian were asleep: I lit the lamp and introduced them to Mustapha Khan. We talked briefly of the journey and decided to climb the pass the following day. Mustapha seemed completely unperturbed by our company and when we arranged our blankets for the night he lay down between Julian and myself as if spending the night with three English-men was the most natural thing in the world for him.

It was still dark when Mustapha Khan woke us and for the next few hours we climbed without a break, except for pauses when jets or spotter planes passed over. By mid-morning we had crossed the mine-field and reached the edge of the plateau where we had camped pre-viously. We stopped for a rest and shared our meat and bread with Mustapha Khan who in turn produced generous supplies of dried mul-berries and *qu'rut* and told us of his exploits as a hunter. One of his closest companions, a skilful hunter like himself, lived in the village over the mountains. On arrival we should ask for a man whose name sounded like "Muddy Sore" who would surely help us.

We reached the top of the pass by mid-afternoon: Mustapha Khan pointed down into the neighbouring valley several thousand feet below at some dark specks at the foot of a grey mountain.

He was eager to return before nightfall so we paid him at once and thanked him for his help. Then we shook hands and he kissed us farewell.

The way down led across a scree of jagged black boulders. It was one of the most uncomfortable and desolate stretches of country I have encountered. Scott's description of the Antarctic—"God this is an awful place!"—fitted it perfectly and when the first flecks of sleet began to sting through the air, my misery was complete.

We found a herd of goats sheltering in a fold of the hills and some villagers watching over them. The man had dispiriting news for us: a few hours earlier Soviet troops had attacked and overrun the village and surrounded the *mujahedin* in their *kargah*. The people had fled to the north of the village and taken refuge in caves and sheepfolds. The men were slow-witted with the cold and the shock of the past few hours, and were unable to help us further. To our right, a cloud of smoke was rising over the crest of a hill. It seemed unwise to spend any more time in conversation so we took the path to our left which the men assured us led toward Nuristan. Half an hour later we came to a huddle of buildings and a boy led us to a small, windowless hut where we slumped down on a straw-covered floor. After a few minutes he returned with some blankets and a lamp which he set in a niche in the wall.

"You are safe here," he said; "the Shuravi are two or three miles away and will not be here before morning, *Insha'allah*. Now I will try to find you something to eat. But we have very little food. Most of our possessions are in the village. We only live here in the summer, when the sheep are in the higher pastures—or when the Shuravi come."

The boy vanished into the night and we settled down to wait. The warmth of the little room and the gentle light of the lamp were deeply soothing. Peter lay down and went to sleep immediately, while Julian and I sat in silence, listening to the wind rustling in the roof of thorns and leaves. There was nothing to be said.

I was woken by the arrival of an old man bringing a plate of eggs and bread which he placed on the floor in front of us. He had the slanting eyes and wispy beard of an Uzbek. He introduced himself as the village headman; his son was the local *mullah* and the building we were staying in was the village mosque. The boy was his grandson and would guide us over the next pass into Nuristan.

While eating we heard the sound of a plane circling overhead and the old man became agitated, wringing his hands and moaning softly to himself.

"Taking infra-red photographs," said Peter. "The *muj* still haven't got used to them. Even if they're undercover, heat concentrations reveal their position. Nothing much they can do about it, except stop lighting fires."

We gave the old man some money for the meal, turned down the lamp and settled down to sleep. I considered briefly what might happen if we were captured, but I was too tired to give it much thought. For the moment it was good to be wrapped in a blanket listening to the wind buffeting outside the door.

⋯⋯⋯⋯⋯

"Quickly! Quickly! Get up! Get up!" The lamp was lit and the old man was standing over us, wrapped in a coat and wearing thick leather boots. In his anxiety, he lapsed from Dari into another dialect which I could not understand, but it was clear from his shaking hands and voice that there was no time to lose. We threw our things together, pulled on our boots and followed the swaying lamp into the darkness.

Outside the boy was waiting for us. The old man handed him the lamp then bent down to hoist a huge bundle of clothes and blankets on to his shoulders; he extinguished the lamp and tied it to the old man's pack, then we set off. At first the old man went ahead, but after a quarter of an hour the path rose more steeply and he began to fall behind. Several times he stopped to ease the pack on his shoulders and finally he came to a halt by the side of the path and unhitched the pack on to a boulder. I offered to take it but when I put my arms through the carrying cords and took the weight of the pack on my back I could hardly stand. My weakness shocked me but there was nothing I could do: it was too heavy for me. The old man tied a few items into a blanket and hid the remainder of the pack under a thorn bush.

We stumbled on through the darkness. Now and again flares shot up over the village behind us, and mortars and artillery reverberated in the hills around us. "*Ay khoda, khoda,*" the old man groaned. "The Shuravi are terrible, terrible, terrible." Half an hour later he left us. We stood in silence and watched the dawn filter into the east: mist and clouds hung suspended against the mountain walls. A thick column of smoke was drifting up from the floor of the valley and the morning air was bitter with the smell of ash. A wind blew across the rocky slope, rattling the branches of some thorn bushes and, in between gusts, there was the sound of a small child crying. The boy was telling me to wait until his grandfather returned when he clutched at his stomach and slipped away behind some boulders. Some time later he staggered into view, still adjusting the cord of his trousers, and mumbled, "*mariz*— sick."

The sun cast a pale yellow light from behind a bank of grey cloud and the high-pitched wailing of the child echoed across the wet stones. The old man reappeared with a bundle of dried mulberries and bread which he pressed into Julian's pack. We gave him as much money as we could afford, and set off after the boy who had already started walking up the pass.

The path was still in shadow and the ground was frozen hard beneath our feet. The boy stopped repeatedly to relieve himself. Eventually he sat down on a rock and called out that he could go no further. We tried to persuade him to go on but it was hopeless: his cheeks were hollow and his eyes were half-closed with exhaustion. We waited for him to recover his strength and the sun grew hot on our shoulders. The boy was lying on a rock: his clothes were in rags and his feet were encased in thin brown plastic shoes, split at the heels, crudely patched with strips of green plastic and tied together with strips of torn cloth. He turned his back to the wind which twitched the loosely wrapped petou from his body, displaying a shirt tail and trousers, streaked with blood and feces.

We ate a few handfuls of mulberries and I bent down to drink at a glistening rivulet of water running between narrow margins of close-cropped grass. It was numbingly cold and the grass and weeds at the water's edge were encased in shining beads of ice.

A helicopter flew over the mountains further down the valley. For a minute or two it hovered on the edge of the cloud of smoke from the burning village, then an explosion erupted beneath it and, as it wheeled away, another darker cloud of smoke and dust climbed into the sky.

"Must have been a big one," said Peter, "probably a thousand-pound bomb."

The boy was still asleep on the rock and I had to shake him by the shoulder to wake him. We had no idea where the pass crossed over into Nuristan: only the boy knew where it was. He was on the verge of unconsciousness and for a quarter of an hour I had to shout and bully him into giving us directions. His mouth was thick with saliva and several times I had to ask him to repeat himself. At last I understood enough to have a reasonable idea of the direction we needed to take. His eyes had closed again and when I put some money into his hand his fingers remained motionless.

Our progress up the pass was heartbreakingly slow. Peter was very weak and we stopped every fifteen minutes. I kept looking back at the place where we had left the boy and finally, to my relief, I saw that he had disappeared from the rock.

The peaks seemed to grow sharper in the bright frosty air and the sky was a cloudless blue. In the middle of the morning several MiG 27s and Su 17s howled overhead in a plunging attack and began bombing the valley below. The attacks went on, intermittently, for the next two hours. But we reached the top of the pass, and sat watching the planes race over the mountains, listening to the monstrous thumping of their bombs. The roaring of demons in the sky and the mountains trembling, fire and terror: how could the people who lived in these remote hills and valleys possibly begin to understand what was happening to them?

From where we were, safe on the heights overlooking the valley, the bombing was so much noise and smoke: just as the battlefields of Troy must have appeared to the inhabitants of Mount Olympus. For a few minutes I ignored the dangers of hubris and considered the similarities between those all-too-human deities and ourselves. Observers from another world, we had passed among the people, seen their suffering and heard their prayers, received their kindness and momentarily known the turbulence of war. But all the while we had been wearing an invisible armour: the knowledge of another life to which we could eventually return.

In front of us, the desolate beauty of Nuristan stretched out toward the majestic range of the Hindu Kush and freedom. Behind us were the mountains and valleys and plains of Afghanistan, and a people who remained captives in their own country. As we began the descent into Nuristan I felt like an escaped prisoner: relief and exhilaration, mixed with guilt and regret for those who could not come with me. We crossed another, mine-strewn plateau and descended into a barren valley where an icy river tumbled past a few, abandoned shelters made of stones and timber. It was late afternoon, the sun had dropped below the mountains and a sharp wind was picking up. The boy had told us of a village an hour's journey over the pass into Nuristan, but we had been walking for three or four hours already and there was still no sign of it. We briefly considered spending the night in one of the shelters but then decided to press on.

An hour later we rounded a bend in the river and saw a thread of smoke drifting from between some large rocks at the bottom of a cliff. The fire belonged to a family from Khunduz who assured us that there was, indeed, a village another hour's walk down the river.

We walked until it grew dark. A figure on horseback approached us out of the twilight. Again we asked how far it was to the next village and again the reply was an hour, or even a little longer. The journey had become unreal and I toyed with the whimsical idea that travellers in search of Shangri-La might well have received the same answer, always the same answer, "Yes, keep on, it isn't far from here, only another hour, another day, you may get there by candlelight . . ." spurring them on toward an unknown end.

The moon was high in the sky by the time we came to the glow of a lamp hanging inside a tent. Some men, refugees from the Panjshir, invited us inside to share their meal and stay the night. We accepted gratefully: we had been travelling almost continuously for more than eighteen hours and were glad to be able to rest at last. As we sat drinking chai I asked one of them, out of idle interest, how far he thought it might be to the next village. I had already guessed the answer and I was not disappointed.

"With a good horse—maybe an hour. *Insha'allah.*"

PART SIX

CLASSIC QUESTERS IN EXTREMIS

We snapped the branch into three pieces, laid them together on the snow, and stood over the twigs until, with the aid of Gibbon's noble prose, they began to burn.

—John Mills

AL PURDY

*Al Purdy has traveled to various parts of the world, but his
extensive travels throughout Canada, ever since riding freight
trains to the west coast in the thirties, have helped map the
country for younger poets influenced by his sense of place
and history. Among his books are* The Cariboo Horses,
North of Summer: Poems from Baffin Island, *and* The
Collected Poems of Al Purdy, *which recently earned him a
second Governor General's Award. In the following Baffin
poem from 1967, the mock-heroic tone discloses none of the
three-day illness that he suffered there with "no one to give
me a pill or needle."*

WHEN I SAT DOWN TO PLAY
THE PIANO

He cometh forth hurriedly from his tent
and looketh for a quiet sequestered vale
he carrieth a roll of violet toilet tissue
and a forerunner goeth ahead to do him honour
yclept a snotty-nosed Eskimo kid
He findeth a quiet glade among great stones
squatteth forthwith and undoeth trousers
"The Irrational Man" by Wm. Barrett in hand
while the other dismisseth mosquitoes
and beginneth the most natural of natural functions
buttocks balanced above the boulders

Then
    dogs[1]
        Dogs[3]
           DOGS[12]
                all shapes and sizes
all colours and religious persuasion
a plague of dogs rushing in
having been attracted by the philosophic climate
and being wishful to learn about existential dogs
and denial of the self with regard to bitches
But let's call a spade a shovel
therefore there I am I am I think that is
surrounded by a dozen dozen fierce Eskimo dogs
with an inexplicable (to me) appetite
for human excrement
                Dear Ann Landers
what would you do?
                Dear Galloping Gourmet
what would you do
                in a case like this?
Well I'll tell you
NOT A DAMN THING
You just squat there cursing hopelessly
while the kid throws stones
and tries to keep them off and out from under
as a big black husky dashes in
swift as an enemy submarine
white teeth snapping at the anus
I shriek
      and shriek
      (the kid laughs)
      and hold onto my pants
      sans dignity
      sans intellect
      sans Wm. Barrett
      and damn near sans anus

Stand firm little Eskimo kid
it giveth candy if I had any
it giveth a dime in lieu of same
STAND FIRM
Oh avatar of Olympian excellence
noble Eskimo youth do your stuff
Zeus in the Arctic dog pound
Montcalm at Quebec
Horatius at the bridge
Leonidas at Thermopylae
Custer's last stand at Little Big Horn
"KEEP THEM DAMN DOGS OFF
YOU MISERABLE LITTLE BRAT!"

Afterwards
Achilles retreateth without honour
unzippered and sullen
and sulketh in his tent till next time appointed
his anus shrinketh
he escheweth all forms of laxative and physick meanwhile
and prayeth for constipation
addresseth himself to the Eskimo brat miscalled
    "Lo tho I walk thru the valley of
              the shadowy kennels
      in the land of permanent ice cream
              I will fear no huskies
              for thou art with me
    and slingeth thy stones forever and ever
              thou veritable David
                      Amen"
P.S. Next time I'm gonna take a gun

Kikastan Islands

RUSSELL BANKS

Born in the United States in 1940, Russell Banks is the author of ten books of fiction, including Searching for Survivors, Success Stories, *and* Affliction. *He has lived and worked in Florida, Jamaica, and other parts of the Caribbean, and now teaches at Princeton. In the following passage from his novel* Continental Drift, *the two main themes, one about New Englander Bob Dubois and the other about Vanise Dorsinville, now fleeing Haiti with her nephew and baby, have converged aboard a fishing boat smuggling aliens into Florida. This horrifying account is the imagined fate of would-be citizens who put their lives in unconscionable hands. The worst journeys today are doubtless the journeys of refugees—movements of the persecuted and unfortunate poor, which remain largely untold but for occasional writers who find it morally imperative to give voice to such migrations.*

··

from CONTINENTAL DRIFT

Their first sight of land is the flash of the lighthouse below Boca Raton, which tells them that the *Belinda Blue* has come out of the Gulf Stream farther to the north than they intended, miles from where they planned to drop off the Haitians and so far from Moray Key that they can't hope to get home before dawn. Tyrone grumbles and blames Bob, who blames the southeast wind and his not being used to running the *Belinda Blue* with so much weight aboard.

It's dark, thickly overcast this close to shore, and the sea is high.

The boat rides the swells, and when she crests, they can see the beach stretching unbroken from the pink glow of Miami in the south to the lights of Fort Lauderdale in the north. Then, when the boat slides down into the belly between the huge waves, they see nothing but a dark wall of water and a thin strip of sky overhead.

Frightened, the Haitians have crawled aft from their lean-to, and peer wide-eyed at the sea. The pitch and roll of the boat tosses them against one another, and several of them begin to cross themselves and pray. The old woman, hiding behind the others, has started to sing, a high-pitched chanting song that repeats itself over and over. The boy Claude is still up on the bridge with Bob, where Tyrone has joined them. Claude, too, is frightened, but he watches the white man's face closely, as if using it to guide his own emotions. Right now, the white man, who is at the wheel, seems angry with his mate, and the mate seems angry also, for they are scowling and shouting at one another in the wind.

"For Christ's sake, we drop them off at Hollywood or Lauderdale now, they won't know where the hell they are! They'll get busted in an hour. They'll stick out like sore thumbs, for Christ's sake! If we take them down to Coral Gables, like we said we'd do, they'll get to cover in Little Haiti right away."

"Too far, Bob! Dem too heavy in dis sea, mon! Got to leave 'em up here, let 'em find dere own way!"

Bob argues a little longer, but he knows the man is right. "All right. Hollywood, then. Be midnight by then, we can drop them by the A-One-A bridge at Bal Harbour. The water's calm there once you get around the point. Christ only knows how they'll get down to Miami from there, though."

"Not our problem, Bob."

"Go down and talk to them," Bob says to Tyrone. "Tell them what's happening, you know? Maybe one of 'em's got family or something can come out with a car. Who knows? At least let 'em know where they're going to get dropped off. Draw a map or something for 'em."

Tyrone shrugs his shoulder and turns away. "Don't make no never mind to dem, mon. Long's dem in America."

"Yeah, sure, but do it anyway." Bob brings the boat around to port, facing her into the waves, and moves the throttle forward. The boat dips and slides down and hits the gully, yaws into the sea and starts to climb again. Tyrone motions for Claude to follow, and the two of them start down from the bridge. When the boat reaches the crest and hangs there for a second before beginning the descent again, Bob looks off to his starboard side and sees the beach like a taut, thin white ribbon and believes that he can hear the waves crashing not a half mile distant. Beyond the beach he can see the lights of houses between the sea and the road to Palm Beach, where here and there cars move slowly north and south—ordinary people going about their night's ordinary business.

Again, the boat rolls a second and starts the drop, pitches across the smooth trough, yaws between waves and rises, and this time, when it reaches the crest of the wave, Bob looks out over the dripping bow and sees the lights of another boat. It's less than two hundred yards off the portside and headed north, and it's a large boat, twice the size of the *Belinda Blue*—that's all Bob can see of her, before the boat disappears from sight, and Bob realizes that they have pitched again and are descending. He yells for Tyrone, who's under the tarpaulin talking to the Haitians, and frantically waves him up to the bridge. "Boat!" he shouts. "Boat!"

Tyrone scrambles up the ladder to the bridge, and when the *Belinda Blue* crests again, Bob points out the lights of the stranger.

"Coast guard," Tyrone says. "Cut de lights."

Bob obeys at once. "Oh, Jesus H. Christ!" he says. "The fucking coast guard." He can hear the twin diesels that power her and can see that, yes, it is a cutter, ninety or a hundred feet long, with the high conning tower and the fifty- and sixty-caliber machine guns bristling at the stern and bow. "I don't think they spotted us," Bob says. But then he realizes that the cutter is turning slowly to port. "Oh, fuck, here they come!"

Tyrone reaches out and cuts the throttle back.

"What the fuck you doing?"

"Bring 'er around, gwan get dem Haitians off," Tyrone says.

"What? What're you saying?" Bob grabs Tyrone's shoulder and flips the man around to face him.

"Dem can get to shore from here, mon!" Tyrone shouts into the wind. "It's not far!"

"Not in this sea, for Christ's sake! We can't *do* that! We can't!"

"Got to, Bob!" The Jamaican turns away and starts to leave.

"Wait, goddammit! *I'm* the fucking captain, you're not!"

Tyrone looks at Bob with cold disgust. "We cut dem fuckin' Haitians loose, den *maybe* we get home tonight. Captain."

"Otherwise?"

Tyrone does not answer.

Bob shouts, "They've got us anyhow, the coast guard! We're caught anyhow!"

"No, dem got to stop to pick up de Haitians. Wid dem gone, de boat fast enough to get us out of here first maybe!"

"Or else we end up in jail, and they go back to Haiti! Right? Right, Tyrone?"

Again, Tyrone says nothing.

Bob says, "All right. Go ahead." Tyrone leaps away and down the ladder.

Bob looks over the rail to the deck below, where the Jamaican frantically, roughly, yanks the Haitians out from under the tarpaulin. He's shouting at them in Creole and Jamaican patois, making it very clear that they must jump into the water, and they must do it now. Every few seconds he points out to where they spotted the coast guard cutter, though Bob can no longer see her, for they're down in the trough between waves again, and Tyrone pulls at their arms, shoving the Haitians toward the starboard rail, but they shake their heads no, and a few start to cry and wail, no, no, they will not go. They cling to one another and to the chocks and cleats and gunwales and look wild-eyed about them, at the towering sea, at Bob up on the bridge, at Tyrone jumping angrily about, at each other, and they weep and beg, No, no, please don't make us leave the boat for the terrible sea.

The *Belinda Blue* rises to the ridge of water, and Bob sees the cutter again, now clearly turning back toward them, and they've got searchlights whipping wands of light across the water. "They're turning, they're gonna try to board us!" he yells down, and he sees Tyrone step from the cabin with a rifle in his hand, the shark gun, a 30-06 with a scope, and Bob says quietly, "Tyrone, for Christ's sake."

The Haitians back swiftly away from Tyrone, horrified. With the barrel of the gun, he waves them toward the rail and tells them once again to jump, but they won't move. The babies are screaming now, and the women and several of the men are openly weeping. Claude's face is frozen in a look of amazed grief.

Tyrone pulls the trigger and fires into the air, and one of the Haitians, the boy Claude, leaps into the water and is swept away. A second follows, and then a woman. Tyrone screams at the rest to jump, and he fires again.

Bob bellows from the bridge, "Tyrone! For Christ's sake, stop! They're drowning!" But the Jamaican is now bodily hurling the Haitians into the sea, one after the other, the old man, the woman with the two small children, Vanise and her child, the old woman. He's clearing the deck of them. They weep and cry out for help from God, from the loas, from Bob, who looks on in horror, and then they are gone, lifted up by the dark waves and carried away toward the shore.

Tyrone scrambles back up to the bridge, the rifle still in his hand, and he wrenches the wheel away from Bob and hits the throttle hard, bringing the boat swiftly around to port and away. Off to the north a few hundred yards, its searchlights sweeping over the water, the cutter has slowed and stopped, for they have apparently spotted the Haitians bobbing in the water. Bob sees that they are dropping a lifeboat from the stern. He follows one of the beams of light out to where it has fixed on a head in the water, one of the young men, and then he sees the man go down. The light switches back and forth, searching for him, then seems to give up and move on, looking for others. "They're drowning!" he cries. "They're drowning!"

Tyrone doesn't answer. He shoves the rifle at Bob and takes the wheel with both hands, bucking the *Belinda Blue* into the waves, driving her against mountains of water and quickly away from shore, heading her straight out to sea.

Bob holds the gun for a moment, looks at it as if it were a bloody ax. Then he lifts it over his head with two hands and hurls it into the sea.

Tyrone looks over his shoulder at Bob and says, "Good idea, mon. Dem prob'ly heard de shootin'. Nobody can say we de ones doin' de shootin' now. Got no gun, got no Haitians," he says, smiling. Then he says, "Better clear de deck of anyt'ing dem lef' behind, mon."

Slowly Bob descends to the deck, and kneeling down, he crawls under the tarpaulin, reaching around in the dark, until he comes up with several battered suitcases, a cloth bundle, a woven bag, and he tosses them overboard one by one, watches them bob on the water a second, then swiftly sink.

················

It's a pink dawn, the eastern sky stretched tight as silk on a frame. Overhead, blue-gray rags of cloud ride in erratic rows, while in the west, over southern Florida, the sky is dark and overcast. A man with white hair leads a nosy, head-diving dog, a blue-black Labrador, from his house and down the sandy walkway to the beach.

The man and the dog stroll easily south, and now and then the man stops and picks up a piece of weathered beach glass for his collection. The dog turns and waits, and when the man stands and moves on, the dog bounds happily ahead.

A quarter mile from where they started, the dog suddenly darts into the water, and the man stops and stares, as a body, a black woman's body, passes by the dog and with the next wave is tossed onto the beach. A few yards beyond, a child's body has been shoved up onto the beach, and beyond that, a pair of men lie dead on the sand.

The man counts five bodies in all, and then he turns and runs back up the beach, his dog following, to his home, where he calls the local police. "Haitians, I'm sure of it. Washing up on the sand, just like last time. Women and children this time, though. It's just awful," he says. "Just awful."

················

A mile south of where the other bodies came to shore at Golden Beach, and five miles south of Hollywood, while ambulance crews are lugging the bodies away from the water and up the beach to the ambulances, a woman struggles through the last few waves to the shore. She is alone, a young black woman with close-cropped hair, her dress yanked away from her by the force of the water, her limbs hanging down like anchors, as she staggers, stumbles, drags herself out of the water and falls forward onto the sand. Her name is Vanise Dorsinville; she is the only Haitian to survive the journey from New Providence Island to Florida on the *Belinda Blue*.

At the same time, possibly at the same moment, for these events have a curious way of coordinating themselves, Bob Dubois brings the *Belinda Blue* in from the open sea, passes under the bridge at Lower Matecumbe Key and heads for the Moray Key Marina. He cuts back the throttle as he enters the marina, letting the boat drift around to starboard so he can reverse her into the slip next to the *Angel Blue*, and he notices that Ave's boat is gone from the slip.

He puts the boat into reverse, and his Jamaican mate jumps onto the deck in the bow, ready to tie her up. Bob is backing the boat skillfully into the slip, when he sees, standing on the pier, apparently waiting for them, two Florida state troopers.

The Jamaican looks up at Bob on the bridge. "Get out, Bob! Reverse de fuckin' boat, mon, and get 'er out of here!"

Bob simply shakes his head no and calmly backs the boat into the slip.

J. M. COETZEE

Born in Cape Town in 1940, J. M. Coetzee was educated in South Africa and the United States and now teaches at the University of Cape Town. Among his novels are Age of Iron, Foe, In the Heart of the Country, *and* Dusklands. *The following fictional journey through a harsh hinterland is taken from* Waiting for the Barbarians. *Coetzee seems able to fashion landscape into archetype without any loss of details, and travel into moral allegory without losing human idiosyncrasy—an ability he would deploy again in his succeeding novel* Life & Times of Michael K, *which won the Booker Prize. The narrator here, the Magistrate, who is returning his native consort to her people, comes to see this girl in a new light as she adapts well to the hard conditions of travel.*

from WAITING FOR THE BARBARIANS

The air every morning is full of the beating of wings as the birds fly in from the south, circling above the lake before they settle in the salty fingers of the marshes. In the lulls of the wind the cacophony of their hooting, quacking, honking, squawking reaches us like the noise of a rival city on the water: greylag, beangoose, pintail, wigeon, mallard, teal, smew.

The arrival of the first of the migrating waterfowl confirms the earlier signs, the ghost of a new warmth on the wind, the glassy translucence of the lake-ice. Spring is on its way, one of these days it will be time to plant.

Meanwhile it is the season for trapping. Before dawn, parties of men leave for the lake to lay their nets. By mid-morning they are back with huge catches: birds with their necks twisted, slung from poles row upon row by their feet, or crammed alive into wooden cages, screaming with outrage, trampling each other, with sometimes a great silent whooper swan crouched in their midst. Nature's cornucopia: for the next weeks everyone will eat well.

Before I can leave there are two documents to compose. The first is addressed to the provincial governor. "To repair some of the damage wrought by the forays of the Third Bureau," I write, "and to restore some of the goodwill that previously existed, I am undertaking a brief visit to the barbarians." I sign and seal the letter.

What the second document is to be I do not yet know. A testament? A memoir? A confession? A history of thirty years on the frontier? All that day I sit in a trance at my desk staring at the empty white paper, waiting for words to come. A second day passes in the same way. On the third day I surrender, put the paper back in the drawer, and make preparations to leave. It seems appropriate that a man who does not know what to do with the woman in his bed should not know what to write.

To accompany me I have chosen three men. Two are young conscripts to whose services on secondment I am entitled. The third is an older man born in these parts, a hunter and horse trader whose wages I will pay out of my own pocket. I call them together the afternoon before we leave. "I know this is not a good time of year to travel," I tell them. "It is a treacherous time, the tail end of winter, spring not yet here. But if we wait longer we will not find the nomads before they start on their migration." They ask no questions.

To the girl I say simply, "I am taking you back to your people, or as near as I can, seeing that they are now dispersed." She gives no sign of rejoicing. I lay at her side the heavy fur I have bought her to travel in, with a rabbitskin cap embroidered in the native fashion, new boots, gloves.

Now that I have committed myself to a course I sleep more easily and even detect within myself something like happiness.

We depart on the third of March, accompanied through the gate and down the road to the lakeside by a ragtag escort of children and dogs. After we pass the irrigation wall and branch off from the river road, taking the track to the right used by no one but hunters and fowlers, our escort begins to dwindle till there are only two stubborn lads trotting behind us, each determined to outlast the other.

The sun has risen but gives off no warmth. The wind beats at us across the lake bringing tears to our eyes. In single file, four men and a woman, four pack animals, the horses persistently backing to the wind and having to be sawed around, we wind away from the walled town, the bare fields, and eventually from the panting boys.

My plan is to follow this track till we have skirted the lake to the south, then to strike out northeast across the desert toward the valleys of the ranges where the northern nomads winter. It is a route rarely travelled, since the nomads, when they migrate with their flocks, follow the old dead riverbed in a vast sweep east and south. However, it reduces a journey of six weeks to one or two. I have never travelled it myself.

So for the first three days we plod south and then eastward. To our right stretches a plain of wind-eroded clay terraces merging at its extremes into banks and red dust clouds and then into the yellow hazy sky. To our left is flat marshland, belts of reeds, and the lake on which the central ice sheet has not melted. The wind blowing over the ice freezes our very breath, so that rather than ride we often walk for long spells in the lee of our horses. The girl winds a scarf around and around her face and, crouching in the saddle, blindly follows her leader.

Two of the pack horses are loaded with firewood, but this must be conserved for the desert. Once, half buried in driftsand, we come upon a spreading moundlike tamarisk which we hack to pieces for fuel; for the rest we have to be content with bundles of dry reeds. The girl and I sleep side by side in the same tent, huddled in our furs against the cold.

In these early days of the journey we eat well. We have brought salted meat, flour, beans, dried fruit, and there are wildfowl to shoot. But we have to be sparing with water. The marshwater here in the shallow southern fingers is too salty to be drinkable. One of the men has to wade twenty or thirty paces in, as deep as his calves, to fill the skins, or, better, to break off lumps of ice. Yet even the melted ice-water is so bitter and salty that it can only be drunk with strong red tea. Every year the lake grows more brackish as the river eats into its banks and sweeps salt and alum into the lake. Since the lake has no outflow its mineral content keeps rising, particularly in the south, where tracts of water are seasonally isolated by sandbars. After the summer flood the fishermen find carp floating belly-up in the shallows. They say that perch are no more to be seen. What will become of the settlement if the lake grows into a dead sea?

After a day of salty tea all of us except the girl begin to suffer from diarrhoea. I am the worst afflicted. I feel keenly the humiliation of the frequent stops, the undressing and dressing with frozen fingers in the lee of a horse while the others wait. I try to drink as little as possible, to the point even that my mind throws up tantalizing images as I ride: a full cask by the wellside with water splashing from the ladle; clean snow. My occasional hunting and hawking, my desultory womanizing, exercises of manhood, have concealed from me how soft my body has grown. After long marches my bones ache, by nightfall I am so tired that I have no appetite. I trudge on till I cannot put one foot in front of the other; then I clamber into the saddle, fold myself in my cloak, and wave one of the men forward to take over the task of picking out the faint track. The wind never lets up. It howls at us across the ice, blowing from nowhere to nowhere, veiling the sky in a cloud of red dust. From the dust there is no hiding: it penetrates our clothing, cakes our skin, sifts into the baggage. We eat with coated tongues, spitting often, our teeth grating. Dust rather than air becomes the medium in which we live. We swim through dust like fish through water.

The girl does not complain. She eats well, she does not get sick, she sleeps soundly all night clenched in a ball in weather so cold I would hug a dog for comfort. She rides all day without a murmur. Once, glancing up, I see that she is riding asleep, her face as peaceful as a baby's.

On the third day the rim of the marshland begins to curve back toward the north and we know that we have rounded the lake. We pitch camp early and spend the last hours of light collecting every scrap of fuel we can while the horses browse for the last time on the meagre marshgrass. Then at dawn on the fourth day we begin the crossing of the ancient lake bed that stretches another forty miles beyond the marshes.

The terrain is more desolate than anything we have yet seen. Nothing grows on this salty lake floor, which in places buckles and pushes up in jagged crystalline hexagons a foot wide. There are dangers too: crossing an unusually smooth patch the front horse suddenly plunges through the crust and sinks chest-deep in foul green slime, the man who leads it standing a moment dumbstruck on thin air before he too splashes in. We struggle to haul them out, the salt crust splintering under the hooves of the flailing horse, the hole widening, a brackish stench everywhere. We have not left the lake behind, we now realize: it stretches beneath us here, sometimes under a cover many feet deep, sometimes under a mere parchment of brittle salt. How long since the sun last shone on these dead waters? We light a fire on firmer ground to warm the shivering man and dry his clothes. He shakes his head. "I always heard, beware of the green patches, but I never saw this happen before," he says. He is our guide, the one man among us who has travelled east of the lake. After this we push our horses even harder, in a hurry to be off the dead lake, fearful of being lost in a fluid colder than ice, mineral, subterraneous, airless. We bow our heads and drive into the wind, our coats ballooning behind us, picking a way over the jagged salt shards, avoiding the smooth ground. Through the river of dust that courses majestically across the sky the sun glows like an orange but warms nothing. When darkness falls we batter the tent pegs into cracks in the rock-hard salt; we burn our firewood at an extravagant rate and like sailors pray for land.

On the fifth day we leave the lake floor behind and pass through a belt of smooth crystalline salt which soon gives way to sand and stone. Everyone is heartened, even the horses, which during the crossing of the salt have had nothing but a few handfuls of linseed and a bucketful of brackish water. Their condition is visibly deteriorating.

As for the men, they do not grumble. The fresh meat is giving out but there remain the salt meat and dried beans and plenty of flour and tea, the staples of the road. At each halt we brew tea and fry little fatcakes, delicious morsels to the hungry. The men do the cooking:

being shy of the girl, unsure of her standing, unsure most of all what we are doing taking her to the barbarians, they barely address her, avoid looking at her, and certainly do not ask for her help with the food. I do not push her forward, hoping that constraint will disappear on the road. I picked these men because they were hardy and honest and willing. They follow me as lightheartedly as they can under these conditions, though by now the brave lacquered armour the two young soldiers wore when we passed through the great gate is strapped in bundles on the pack-horses and their scabbards are full of sand.

The sand flats begin to modulate into duneland. Our progress slows as we toil up and down the sides of the dunes. It is the worst possible terrain for the horses, which plod forward a few inches at a time, their hooves sinking deep in the sand. I look to our guide, but all he can do is shrug: "It goes on for miles, we have to cross it, there is no other way." Standing on a dune top, shielding my eyes, staring ahead, I can see nothing but swirling sand.

That night one of the pack horses refuses its feed. In the morning, even under the severest flogging, it will not rise. We redistribute the loads and cast away some of the firewood. While the others set out I stay behind. I can swear that the beast knows what is to happen. At the sight of the knife its eyes roll. With the blood spurting from its neck it scrambles free of the sand and totters a pace or two downwind before it falls. In extremities, I have heard, the barbarians tap their horses' veins. Will we live to regret this blood spent so lavishly on the sand?

On the seventh day, with the dunes finally behind us, we make out against the dull grey-brown of the empty landscape a strip of darker grey. From nearer we see that it stretches east and west for miles. There are even the stunted black shapes of trees. We are lucky, our guide says: there is bound to be water here.

What we have stumbled on is the bed of an ancient terminal lagoon. Dead reeds, ghostly white and brittle to the touch, line what were its banks. The trees are poplars, also long dead. They have died since the underground water receded too far to be reached by their roots years and years ago.

We unload the animals and begin to dig. At two feet we reach heavy blue clay. Beneath this there is sand again, then another stratum of clay, noticeably clammy. At a depth of seven feet, with my heart pounding and my ears ringing, I have to refuse my turn with the spade. The three men toil on, lifting the loose soil out of the pit in a tent cloth tied at the corners.

At ten feet water begins to gather around their feet. It is sweet, there is no trace of salt, we smile with delight at each other; but it gathers very slowly and the sides of the pit have continually to be dug out as they cave in. It is only by late afternoon that we can empty out the last of our brackish lakewater and refill the waterskins. In near dark we lower the butt into our well and allow the horses to drink.

Meanwhile, now that there is an abundance of poplarwood the men have dug two little ovens back to back in the clay and built a roaring fire on top of them to bake the clay dry. When the fire abates they can rake the coals back into the ovens and set about baking bread. The girl stands watching all this, leaning on her sticks to which I have fastened discs of wood to help her in the sand. In the free and easy camaraderie of this good day, and with a day of rest promised, talk flows. Joking with her, the men make their first overture of friendship: "Come and sit with us and taste what men's baking is like!" She smiles back at them, lifting her chin in a gesture which perhaps I alone know is an effort to see. Cautiously she sets herself down beside them to bathe in the glow from the ovens.

I myself sit farther away sheltered from the wind in the mouth of my tent with one of the oil lamps flickering beside me, making the day's entry in the logbook but listening too. The banter goes on in the pidgin of the frontier, and she is at no loss for words. I am surprised by her fluency, her quickness, her self-possession. I even catch myself in a flush of pride: she is not just the old man's slut, she is a witty, attractive young woman! Perhaps if from the beginning I had known how to use this slap-happy joking lingo with her we might have warmed more to each other. But like a fool, instead of giving her a good time I oppressed her with gloom. Truly, the world ought to belong to the singers and dancers! Futile bitterness, idle melancholy, empty regrets! I blow out the lamp, sit with my chin on my fist staring toward the fire, listening to my stomach rumble.

GRAHAM GREENE

Famous for such novels as Brighton Rock, The Power and
the Glory, The End of the Affair, The Quiet American,
and The Human Factor, *Graham Greene took his place in
the company of Evelyn Waugh, Peter Fleming, and Robert
Byron as a distinguished travel writer of the thirties with the
1936 publication of* Journey Without Maps, *a narrative of
his ruinous West African trek by foot through two hundred
miles of seediness and mosquitoes, during which he contracted malaria. He followed this book three years later with*
The Lawless Roads, *an account of his unhappy journey in
Mexico, a country where he was unable to experience much,
if any, pleasure.*

---

from THE LAWLESS ROADS

THE LONG RIDE

I left my suitcase behind, and because it seemed absurd to think of rain
I foolishly abandoned my cape and took only the net, a hammock, and
a rucksack.

At a quarter past four I got up and dressed by the light of my
electric torch, folded up the huge tentlike mosquito net. Everybody in
Salto was asleep but my guide—a dark, dapper young man of some
education who had come from Las Casas by way of Yajalon—and his
father, who had prepared us coffee and biscuits in his home. It was the
cool and quiet beginning of one of the worst days I have ever spent.
Only the first few hours of that ride were to provide any pleasure—

riding out of Salto in the dark with one sleepy mongrel raising its muzzle at the clip clop of the mules, the ferry across the river in the earliest light, the two mules swimming beside the canoe, with just their muzzles and their eyes above the water like a pair of alligator heads, and then the long banana plantations on the other bank, the fruit plucked as we rode tasting tart and delicious in the open air at dawn.

The trouble was, the way to Palenque lay across a bare exposed plateau, broken only occasionally by patches of forest and shade, and by nine in the morning the sun was blindingly up. By ten my cheap helmet bought in Veracruz for a few pesos was just the damp hot cardboard it had pretended not be be. I had not ridden a horse for ten years; I had never ridden a mule before. Its trot, I imagine, is something like a camel's: its whole back heaves and strains. There is no rhythm you can catch by rising in the stirrups; you must just surrender yourself to the merciless uneven bump. The strain on the spine to the novice is appalling: the neck stiffens with it, the head aches as if it had been struck by sun. And all the time the nerves are worn by the stubbornness of the brute; the trot degenerates into a walk, the walk into an amble, unless you beat the mule continually. "*Mula. Mula. Mula. Echa, mula,*" the dreary lament goes on.

And all the time Palenque shifted like a mirage; my guide had never been there himself: all he could do on the wide plain was to keep a rough direction. Ten hours away the storekeeper had said, and after four hours I thought I could manage that quite easily, but when we stopped at an Indian's hut about eleven in the morning (six hours from Salto) and heard them talk as if it were now not quite halfway, my heart sank. A couple of wattle huts like those of West African natives, chickens and turkeys tumbling across the dusty floor, a pack of mongrels and a few cows listless in the heat under some thorny trees—it was better than nothing on that baked plateau, and I wished later we had stayed the night. They swung a string hammock up and I dismoutned with immense difficulty. Six hours had stiffened me. They gave us tortillas—the flat, dry pancake with which you eat all food in the Mexican country—and an egg each in a tin mug, and coffee, delicious coffee. We rested half an hour and then went on. Six hours more, I said, with what I hoped was cheerfulness to my guide, but he scouted the notion. Six hours—oh, no, perhaps eight. Those people didn't know a thing.

I can remember practically nothing of that ride now until its close; I remember being afraid of sunstroke my head ached so—I would raise my hat for coolness, and then lower it from fear; I remember talking to my guide of the cantinas there would be in Palenque and how much beer and tequila we would drink. I remember the guide getting smaller and smaller in the distance and flogging at my mule (*"Mula. Mula. Echa, mula"*) until I overtook him at a trot that wrenched the backbone. I remember that we passed a man with the mails traveling on a pony at a smart canter and he said he'd left Palenque in the night. And then somewhere on that immense rolling plain, in a spot where the grass grew long, the mule suddenly lay down under me. The guide was a long way off; I felt I could never get up on that mule again; I sat on the grass and tried to be sick and wanted to cry. The guide rode back and waited patiently for me to remount, but I didn't think it was possible—my body was too stiff. There was a small coppice of trees, some monkeys moved inquisitively, and the mule got on its feet again and began to eat.

Can't we stay the night somewhere, I said, in some hut, and go on tomorrow? But the guide said there wasn't a single hut between here and Palenque. It was two o'clock in the afternoon; we had been riding for nine hours, with half an hour's break; Palenque was, he said, about five hours away. Couldn't we string our hammocks up to the trees and sleep here? But he had no hammock and besides, there was no food, no drink, and lots of mosquitoes, perhaps a leopard. I think he meant a leopard—they call them tigers in Chiapas—and I remember how Victorian Dr. Fitzpatrick had met one on his ride across these mountains, standing across his path. It is rather terrifying to believe you cannot go on, and yet to have no choice. . . .

I got back into the saddle, thanking God for the big Mexican pommel which you can cling to with both hands when all else fails, and again the ride faded into obscurity—I didn't talk so much now about the cantina, I grumbled to myself in undertones that I *couldn't* make it, and I began to hate the dapperness of my guide, his rather caddish white riding-breeches—it was nothing to him, the ride; he rode just as he would sit in a chair. And then the mule lay down again; it lay down in the end four times before we saw, somewhere about five o'clock when the sun was low, a little smoke drifting over the ridge of the down. "Palenque," my guide said. I didn't believe him, and that was lucky, because it wasn't Palenque, only a prairie fire we had to ride around, the mules uneasy in the smoke. And then we came into a patch of forest and the ways divided; one way, the guide said—on I don't know whose authority, for he had never been here before—led to the German *finca*, the other to Palenque. Which were we to take? I chose Palenque: it was nearer and the lodging more certain, above all the drink. I didn't really believe in the German and his lovely daughter, and when after we'd been going a quarter of an hour we just came out on the same path, I believed less than ever in them. As the sun sank, the flies emerged more numerous than ever; they didn't bother to attack me; great fat droning creatures, they sailed by and sank like dirigibles on to the mule's neck, grappled fast, and sucked until a little stream of blood flowed down. I tried to dislodge them with my stick, but they simply shifted their ground. The smell of blood and mule was sickening. One became at last a kind of automaton, a bundle of flesh and bone without a brain.

And then a little party of riders came out of a belt of forest in the last light and bore news—Palenque was only half an hour distant. The rest of the way was in darkness, the darkness of the forest and then the darkness of night as well. That was how we began and ended. The stars were up when we came out of the forest, and there at the head of a long parklike slope of grass was a poor abandoned cemetery, crosses rotting at an angle and lying in the long grass behind a broken wall, and at the foot of the slope lights moved obscurely up towards a collection of round mud huts thatched with banana leaves as poor as anything I ever saw in West Africa. We rode through the huts and came into a long wide street of bigger huts—square ones these, raised a foot from the ground to avoid ants, some of them roofed with tin—and at the head of the street on a little hill a big plain ruined church.

My guide apparently had learned where we could get food, if not lodging—a woman's hut where the school teacher lived, and while food was prepared we staggered out on legs as stiff as stilts to find the drink we had promised ourselves all the hot day. But Palenque wasn't Salto; the Salto cantina loomed in memory with the luxury of an American bar. In the store near the church they had three bottles of beer only—warm, gassy, unsatisfying stuff. And afterwards we drank a glass each of very new and raw tequila; it hardly touched our thirst. At the other end of the village was the only other store. We made our way there by the light of electric torches, to find they sold no beer at all: all we could get was mineral water coloured pink and flavoured with some sweet chemical. We had a bottle each and I took a bottle away with me to wash down my quinine. Otherwise we had to try and satisfy our thirst with coffee—endlessly; a good drink, but bad for the nerves. The school teacher was a plump complacent young half-caste with a patronising and clerical manner and a soft boneless hand: that was what the village had gained in place of a priest. His assistant was of a different type: alert, interested in his job for its own sake and not for the prestige it gave him, good with children, I feel sure. After we had eaten, he led us up the street to his own room, where we were to sleep. It was a small room in a tin-roofed hut beside the ruined church, which they used now as a school. He insisted that I should take his bed, my guide took my hammock, and our host tied up another for himself from the heavy beams.

I think the hut had once been a stable; now it seemed to be divided by thin partitions into three. In one division we slept, in another small children cried all night, and behind my head, in the third, I could hear the slow movements and the regular coughing of cows. I slept very badly in my clothes—I had cramps in my feet and a little fever from the sun. Somewhere around midnight there was the sound of a horse outside and a fist beat on the big-bolted barn door. Nobody moved until a voice called, *"Con amistad"* (with friendship), and then the stranger was let in. I put on my electric torch and he moved heavily round the little room tying up a hammock; then he took off his revolver holster and lay down, and again I tried to sleep. It seemed to me that a woman's voice was constantly urging me to turn my face to the wall because that way I lay closer to Tabasco, the Atlantic, and home. I felt sick, but I was too tired to go outside and vomit. The hammocks creaked and something fluttered in the roof and a child wailed. There was no ventilation at all.

VISITING THE RUINS

Fate had got me somehow to Palenque, and so I thought I had better see the ruins, but it was stupid, after the long ride and the feverish night, to go next morning. And it was stupid, too, to start as late as seven, for it was nearly half-past nine before we reached them and the tropical sun was already high. It wasn't so much stiffness that bothered me now: it was the feel of fever, an overpowering nausea without the energy to vomit, a desire to lie down and never get up again, a continuous thirst. I had tried to get some mineral water to take with me, but our purchases had cleared the store right out, and all the time, if only I had known it, I was in one of the few places in Mexico where it was safe to drink the water. Springs rose everywhere; as we climbed through the thick hot forest they sparkled between the trees, fell in tiny torrents, spread out, like a Devonshire stream, over the pebbles in a little clearing. But I didn't drink, merely watched with sick envy the mules take their fill, afraid that the streams might be polluted farther up by cattle, as if any cattle could live in this deep forest: we passed the bleached skeleton of something by the path. So one always starts a journey in a strange land—taking too many precautions, until one tires of the exertion and abandons care in the worst spot of all. How I hated my mule, drinking where I wanted to drink myself and, like the American dentist, chewing all the time, pausing every few feet up the mountainside to snatch grasses.

Nobody had properly opened up the way to Palenque; sometimes the guide had to cut the way with his machete, and at the end the path rose at a crazy angle—it couldn't have been less than sixty degrees. I hung on to the pommel and left it all to the mule and anyway didn't care. And then at last, two hours and a half from the village, the ruins appeared.

I haven't been to Chichen Itzá, but judging from photographs of the Yucatán remains they are immeasurably more impressive than those of Palenque, though, I suppose, if you like wild nature, the setting of Palenque is a finer one—on a great circular plateau halfway up the mountainside, with the jungle falling precipitously below into the plain and rising straight up behind; in the clearing itself there is nothing but a few Indian huts, scrub and stone and great mounds of rubble crowned with low one-storey ruins of grey rock, so age-worn they have a lichenous shape and look more vegetable than mineral. And no shade anywhere until you've climbed the steep loose slopes and bent inside the dark cool little rooms like lavatories where a few stalactites have formed and on some of the stones are a few faint scratches which they call hiero-glyphics. At first you notice only one of these temples or palaces where it stands in mid-clearing on its mound with no more importance than a ruined stone farm in the Oxford countryside, but then all round you, as you gaze, they open up, emerging obscurely from the jungle—three, four, five, six, I don't know how many gnarled relics. No work is in progress, and you can see them on the point of being swallowed again by the forest; they have looked out for a minute, old wrinkled faces, and will soon withdraw.

Well, I had told people I was here in Chiapas to visit the ruins and I had visited them; but there was no compulsion to see them, and I hadn't the strength to climb more than two of those slopes and peer into more than two of the cold snaky chambers. I thought I was going to faint; I sat down on a stone and looked down—at trees, and nothing but trees, going on and on out of sight. It seemed to me that this wasn't a country to live in at all with the heat and the desolation; it was a country to die in and leave only ruins behind. Last year Mexico City was shaken more than two hundred times by earthquake. . . . One was looking at the future as well as at the past.

I slid somehow down on to the ground and saw my guide set off with the Indian who guards the site towards another palace; I couldn't follow. With what seemed awful labour I moved my legs back toward the Indian huts; a kind of stubbornness surged up through the fever— I wouldn't see the ruins, I wouldn't go back to Palenque, I'd simply lie down here and wait—for a miracle. The Indian hut had no walls; it was simply a twig shelter with a chicken or two scratching in the dust, and a hammock and a packing case. I lay down on my back in the hammock and stared at the roof; outside, according to authorities, were the Templo de las Leyes, the Templo del Sol, the Templo de la Cruz de Palenque. I knew what they could do with their temples. . . . And farther off still England. It had no reality. You get accustomed in a few weeks to the idea of living or dying in the most bizarre surroundings. Man has a dreadful adaptability.

I suppose I dozed, for there were the Indian and the guide looking down at me. I could see the guide was troubled. He had a feeling of responsibility, and no Mexican cares for that. It's like a disused limb they have learned to do without. They said if I'd move into the other hut they would get me coffee. I felt that it was a trap: if they could make me move, they could make me get on that mule again and then would begin the two-and-a-half hour ride back to Palenque. An hour had lost meaning; it was like a cipher for some number too big to comprehend. Very unwillingly, very slowly, I shifted a dozen feet to another open hut and another hammock. A young Indian girl with big silver ear-rings and a happy sensual face began to make corn coffee— thin grey stuff like a temperance drink which does no harm. I said to the guide, without much hope, "Why shouldn't we sleep here?" I knew his answer—mosquitoes; he was a man who liked his comforts. He brought up again that dream of a German with a beautiful daughter; I lay on my back, disbelieving. The *finca*, he said, was only a little way from Palenque. We'd go there tonight in the cool. I went on drinking corn coffee, bowl after bowl of it. I suppose it had some tonic effect, for I have a dim memory of suddenly thinking, "Oh, hell, if I'm going to collapse, I may as well collapse in the village where the damned guide won't worry me. . . ." I got on the mule and when once I was up it was as easy—almost—to sit there as in a hammock; I just held on to the pommel and let the mule do the rest. We slid down slowly over the tree roots toward the plain. I was too exhausted to be frightened.

And when time did somehow come to an end, I fell off the mule and made straight for the schoolmaster's hammock and lay down. I wanted nothing except just not to move. The plump complacent school-master sat on the steps and had a philosophical talk with a passing peasant—"The sun is the origin of life," a finger pointed upwards. I was too sick to think then of Rivera's school teachers in snowy-white blessing with raised episcopal fingers the little children with knowledge, knowledge like this. "That is true. Without the sun we should cease to exist." I lay and drank cup after cup of coffee; the school teachers had lunch, but I couldn't eat, just went on drinking coffee, and sweating it out again. Liquid had no time to be digested; it came through the pores long before it reached the stomach. I lay wet through with sweat for four hours—it was very nearly like happiness. In the street outside nobody passed: it was too hot for life to go on. Only a vulture or two flopping by, and the whinny of a horse in a field.

ERIC HANSEN

Born in 1948, Eric Hansen is a graduate of the University of California at Berkeley, and has traveled extensively in the Middle East and Asia. In 1982 he spent seven months walking across Borneo and back. What follows is a crucial part of this intrepid expedition when, mistaken for a bali saleng, *or a collector of blood offerings for coastal construction projects, Hansen encounters trouble among village people in the Kayan River valley.*

---

from STRANGER IN THE FOREST

"The people are afraid," Pa Biah warned me. "Don't travel by yourself; it is not safe. The people know you have come to the valley. They may hurt you if they see you alone in the jungle."

The red glow from Pa Biah's cheroot gradually faded, and as he coaxed the fire back to life with his foot, we sipped hot bitter tea from chipped enamel mugs. Ibu Iting, his wife, sat nearby. She was making thread by pulling strands of cotton from the edge of an old piece of fabric. While holding the ends of two strands in her left hand, she twisted them together by rubbing them between her right hand and thigh. She threaded her needle and continued to listen to our conversation as she patched a well-worn pair of trousers.

"Last year," Pa Biah continued, "*bali saleng* was described as a brown-skinned man with long black hair and pointed teeth. He wore a powder blue, short-sleeved, military-type shirt with matching shorts. He had a special set of spring-powered shoes that enabled him to jump four meters in the air and ten meters away in a single bound. He could spring through the air to cover long distances quickly and capture people by surprise. After tying up his victim with strips of rattan, he would take the blood from the wrist or the foot with a small knife and a rubber pump. The corpse would then be hoisted with vines up into the jungle canopy so that searchers could not find it."

Listening attentively, I tried to imagine a police department's composite sketch of such an individual. The image of *bali saleng* was still too farfetched for me to take seriously.

"A *bali saleng* cannot be killed by man," Pa Biah continued. "Bullets bounce off him, spears cannot pierce his body, and when he gets old he will take on a young man without family and train him."

Pa Biah went on to tell me that the year before a pregnant woman was reported to have been killed by a *bali saleng* near the village of Long Ampung. Pregnant women are considered prime targets because they contain the blood of two people.

That night the people of Long Nawang locked themselves into their family quarters and did not open their doors until daybreak.

I listened to Pa Biah's stories with interest, but I failed to recognize my own imminent danger. I was placing too much confidence in my knowledge of the language and too little importance on the power of fear. Instead of accepting the people's beliefs as something real and adjusting my behavior accordingly, I was relying on a false sense of security. With nearly eighteen hundred jungle miles behind me, I had become careless.

The next morning I got up and left at dawn—alone. I didn't get far. Four hours up the valley, as I followed the Kayan River southeast from Long Nawang, I was attacked in the village of Long Uro. The first thing I heard was the frantic pounding of children's feet along hardwood planks of the longhouse porch. There were a few startled cries from the women then the sound of men's voices. It all happened very quickly. It took me a moment to realize that I was the cause of the commotion.

A group of about two dozen men, some armed with spears, came down to the trail where I was standing. After some excited questioning and gesturing (not all of which I understood), I felt their hands on me. I was stripped of my pack and forced to the ground. I didn't resist. I sat in the dirt with my back to a drainage ditch as the men formed a tight semicircle in front of me. For the next two hours they fired accusations at me in Indonesian. I was repeatedly questioned and cross-examined. My mind became alert, and I was careful not to show any fear. They wanted to know why I was by myself, why I didn't have a cooking pot, what I was doing in the Kayan River valley, and how I had come over the mountains from Sarawak. My answers didn't sound very convincing, and I soon realized how vulnerable I was. The experience of facing so many frightened people was intimidating. My belongings were ransacked; shotgun shells, diaries, salt, clothing, and half-finished letters to friends littered the ground. I was repeatedly asked about the contents of my pack. After two men had gone through everything, I realized that they had been looking for spring-powered shoes, the small blood knife, and the rubber pump.

Over and over they repeated two questions: "Why do you walk by yourself?" and "Why aren't you afraid of *bali saleng?*"

The fact is that no one in Borneo walks by himself in the jungle. It is too easy to fall down or to get lost or sick. Every year people disappear in the rain forest without a trace. Solo travel isn't done except by the spirits. It was difficult to explain to these villagers why I had no fear. By now hours had passed, and I felt my energy fading. These frightened, angry people, with their excited sing-song manner of speaking, were exhausting me. Here in a village of practicing animists was a middle-class Westerner arguing about evil spirits in their jungle. By consistently basing my answers on logic and reasoning, I was only making the situation worse. I would have merely increased their suspicions if I had claimed not to believe in spirits. How could I possibly be convincing? I asked myself. It became irrelevant and unimportant to me whether they understood who I really was. By this time I wanted only one thing: to be able to leave the village safely. I realized that I had to accept their fear and deal with it on their terms. It was absurd for me to try to convince them that one of their greatest fears was unfounded. A solution came to me unexpectedly.

The Kenyah, as do all the inland people, have a tradition of amulets, charms, and spell-breakers. The collective term for these items is *jeemat*. A *jeemat* can be made from a wide assortment of materials;

the most common are seedpods, bones, wood shavings, crushed insects, beeswax, cowrie shells, and odd-shaped black pebbles known as hook stones. A *jeemat* can be made by man or found, but the most powerful ones (the hook stones) are given by a spirit or ghost. Directions for their use are revealed during a dream. It is very bad luck to lose or give away a charm that has come from the spirits. *Jeemats* are usually worn around the neck or wrist and are an important part of one's personal adornment. They are visible proof of one's faith in the power of the spirit world.

With this in mind, I remembered I was wearing a small, stuffed fabric banana pin that a friend had given me before I started my trip. The pin was about three inches long and had a bright yellow, polka-dot peel. The banana was removable. It could be dangled at the end of a short safety string. Until that moment in Long Uro, I had used the pin only to amuse people.

"This," I said, gesturing to the pin, "is my *jeemat*. It protects me from *bali saleng*." It caught them off guard; it also aroused their interest. One of the men came forward to touch the banana, but I cautioned him not to. He stopped three feet away from me.

"It has very strong *obat*," I said. *Obat* has many definitions: magic, power, or medicine. "Be careful, this charm was made especially for me by a spirit. That is why I'm not afraid to walk alone in the jungle." The mood of the interrogation changed as interest shifted to my banana pin.

"Where did it come from?" "What is it made of?" "Do you have more?" "How much would one cost?" they wanted to know.

I did not concoct my banana-pin story because I thought my tormentors were simple-minded or childish. Quite the opposite. The Kenyah have a highly developed relationship with the spirit world. I couldn't think of any other story they might believe. From generations of experience, they know how to coexist with both good and bad spirits. Firmly rooted in the twentieth century, I certainly didn't have anything to teach them. I was the outsider, the ignorant one. I had great respect for all the inland people. With their unique forms of architecture, social organization, and sophisticated farming techniques, they have estab-lished themselves in an incredibly difficult environment. The decision to present the banana pin as a powerful charm not only helped save me in this situation, but also forced me to reconsider how I was responding to the people. I stopped being the observer and began to accept their supernatural world, and my journey was never the same. In that single moment I grew much closer to my experiences.

The tension eased after I had revealed the power of the banana-pin charm. A few obstinate older men insisted on going over the fine points of my story, but the rest seemed to think I was probably harmless. I was flushed with relief. The blood and adrenaline pounded through my body and made my fingertips and toes ache. I felt light-headed and blessed to have survived this incident unharmed.

I was free to go, but it was too late to continue up the valley to my original destination—Long Sungai Barang. I had to spend the night in Long Uro. Dozens of eyes stared at me through knotholes and cracks in the rough wooden walls as I ate a miserable and lonely dinner. I was served half-rotten fish pounded in a mortar, bones and all. Having finished my meal, I strung my mosquito net in a filthy corner, unrolled my mat, and escaped into an exhausted sleep.

During the night there must have been more discussion because in the morning, just after I left the village, I came upon a young man standing at the side of the pathway. He was barefoot, well muscled, and dressed in blue shorts. He wore white gloves and held a large unsheathed parang at his side. He didn't respond to my greeting as I approached, but as I passed he fell into step a few feet behind me. I continued on for a short while then decided it would be better to confront him. I turned to speak, but he had vanished into the undergrowth. I knew that he could be no more than fifty feet from where I stood, but I couldn't see him. For months this jungle had seemed so benign and giving. How quickly it had become frightening. It was clear to me that at any moment I might be ambushed and killed.

Farther up the valley I passed abandoned farm huts and stopped briefly in the village of Lidung Payau to ask directions to the village of Long Sungai Barang. On the far side of Lidung Payau, I saw what I soon realized was a cage fashioned out of logs six inches in diameter. The structure was raised off the ground and had a slat floor that let excrement out and the flies in. The cage measured six feet by five feet by four feet and had a shingled roof. It was "home" not to an animal, but to a man. There were no doors or windows. I later learned that the inhabitant, barely visible between the gaps in the horizontal logs, had lived in the cage for more than two years. I don't know what his crime was. The cloud of furiously buzzing blackflies must have driven him mad. I looked upon this wretched man as a fellow sufferer, but when I tried to speak with him, he moved to the far side of his cage, and I could sense his fear of my presence.

I no longer had my sense of security and self-confidence. I lost track of time. As my anxiety mounted, a few hundred yards began to seem like miles. My thinking became erratic and unsound. There was no turning back, and for the first time since leaving Long Sungai Anai three days earlier, I began to panic. I sensed that I was being watched. Soaked in perspiration, I paused frequently to look over my shoulder and listen for the sound of human voices or of jungle knives slashing through the undergrowth. I scanned the surrounding walls of impenetrable green and brown foliage, but I could detect nothing. There were only the normal sounds of the jungle: the wind, the flutter of leaves, dripping water, and rubbing branches. I could see black hornbills perched nearby, so I called to them. I wanted to hear something friendly and reassuring, but their calls came back to me sounding like strangled pleas.

I hurried on to Long Sungai Barang, hoping that word of the incident in Long Uro hadn't preceded me. I wanted a fresh start. I now realized the full extent of my naiveté, my incredible stupidity. I was completely alone and vulnerable. I didn't know what else to do except to keep walking and to try to relax. I stopped frequently, considered going back, couldn't decide, then continued on. Whenever I sat down to rest and clear my mind, a new wave of anxiety would engulf me.

I knew that Long Sungai Barang was the last village in the upper Kayan River valley. If the people there weren't friendly, I would be trapped. Four hundred miles of primary rain forest separated me from the most accessible coast.

It was late afternoon by the time I entered the longhouse at Sungai Barang. I was disoriented and confused, and my legs were bleeding freely from the leeches and barbed vines. I was led to the headman's room. While he was being summoned, I was surrounded by about a dozen Kenyah men. I could feel the deep, painful grooves that the straps of the rattan pack had cut into my shoulders. My shirt was pasted to my back from the heat of the day. The men seemed relaxed and curious, but I felt they looked right through me and sensed my uncertainty.

We talked about the approaching rice harvest for perhaps ten minutes; then to my left I heard the familiar creak and slam of a sapling-powered hardwood door. In midsentence I looked up, expecting to see the headman, but there before me stood a young, white-skinned woman with golden hair. She was dressed in a flowered sarong and a blouse. She was barefoot, pretty, and smiling. I was completely unnerved. It just wasn't possible for her to be there. I became incredulous and even more confused. Finally I just smiled back and felt my pent-up fears and anxieties begin to dissolve.

The first thing I noticed as she stood there was the fragrance of her skin. It wasn't the scent of soap or perfume; it was the scent of another culture, another world, a fresh, wonderful smell that made me question my attraction to smoky jungle campfires and eating wild animals. We spoke Indonesian. There was no urgency to our voices. In Kenyah fashion we began with trivial matters in order to mask the real intent of our conversation, and gradually we led up to the important questions. More people came into the room. They sat quietly, watched, and listened. Eventually the temptation to speak our own language was overwhelming. The woman smiled again and in perfect English said, "I'm Cynthia. I live next door. The headman won't be back until late tonight. Would you like to come over to my place for a visit?"

REDMOND O'HANLON

Redmond O'Hanlon was born in Dorset in 1947 and edu-
cated at Marlborough and Oxford. His doctoral thesis com-
bined his interests in nature and the English novel, and in
1984 he published Joseph Conrad and Charles Darwin. *In*
that year he also published his first travel book, Into the
Heart of Borneo. *In his second,* In Trouble Again: A Journey
Between the Orinoco and the Amazon, *he can be seen*
traveling in South America in the same ironical, bug-infested
tradition as Evelyn Waugh and the wandering naturalists
of the nineteenth century. O'Hanlon is a Fellow of the Royal
Geographic Society and lives with his wife and children near
Oxford.

---

from *IN TROUBLE AGAIN*

The Baria is not the easy waterway which Spruce imagined it to be.
Four days into its dendritic delta it seemed the most difficult place on
earth. The yelping toucans, the big Amazon parrots, the paired flights
of macaws, the rattling cry of the ringed kingfisher, the giant herons,
the anhingas, the swallow-tailed kites—all the birds of the open river
had long since disappeared. Even the big blue morpho butterflies and
the bats, the tiny grey bats that fluttered in flocks like blown woodsmoke
from one dead branch to another as we approached—even they had
gone. The trees in the labyrinth met overhead, knotted together with
lianas, their foliage thickened with epiphytic orchids and umbrella-
leaved bromeliads. The sun only reached the black-water channels of
the Baria when a storm or old age or a collapsing bank had felled a
tree and left a gap in the canopy.

Woken at four-thirty in the morning by the one clock still functioning, a cheap Classa alarm which I kept in a plastic bag, I shone my torch across the leaf litter and carefully noted the positions of two scorpions. Small, mean and black, with a serious-looking whip-over sting, there would be a scorpion, I had calculated, under every eleventh leaf. They, too, caught by the rising water, had to camp with us on islands that were never more than ten yards by twenty. We had to share these small outcrops with all the refugees from the jungle floor. I changed fast out of my dry clothes, made a brief tick check by torchlight, pulled on my wet clothes and steeled myself for the first personal trauma of the day. In my own utopia I would elect to shit only in a lead-lined chamber half-a-mile underground, safe from enemy radar. Shitting two yards from Simon and five yards from Chimo was, I found, difficult. I hung on to a sapling with one hand, switched off my torch, took down my trousers and squatted over the black, swirling water.

"Don't look," I said.

"Who's interested?" said Simon, leaning out of his hammock and pointing his torch straight at me.

"Push!" yelled Chimo.

"Bit runny today," said Simon.

<hr />

Dawn filtered down. Frogs and cicadas began to call. The mosquitoes scrambled. And, as we folded up the wet tarpaulins, there came four loud blasts on a whistle, followed by a noise of sucking, then clickings of disapproval.

"Viudita carablanca," said Chimo, putting his fingers to his cheeks, drawing in his breath, and making sucking and clicking noises in his turn. There was no reply. Somewhere up in the green tangle, a troop of White-faced sakis were watching us.

Chimo, Culimacaré and Pablo cut fresh poles and we set off, punting the heavy canoes slowly forward. It was not easy to find a purchase for the ten-foot-long poles—the channels, although never more than six to fifteen feet wide, were far too deep for us to touch bottom—so we pushed against submerged branches or roots on the soft bank. Most of the time we could not punt at all, but pulled the boats forwards, standing on submerged branches up to our waists or necks, easing the hull over fallen trees, hacking a way through their dense, upstanding, lateral shoots.

At such times, when standing out of the water, the main discomfort was the ants, not the dangerous veinte-cuatro and catanare who seemed to confine themselves to well-marked territories on shore, and not the army ants, but just thousands of ordinary biting ants (I counted fourteen different species) which went for your head and neck and fastened onto your back inside your shirt. "Hormiga! Hormiga!" Culimacaré would shout when he struck a particularly ant-rich bush, but there was not much you could do to avoid them. At other times we would crouch low, easing the dugouts beneath larger trees which had fallen, but which were still supported lengthwise above the ground and the river by their broken branches, forming bridges for leaf-cutter ants. I grew fond of these fundamentally non-homicidal insects, fully engaged in their perpetual harvest: neatly clipped leaf-sections, held upright, jerkily processed above our heads.

One species of wasp and one species of hornet, in small separate colonies, hung their nests from twigs or fixed them to the backs of leaves suspended over the water. As we cleared a passage with our machetes it was impossible to spot their yellow-brown upended cones. One tremor along a branch, one near cut, and they ejected through the entrance at the base, coming for us with extraordinary speed and concentration. A cry of "Avispa!" really galvanized your limbs: wherever you were, you dived for the water and held your hat across your face to protect your eyes. A wasp sting on the back was tolerable, one on the neck was very painful; five wasp stings on the back equalled one hornet sting on the back. Simon, who disliked the cold, black water on principle and tried to keep his clothes dry for as long as possible each day, moved a fraction slower than the rest of us and, as the last available target, was often stung on the back of the head.

At water level, there were a surprising number of hunting spiders, no bigger, in total extent, than the palm of your hand, which jumped across the surface. Tiny tree frogs, a bright, translucent green as if fashioned in glass, some with little red eyes and feet, dislodged from the foliage as we passed, would fall into the boat or the current, and, pausing to collect themselves, hop or swim to shore; and about twenty times a day we would see the cazadora, the hunter, the long, thin green vine snake, its slim head raised above the water, towing its Vs of ripples.

At normal eye level, we edged past the bases of a seemingly endless variety of tree species, their trunks wrapped with lianas and furry with lichens, their bark smooth or ridged or ringed with spines, and supported on the ground with mats of root fibres, or buttresses, or prop roots like wigwam frames or birdcages, or, occasionally, they were themselves dead or imprisoned in the grasp of a buttressed, hollow, parasitic fig tree which grows from a seed wiped from a bird's beak on some high branch, puts down the slow roots like giant fingers, and throttles its host.

About two hundred yards downstream from our campsite, after an hour and a half of travelling, we met our first serious obstacle: a trunk across the channel which was so large its mass descended some two feet below the water surface and rose about four feet above it. But the tree was big enough, and had fallen recently enough, to open a clearing in the canopy. In the sudden warmth, our clothes began to steam slightly. A screaming piha was calling, unseen, as it did all day, every day.

"And that's another thing," said Simon, lying back on our shared thwart against our packs under the tarpaulin, stretching in the sun and putting his hands over his ears, "just when that moronic bird stops going *hum hum hum up your bum* all night, this bloody idiot starts whistling "

"It's sex," I said, "they're telling the girls they've got their patch."

"Leave it out," said Simon, "you're going soft in the head."

Pablo brought the second dugout up and Culimacaré started clearing the mass of shoots and shrubs from one end of the tree trunk, whilst Chimo and Pablo laboured at the other.

A tiny blue-black hummingbird, perhaps a fork-tailed wood-nymph, suddenly appeared above us; it whirred to and fro like a dandelion seed in a thermal and then hovered purposefully, obviously curious, repeating the manoeuvre, drawing closer.

"Quick, Simon, where's your camera?" I said.

Simon drew the body with the long lens on it out of a plastic bag beneath the tarpaulin, and the bird flew off like a bumblebee.

"Mira!" yelled Chimo, pointing at the leaves in front of him. "Mira! Mira!"

Pablo and Culimacaré stopped cutting. It was a startling picture.

It was a full frontal. It was a short, dangerous, angry coral snake, banded bright red and black to warn its predators, a pattern which even at night tells everyone how deadly it is: and it hung down from its twig-coiled tail, its head up, its white mouth open, hissing.

"For Christsake, take that!" I said.

Simon thrust himself right back against the tarpaulin, his camera clutched across his chest for protection.

"I ain't taking no fucking pictures of no fucking snakes," he shouted, *"They give me the creeps."*

Valentine ran forward and knocked it into the river with a punt pole.

Culimacaré, Pablo and Chimo took it in turns to axe through the tree. I went ahead with my machete and hacked at the easy vegetation. I felt eaten up inside with little white maggots of rage.

••••••••••••••••

Two hours later, sitting together down a clearish straight stretch, Simon reached into another plastic bag and drew out his tape recorder diary. He clicked down the record button and put the machine to his mouth: "Dateline May 14th. Place: Baria river. What's new? I ask myself. No rain today, *that's* what's new I tell myself. Hear that—he held the machine over the side of the boat—"Right? No endless thundering buckets of piss crashing down on my head all day. Well, you can take it from me, Angel-drawers, the whole ghastly business will start again tomorrow. Up-to-the-minute report: only three wasp stings this morning. No more than 10,000 ants. No hornets. Blissikins, you might say. Oh yes—one more thing before I mosey on out to my favourite pub: Fatso's got the right needle with me just because I wouldn't take a picture of some frigging horrible snake. And how do I know Fatso's got the right needle with me? I know Fatso's got the right needle with me cos he hasn't spoken to me for *two whole hours."*

The rage eased. I laughed. I must fight this anger, I thought; such feelings were as dangerous as they would be in a prison cell. It was an effective weapon, that recorder. I rather wished the mould had grown in it as thoroughly as it had colonised his cameras. I only half-treasured the memory of part of last night's entry, for instance, on which I had eavesdropped from my hammock whilst pretending to be asleep: "In all honesty, Angel," I heard him say, *sotto voce*, "to be perfectly frank with you, Redmond is a selfish bastard. He pretends he likes it here. The Indians, of course, poor geezers, don't know any better. And that Juan is just a nasty little dago who treats me like a moron. Good night. I bite your bum. I miss you. Simon."

••••••••••••••••

The normal dank, rotting smell of the river bank—or rather the endless series of little islands and interflowing creeks—was displaced by the powerful, musky odour of otter scent and droppings and urine. We passed a muddy patch of firm ground, big enough to camp on, which had been entirely cleared of its undergrowth of shoots and of the usual plants with thick pointed-shovel-shaped leaves; it was a piece of giant otter advertisement which we met three or four times a day.

"The pong those guys make," said Simon. "It's about as close as you get to comradeship around here. There's not a lot else on offer, not so as you'd notice."

We rounded a bend and came to a small pool where four little streams met, and there, barring the way, were the otters themselves. Five large, dark-brown, tightly furred heads, flattened on top, stuck out of the water in a line.

"Ha! Ha! Uh! Uh! Oof!" they said.

Chimo imitated their chatter and they grew agitated, looking at each other, at the boats, then diving and surfacing right beside us.

"Jesus," said Simon, "knock it off, will you Chimo? They're huge. There's no room in here. *I don't want my nuts nicked off.*"

They had small, laid-back ears, large brown eyes, blotches of white on their big chests, and efficient-looking teeth. Drops of water slid off their long side-whiskers.

"Go on boys," said Simon, waving his arms at them, "piss off and scrag a fish."

The otters submerged and reappeared in a creek to the left.

"Christ," said Simon, getting his cigarettes out of the plastic bag.

"They grow to six foot long," I said.

"Surprise me," said Simon, inhaling.

"They're just curious," said Juan, laughing, "they've never seen people."

"That's why they thought we were fish," said Simon.

We ate our manioc-and-water on a strip of sandy mud beneath another sudden gap in the canopy, where a legume tree lay across the stream: it must have fallen in the storms of the last few days because its outsize, broad beanlike seed-pods were still fresh. Everyone except Simon gathered handfuls, brushed off the ants and opened the long, green, knobbly cases with a thumb; we sucked the sweet, white, protective fur from each bean, spitting out the bean itself.

"No wonder you've got the shits," said Simon, turning away to pee on the sand.

Several round-winged, yellow butterflies settled on his slightly steaming urine; and almost at once they were joined by a solitary kite swallowtail which jostled its way to the centre of the patch: its triangular wings were a filmy white translucence, edged with black, and striped across their veining with black lines of varying lengths, some fringed with scarlet, some with a light green, some running from the leading edge to the scalloped rear and continuing down the long blades of its two swordlike tails.

"Bit like you," said Simon, sitting on a fallen branch, rubbing the scabs on the back of his neck, and watching the butterfly with distaste. "Looks all right to start with—you'd never guess it had such nasty habits. You'd never think it would eat bird-gut soup with froth on top, piss, anything."

The swallowtail pumped up the warm liquid in its proboscis at one end and jetted it out again, in little spurts, from its anus. It was so exposed, so obvious a target for any passing antbird or gnatwren or tanager that I wondered idly if its warning colours were a copy of some poisonous, plant-feeding species; perhaps it was a party to that Darwinian bluff, Batesian mimicry, which Bates had discovered on his travels in the Amazons to the south.

Culimacaré, Pablo and Chimo, working in relays, took an hour to axe through the legume tree and clear our passage back into the dark tunnel ahead of us. And three trees later, in the early evening, as Chimo looked in vain for an island in the black maze of streams which might be large enough to camp on, we emerged, without warning, into an open river.

"Told you so!" said Chimo, lying through his gums and so pleased with himself that he forgot his ritual greeting. "The Maguarinuma!"

Released into space, sky, clouds, a land with horizons, we were silent, allowing our eyes to roam. A pair of swallow-tailed kites were gliding low over the palms of the left bank and eight black vultures were stacked above us, wheeling overhead, the highest only just visible. We laid our poles down the edge of the tarpaulins; Chimo and Pablo tilted the hitched-up engines back into the water, pulled their strings and opened up the throttles. We rounded a couple of bends—and there, straight in front of us, were the dark, lowering, canyon sides of the mountain, three-quarters wrapped in cloud.

The light began to fade; the bushes and then the trees on the bank darkened. The clouds, hanging like slow eruptions of steam from the great peaks to our right, turned pink along their undersides and spread their reflections across the water. To our left the high cliffs and the gullied slopes beneath them grew purple, seemed to increase in size and, as night fell, moved toward us until their shadow finally engulfed the jungle and the river in a massy blackness.

WILFRED THESIGER

Wilfred Thesiger was born in Addis Ababa in 1910 and educated at Eton and Oxford. During the war he served in Abyssinia, Syria, and the Western Desert. Since then he has traveled endlessly, by foot, animal, and boat in such remote regions of the world as Southern Arabia, Kurdistan, the Marshes of Iraq, the Hindu Kush, and northern Kenya. He is the recipient of many honors and awards and his books include The Marsh Arabs *and* The Life of My Choice. *In the desert-traveling tradition of C. M. Doughty before him and Michael Asher after him,* Arabian Sands *recounts his journeys in Arabia from 1945 to 1950. In late 1946 he set out on his first crossing of the parched Empty Quarter, the unexplored desert-within-a-desert virtually unknown to Europeans. His name among the Arabs here was Umbarak.*

....

from ARABIAN SANDS

To rest the camels we stopped for four hours in the late afternoon on a long gentle slope which stretched down to another salt flat. There was no vegetation on it and no salt bushes bordered the plain below us. Al Auf announced that we would go on again at sunset. While we were feeding I said to him cheerfully, "Anyway, the worst should be over now that we are across the Uruq al Shaiba." He looked at me for a moment and then answered, "If we go well tonight we should reach them tomorrow." I said, "Reach what?" and he replied, "The Uruq al Shaiba," adding, "Did you think what we crossed today was the Uruq al Shaiba? That was only a dune. You will see them tomorrow." For a moment, I thought he was joking, and then I realized that he was serious, that the worst of the journey which I had thought was behind us was still ahead.

It was midnight when at last al Auf said, "Let's stop here. We will get some sleep and give the camels a rest. The Uruq al Shaiba are not far away now." In my dreams that night they towered above us higher than the Himalayas.

Al Auf woke us again while it was still dark. As usual bin Kabina made coffee, and the sharp-tasting drops which he poured out stimulated but did not warm. The morning star had risen above the dunes. Formless things regained their shape in the first dim light of dawn. The grunting camels heaved themselves erect. We lingered for a moment more beside the fire; then al Auf said "Come," and we moved forward. Beneath my feet the gritty sand was cold as frozen snow.

We were faced by a range as high as, perhaps even higher than, the range we had crossed the day before, but here the peaks were steeper and more pronounced, rising in many cases to great pinnacles, down which the flowing ridges swept like draperies. These sands, paler coloured than those we had crossed, were very soft, cascading round our feet as the camels struggled up the slopes. Remembering how little warning of imminent collapse the dying camels had given me twelve years before in the Danakil country, I wondered how much more these camels would stand, for they were trembling violently whenever they halted. When one refused to go on we heaved on her head-rope, pushed her from behind, and lifted the loads on either side as we man-handled the roaring animal upward. Sometimes one of them lay down and refused to rise, and then we had to unload her, and carry the water-skins and the saddlebags ourselves. Not that the loads were heavy. We had only a few gallons of water left and some handfuls of flour.

We led the trembling, hesitating animals upward along great sweeping ridges where the knife-edged crests crumbled beneath our feet. Although it was killing work, my companions were always gentle and infinitely patient. The sun was scorching hot and I felt empty, sick, and dizzy. As I struggled up the slope, knee-deep in shifting sand, my heart thumped wildly and my thirst grew worse. I found it difficult to swallow; even my ears felt blocked, and yet I knew that it would be many intolerable hours before I could drink. I would stop to rest, dropping down on the scorching sand, and immediately it seemed I would hear the others shouting, "Umbarak, Umbarak"; their voices sounded strained and hoarse.

It took us three hours to cross this range.

On the summit were no gently undulating downs such as we had met the day before. Instead, three smaller dune-chains rode upon its back, and beyond them the sand fell away to a salt-flat in another great empty trough between the mountains. The range on the far side seemed even higher than the one on which we stood, and behind it were others. I looked round, seeking instinctively for some escape. There was no limit to my vision. Somewhere in the ultimate distance the sands merged into the sky, but in that infinity of space I could see no living thing, not even a withered plant to give me hope. "There is nowhere to go," I thought. "We cannot go back and our camels will never get up another of these awful dunes. We really are finished." The silence flowed over me, drowning the voices of my companions and the fidgeting of their camels.

We went down into the valley, and somehow—and I shall never know how the camels did it—we got up the other side. There, utterly exhausted, we collapsed. Al Auf gave us each a little water, enough to wet our mouths. He said, "We need this if we are to go on." The midday sun had drained the colour from the sands. Scattered banks of cumulus cloud threw shadows across the dunes and salt flats, and added an illusion that we were high among Alpine peaks, with frozen lakes of blue-and-green in the valley, far below. Half asleep, I turned over, but the sand burnt through my shirt and woke me from my dreams.

Two hours later al Auf roused us. As he helped me load my camel, he said, "Cheer up, Umbarak. This time we really are across the Uruq al Shaiba," and when I pointed to the ranges ahead of us, he answered, "I can find a way through those; we need not cross them." We went on till sunset, but we were going with the grain of the country, following the valleys and no longer trying to climb the dunes. We should not have been able to cross another. There was a little fresh *qassis* on the slope where we halted. I hoped that this lucky find would give us an excuse to stop here for the night, but, after we had fed, al Auf went to fetch the camels, saying, "We must go on again while it is cool if we are ever to reach Dhafara."

We stopped long after midnight and started again at dawn, still exhausted from the strain and long hours of yesterday, but al Auf encouraged us by saying that the worst was over. The dunes were certainly lower than they had been, more uniform in height and more rounded, with fewer peaks. Four hours after we had started we came to rolling uplands of gold and silver sand, but still there was nothing for the camels to eat.

A hare jumped out from under a bush, and al Auf knocked it over with his stick. The others shouted "God has given us meat." For days we had talked of food; every conversation seemed to lead back to it. Since we had left Ghanim I had been always conscious of the dull ache of hunger, yet in the evening my throat was dry even after my drink, so that I found it difficult to swallow the dry bread Musallim set before us. All day we thought and talked about that hare, and by three o'clock in the afternoon could no longer resist stopping to cook it. Mabkhaut suggested, "Let's roast it in its skin in the embers of a fire. That will save our water—we haven't got much left." Bin Kabina led the chorus of protest. "No, by God! Don't even suggest such a thing"; and turning to me he said, "We don't want Mabkhaut's charred meat. Soup. We want soup and extra bread. We will feed well today even if we go hungry and thirsty later. By God, I am hungry!" We agreed to make soup. We were across the Uruq al Shaiba and intended to celebrate our achievement with this gift from God. Unless our camels foundered we were safe; even if our water ran out we should live to reach a well.

Musallim made nearly double our usual quantity of bread while bin Kabina cooked the hare. He looked across at me and said, "The smell of this meat makes me faint." When it was ready he divided it into five portions. They were very small, for an Arabian hare is no larger than an English rabbit, and this one was not even fully grown. Al Auf named the lots and Mabkhaut drew them. Each of us took the small pile of meat which had fallen to him. Then bin Kabina said,

"God! I have forgotten to divide the liver," and the others said, "Give it to Umbarak." I protested, saying that they should divide it, but they swore by God that they would not eat it and that I was to have it. Eventually I took it, knowing that I ought not, but too greedy for this extra scrap of meat to care.

MICHAEL ASHER

Born in Great Britain in 1953, Michael Asher was a teacher in the Sudan from 1979 to 1982, where his interest in the nomadic tribes of the Sahara was born. His In Search of the Forty Days Road *is based on his journeys there with the nomads. In the following excerpt from his second book,* A Desert Dies, *he is attempting to travel through the desert by camel to visit some Kababish families in Abu Tabara with his guide, Jibrin. A devastating drought has displaced thousands of nomads in the Sudan by December 1984, where it is much hotter than normal and the grazing has vanished. At this point the two men have been riding six days and are suffering from a severe shortage of water.*

---

from A DESERT DIES

That evening we camped on a rock shelf beyond the ridge. We cooked porridge, but our mouths were too dry to enjoy it. As the next day dawned I saw to the north a long wall of black rock. It looked no more than ten kilometres away, and had two rock chimneys rising above it. I guessed that it was the southern edge of the legendary Jabal Abyad "The White Mountain," where Kababish herds had grazed in past times. There was a high peak marked on the map as Burj al Hatab, but this was nowhere to be seen. The country to the west was hammada with patches of sand rising to naked peaks of basalt here and there. The day was another hot one, without the solace of a cloud to veil the full power of the sun. We had been riding for six days, most of them under summer conditions, and the camels were tired and thirsty. Working in these temperatures they needed to drink every three or four days, and the grain we fed them increased their thirst. As the day grew hotter, I felt my spirits sink. The lining of my stomach felt tight with a sick, acid sensation. I could think of nothing but water. The thirst was an acute pain, like a nagging toothache that all my powers of concentration could not dismiss. We rode through a region where the rocks were weathered into the shapes of nightmare creatures and strange deformed reptiles. It was a dead, dry, moonscape world where men did not belong. By the middle of the morning, on that sixth day, I was almost dropping from my camel with thirst, my body bent and hunched up over the saddle horns. I guessed Jibrin felt the same, for he had assumed the same hunched position. I knew now that the ability to resist thirst was psychological, not physiological. Experiments had proved that an acclimatized European has exactly the same requirements in the desert as a nomad. One had to have the will to endure it.

Jibrin exclaimed, "By God, it is hot!"

"Let's drink," I said. We couched our camels and drew a single mug of water, half each. At once I felt the moisture seeping into my blood and reactivating my cells and muscles, uncloying and lubricating the tight walls of my stomach that had seized up and fused together.

"Let's go," Jibrin said, and on we went, crossing the huge boulder-strewn plain, two tiny black specks in its midst.

Once we came across the tracks of two men and eight camels. Jibrin grew excited. "These are the tracks of my relations!" he said. We followed them a short way, but they veered drunkenly from side to side in great sweeps and soon petered out amongst the rocks. Still, it was cheering to know that we were on the right trajectory, and our spirits rose a little. But by the time the darkness came our optimism had faded.

The night closed in around us. We ate porridge, chewing it mechanically and retching from its dryness. We drank a little water afterwards, but not enough to quench our thirst. I looked at our remaining supply. Both waterskins were empty and there remained about a gallon in the jerrycan. I could hardly believe that we had used so much. That gallon would last us for the next morning; it might last us all day if we did not eat. That meant that it was essential to find Abu Tabara sometime during the next day. We had no leeway. The chances would be firmly against us, even if the weather changed.

In all my travels in the desert by camel, I had never been in a position as serious as this. I had been thirsty before; I had gone for days without drinking, but then the temperature had been relatively low and our navigation assured. I thought longingly of the bulging skins I had seen in Ed Debba. Why had I not persuaded someone to sell me one? I remembered bathing in the shallow inlets on the waterfront at Debba, and thought of the water pots the river people left outside their houses. I could think of nothing else. I said to Jibrin, "If we do not find Abu Tabara tomorrow we are in big trouble!"

"We shall all die when it is time for us to die," the Arab said. "God is generous."

I rolled over on to my stomach and switched on my torch. The way ahead looked grim, and I felt angry with myself. My navigation had failed. My map had failed. Even Jibrin's knowledge had failed. How on earth could we find Abu Tabara? Now all we could do was to resign ourselves to what came, or fight back. Jibrin, true to his culture, had chosen resignation. I, true to mine, wrote in my journal: "As long as there is the will in me, I shall struggle to survive."

Later we curled up in our blankets. After about half an hour I was still awake when I heard the distant growl of a motor vehicle. The sound swelled and died, then swelled again. It sounded like a truck that had got bogged down in the sand. I jumped up and woke Jibrin. He sat up reluctantly. The sound came again, unmistakably. "Don't you hear it?" I asked him. "No," he replied dully. The sound suddenly ceased, and the desert was quiet again. "There is nothing," my companion said. "You imagined it. It is strange what thirst will do. Go back to sleep. You will need your sleep if we are to find Abu Tabara tomorrow." I lay down straining my ears. There was no sound but the humming breath of the camels. Perhaps I had imagined it after all. I reasoned that Jibrin's senses must be more acute than mine. I did not know that he had suffered mumps as a boy, and was deaf in one ear.

Our departure next morning was grim and silent. We moved off, walking as usual through the mystical landscape of moulded rock and drifting sand. My eyes had become accustomed to the washed-out, pastel hues of the desert scenery, so when my gaze swept over the landscape ahead, I picked out a brilliant yellow-and-silver shape amongst the rocks. I was drawn to it like a magnet. A few paces farther on I realized that it was certainly something man-made. Then Jibrin said, "It *is* a trick, by Almighty God! There are two of them!"

As we approached, we saw that there were two silver-grey Fiats parked amongst the boulders. They were loaded with sacks and carried yellow covers. There were six men with the vehicles, who gathered together to stare at us when we approached. We left our camels hobbled at some distance and went to greet them.

The two drivers were fat townsmen with black faces and fuzzy hair. Their faces dropped in amazement when they realized I was a European. I greeted them formally in the manner of the nomads and ignored their expressions. This was enough to prevent too many tedious questions. They were friendly and called for tea. They told us that they had come from El 'Atrun and were taking rock salt for sale in Dongola. They had not been to Abu Tabara, but they thought it was ahead.

"What grazing have you seen on the way?" Jibrin asked. I was dying to ask for water and could hardly stand the tension, but I thought it better to let my companion talk.

"Well, there was some grass and trees about half an hour from here," said one of the drivers.

"What kind of trees?" Jibrin asked.

"Thorny ones," answered the other.

I saw Jibrin smile almost pityingly. We drank the tea that the lorry-boys brought us and squatted down in the hearth with them. Jibrin behaved formally and with great dignity. He sipped his tea as if it were his fifth cup. I took my cue from him, even though I was desperate. I realized that it would be a disgrace to display thirst before these townsmen. After we had drunk, Jibrin casually mentioned that we needed some water. The driver told one of the boys to half fill one of our skins. The squelching vessel was laid in front of us. I tried to avoid looking at it. Instead I thanked the men and told them our names.

"Why don't you travel by lorry? It's much easier!" said one of the drivers.

"You can't learn anything in a lorry," I told him. "If you are in a lorry you are not in the desert." He looked at me in bewilderment, but Jibrin's eyes glowed in understanding.

The men climbed aboard the great machines and started the

engines. The desert was filled with the sound of their buzzing, and with fumes of oil. The drivers waved and wished us good luck, and we thanked them again. We grabbed the headropes of our camels to prevent them bolting as the vehicles lumbered off, billowing smoke, slowly gathering speed until they disappeared into the landscape.

Then Jibrin poured out a mugful of water and held it out to me. I was too thirsty to worry about protocol. I drank it down greedily in steady gulps. It tasted like cream. When it was finished, I exclaimed, "Praise be to God!" and meant it. Then Jibrin drank. As we reloaded the camels, he muttered, "Those people don't even know they are travelling. There are some trees here . . . some grass there . . . 'thorny ones' indeed! They know nothing of the desert!"

"You cannot know the desert if you travel by motor vehicle," I said.

"Yes," he agreed. "There is nothing better than a camel in the desert. The lorry is fast but you cannot enjoy it." I had always hated motor vehicles, yet I knew that this time they had saved my life.

We walked for almost four hours over the carcass of the desert. Soon the rocks gave way to a basin of brown dust with a great edifice of jagged black rock on the horizon. We mounted up as the time passed, not daring to halt, for the half skin of water would soon be used up and we could waste no time. In the middle of the plain was a withered *tundub* and at its base lay the tangled skeleton of a camel, the dry hide twisted around the bones. There were a few leaves on the tree and we let our camels browse. Jibrin joked, "Was this camel a male or a female? It doesn't matter much now does it! Was it brown or red? Who cares anyway!"

We pressed on, but now the camels were faltering. "This one will be dead soon if we do not find water!" Jibrin declared. At midday we crossed a dune and saw from the top a depression filled with massive slabs of rock, black and silver, weathered and carved into weird figures and half-buried by furrows of sand. The sun was so hot it took our breath away. As we descended the dune slope, Jibrin said, "It must be here."

I knew he was right. This was the lowest land as far as I could see, and the water course must be in a depression. Then we saw a trail of droppings scattered in the sand. They looked very old. We moved on, weaving in and out of the boulders. There were no other signs of humans or herds, and I was beginning to wonder if this was really the place when Jibrin cried, "See the last of the tents! This is it!" Looking down, I saw many pieces of torn *shuggas*, half covered in sand, with broken pots, useless leather buckets, split saddlebags. "This is Abu Tabara," Jibrin said, smiling. We climbed a hump of sand, and he showed me the single well, covered in flat stones. "They have all gone," he said. "They must have left only days ago." It was disappointing to find the place uninhabited, but the survival instinct was stronger: I was overjoyed to find water.

Near the well we spied an immense block of granite that had split in half. The fissure was easily large enough to take us and all our luggage. As we sat down in the shade both of us said, "Praise be to God!" and were silent for a moment. Jibrin exclaimed "By Almighty God! This is where we were, all that time ago! There were Awlad Huwal and Hamdab here then. I wonder what happened to them all!"

I walked down to the well head. There was a basin of dried clay, and the well was covered with five flat stones. I crouched down and removed them carefully. Then I dropped a pebble into the gaping hole. The "plunk!" and the rippling of water was a holy sound in this appalling dryness. Abu Tabara was a holy shrine devoted to this end. Jibrin brought the well bucket and hoisted up some of the liquid. It was clean and clear and its taste as untainted as the desert wind. It seemed like a miracle. Here, in the middle of the most dangerous desert on earth, there was water. Here there was life.

ERIC NEWBY

Eric Newby was born in London in 1919 and educated at St. Paul's School. In World War II he was captured off the coast of Sicily on a secret mission and was kept a prisoner-of-war from 1942 to 1945. His many books of adventure and travel include The Last Grain Race, Slowly Down the Ganges, Love and War in the Apennines, The Big Red Train Ride, *and* A Traveller's Life. A Short Walk in the Hindu Kush *narrates the story of his amateur mountain-climbing experiences in Asia with his friend Hugh Carless. In the following passage they are attempting to scale the summit of Mir Samir in Nuristan, having already taken five hours instead of two just to reach their present position on a ridge, only to find that the summit is still invisible. We are reminded of Wilfred Thesiger's observation: "Who, after all, would dispute that it is more satisfying to climb to the top of a mountain than to go there in a funicular railway?" Mr. Thesiger, of course, was in the desert.*

....

from A SHORT WALK IN THE HINDU KUSH

First we tackled the castlelike knob to our left, going up the north side. It had all the attributes of an exposed face, together with a truly awe-inspiring drop of three thousand feet to the east glacier, and it was bitterly cold; like everywhere else we had so far been on this aggravating mountain there were no good belays. Up to now in the most difficult circumstances we had managed a few grim little jokes, but now on the face of this abominable castle our capacity for humour finally deserted us.

From the top of the castle there was the choice of the north side which was cold and grim or the south, a labyrinthine chaos of rock, fitted with clefts and chimneys too narrow to admit the human frame without pain. In one of these clefts that split a great boulder twenty feet long, we both became wedged and only extricated ourselves with difficulty. Sometimes exasperated with this lunatic place we would force a way over the ridge through the soft snow only to find ourselves, with no way of going on, forced to return by the way we had come.

But as we advanced, the ridge became more and more narrow and eventually we emerged on to a perfect knife edge. Ahead, but separated from us by two formidable buttresses, was the summit, a simple cone of snow as high as Box Hill.

We dug ourselves a hole in the snow and considered our position. The view was colossal. Below us on every side mountains surged away it seemed for ever; we looked down on glaciers and snow-covered peaks that perhaps no one has ever seen before, except from the air. To the west and north we could see the great axis of the Hindu Kush and its southward curve, from the Anjuman Pass around the northern marches of Nuristan. Away to the east-northeast was the great snow-covered mountain we had seen from the wall of the east glacier, Tirich Mir, the twenty-five-thousand-foot giant on the Chitral border, and to the southwest the mountains that separated Nuristan from Paryshir.

Our own immediate situation was no less impressive. A stone dropped from one hand would have landed on one of the upper glaciers of the Chamar Valley, while from the other it would have landed on the east glacier. Hugh, having determined the altitude to be 19,100 feet, now gave a practical demonstration of this by dropping the aneroid, which fell with only one bounce into the Chamar Valley.

"Bloody thing," said Hugh gloomily. "I don't think it was much use anyway." Above us choughs circled uttering melancholy croaking noises. "We've got to make a decision about going on," he said. "And we've got to be absolutely certain it's the right one, because our lives are going to depend on it."

Anywhere else such a remark would have sounded over dramatic. Here it seemed no more than an accurate statement of fact.

"How long do you think it will take to get to the top?"

"All of four hours and then only if we don't go any slower."

It was now one-thirty; we had been climbing for nine hours.

"That means five-thirty at the summit. Going down, four hours at least to the Castle, and then twenty minutes to the *col* on the ridge. It'll be nine o'clock. Then there's the ice slope. Do you think we can manage the *col* to the camp in the dark?"

"The only alternative is to sleep on the ridge. We haven't got any sleeping-bags. I'm afraid we wouldn't last out. We can try if you like."

For a moment we were dotty enough to consider going on. It was a terrific temptation: we were only seven hundred feet below the summit. Then we decided to give up. Both of us were nearly in tears. Sadly we ate our nougat and drank our cold coffee.

The descent was terrible. With the stimulus of the summit gone, we suddenly realized how tired we were. But, although our strength and morale were ebbing, we both agreed to take every possible precaution. There was no mountain rescue service on this mountain. If anything happened to one of us, a bad sprain would be enough, it would be the end for both. As we went down I found myself mumbling to myself again and again, "One man's death diminishes mee, one man's death diminishes mee."

Yet, though we were exhausted, we felt an immense sense of companionship. At this difficult moment the sense of dependence on one another, engendered perhaps by the fact that we were roped together and had one another's lives in our hands, produced in me a feeling of great affection for Hugh, this tiresome character who had led me to such a spot.

At six we were at the *col* below the Castle, exactly as he had prophesied. The conditions were very bad. All the way down from the Castle a tremendous wind had been blowing and the mountainside was flooded in a ghastly yellow light as the sun went down. As the clouds came up the wind became a blizzard, a howling gale with hail and snow battering us. We had come down from the Castle without crampons. Now to cross the head of the *col* in this wind on the frozen snow, we had to put them on again. Still wearing them, we lowered ourselves one by one over the overhanging crest into a gully on the south face.

The south face was a grey desolation and the gully was the wrong one. It was too wide for an easy descent and was smooth ice the whole way for two hundred feet.

Twice we had to take off and put on our crampons, almost blubbering with fatigue and vexation, as the straps were frozen and adjusting them seemed to take an eternity. Worst of all the wind on the ridge was blowing snow into the gully, half blinding us and sending down big chunks of rock. One of these hit Hugh on the shoulder, hurting him badly, and I thought he was going to faint. The gully was succeeded by a minute chimney full of ice, down which I glissaded on my behind for twenty feet until Hugh pulled me up. Very stupidly I was wearing my crampons attached to a sling round my middle and I sat on them for the full distance, so that they went in to the full length of the spikes, scarring me for life in a most interesting manner.

By now it was quite dark. We had an hour on the rocks, now covered with a fresh sheet of ice, that I shall remember for the rest of my life. Then we were home. "Home" was just the ledge with the two sleeping bags, some food and the stoves, but we had thought of nothing else for hours.

As we stumbled on to it, a great dark shape rose up and struck a match, illuminating an ugly, well-known face with a wart on its forehead. It was Shir Muhammad, most feckless and brutal of drivers, come up to find us.

"I was worried about you," he said simply, "so I came."

It was nine o'clock; we had been climbing for seventeen hours.

By now we were beyond speech. After a long hour the contents of both cooking pots boiled simultaneously, so we drank tea and ate tomato soup at the same time. It was a disagreeable mixture, which we followed with a pot of neat jam and two formidable-looking sleeping-pills that from their size seemed more suitable for horses than human beings.

"I don't approve of drugs," were Hugh's last words before we both sank into a coma, "but I think that under the circumstances we're justified."

We woke at five. My first thought as I came to was that I had been operated on, an illusion heightened by the sight of Hugh's bloody bandaged hands gripping the mouth of his sleeping bag. Mine were now in the same condition as Hugh's had been two days previously; his were worse than ever.

It took us both a long time to dress and Shir Muhammad had to button our trousers, which was a difficult operation for someone who had never had fly buttons of his own. It was the only time I ever saw him laugh. Then he laced our boots.

As soon as I started to move I realized that my feet were beyond boots, so I decided to wear rubber shoes.

By the time we left the platform it was like a hot plate. Shir Muhammad went first, skipping downhill like a goat bearing a great load. Soon he became impatient with our funereal progress and left us far behind.

At the head of the glacier Hugh stopped and took off his pack.

"What's the matter?"

"Rope," he croaked. "Left a rope. Got to go back."

"Don't be an ass."

"Might need it . . . another try."

"Not this year."

It was useless to argue with him. He was already crawling uphill. My return to fetch the karabiner on the other glacier had created an impossible precedent.

The glare of the small snowfield was appalling. My goggles were somewhere in my rucksack, but I had not the will power to stop and look for them. Soon I developed a splitting headache. With my rubber shoes on I fell continuously. I found myself becoming very grumpy.

At the top of the *moraine* Abdul Ghiyas was waiting for us. He had passed Shir Muhammad without seeing him, somewhere in the labyrinth on the lower slopes of this provoking mountain, and was clucking to himself anxiously.

"Where is Carless *Seb?*"

"Up."

"He is dead?"

"No, he is coming."

"You have climbed the mountain?"

"No."

"Why is Carless *Seb* not with you?"

It was only after much pantomime that I was able to convince him that Hugh was not dead, sacrificed to my own ambition, and he consented to follow me down, carrying my load.

But at the camp we waited an hour, two hours for Hugh; there was no sign of him. I began to be worried and reproached myself for not having waited. The three drivers, huddled over the fire preparing a great secret mess in honour of our arrival, were mumbling, "Carless *Seb*, Carless *Seb*, where is Carless *Seb*?" droning on and on.

Finally Hugh appeared. With his beard full of glacial cream and his cracked lips, he looked like what he in fact was, the survivor of a spectacular disaster.

"Where have you been? We've been worried stiff."

"I got the rope," he said, "then I went to sleep under a rock."

PETER MATTHIESSEN

Peter Matthiessen graduated from Yale in 1950 and helped found The Paris Review *the following year. Among his novels are* At Play in the Fields of the Lord, Far Tortuga, *and most recently,* Killing Mr. Watson. *His numerous nonfiction works include* The Cloud Forest, Wildlife in America, *and* Men's Lives. *In 1973 he set out from Pokhara, Nepal, and walked for five weeks across the snowy Himalaya to reach the Crystal Mountain on the Tibetan plateau, where he and his friend and fellow traveler, biologist George Schaller, hoped to glimpse the rarest of great cats, the snow leopard. His account of that journey, including his return through the high passes, is an often stark and sometimes luminous record of an accompanying search for inner peace. It won the National Book Award.*

············ ·····························

from THE SNOW LEOPARD

The camp is less than a thousand feet below the Namdo Pass, and so this morning there is biting cold, with no warmth in the frozen sun when it appears over the eastern rim. This canyon plunges eventually into a maelstrom of narrow, dark ravines that must emerge into that eastern arm of Phoksumdo that we saw on October 25, for there is the aura of a void between one spine of summits and the next where the turquoise lake of the great demoness lies hidden.

Despite the cold, Tende and Chiring Lamo sit near naked on a sheepskin by their daybreak fire, the child's head laid amongst the beads and amulets and cold silver on Tende's round brown breasts. But Dawa is sick this morning; through Tukten, he tells me that even before leaving Shey, he suffered from dysentery and internal bleeding. That last is worrisome; it might well lead to worse. Perhaps he should rest, but we cannot stay in this wild place between high passes. And of course it is only luck that he came out with us; had it not been for Gyaltsen's fear of Tukten, Dawa might have remained behind and died there, without ever speaking up, less out of fortitude than in that peasant apathy and fatalism that is so often taken for stupidity.

I give him something for his dysentery; it may kill him. In his weakened state, Dawa longs to be taken care of; it pleases him to be reminded that he must wear a snow mask, so as not to complicate his sickness with snow blindness. He stands before me in knee britches, big head hanging, like a huge disobedient child.

The yak route descends into night shadows, crossing the ice rivers of this canyon and emerging again on sunny mountainside. Here where sun and shadow meet, a flock of Himalayan snow cock sails away down the steep mountain. To the north and west, across the canyons, the thorn-scrub slopes are cut by cliffs, and soon blue sheep come into view, two far pale bands, one of nine, and the other of twenty-six. I search in vain for sign of the snow leopard.

Down in the shelter of a gully, a yak caravan is preparing to set out; two men strap last loads on the balky animals. Before long, there appears another caravan, this one bound north; having discharged its salt and wool, it is headed home with a cargo of grain, lumber, and variegated goods, its yaks rewarded for their toil with big red tassels on their packs and small orange ones decking out their ears. The dark shapes of the nomads glint with beads and earrings, amulets, and silver daggers; here are the Ch'ang Tartars of two thousand years ago. With their harsh cries and piercing whistles, naked beneath filthy skins of animals, these wild men bawling at rough beasts are fit inhabitants of such dark gorges; one can scarcely imagine them anywhere else. The Redfaced Devils are inquisitive, and look me over before speaking out in the converse of the pilgrim.

Where do you come from?

Shey Gompa.

Ah. Where are you going?

To the Bheri.

Ah.

And so the wary dogs skirt past, we nod, grimace, and resume our paths to separate destinies and graves.

················

Winding around beneath towers of rock that fall away into abyss after abyss, the path wanders randomly in all directions. In the cold shine of its ice, this waste between high passes is a realm of blind obliterating nature. The labyrinth is beautiful, yet my heart is touched by dread. I hurry on. At last the ledge trail straightens, headed south, and I reach the foot of the last climb to the pass just before noon. On a knoll, there is a prayer wall and a stock corral for those who come too late in the day to start the climb. Plainly, we shall not reach Murwa before nightfall, despite Karma's assurances to the contrary; we shall have to press hard just to cross the pass and descend far enough below the snows to find brushwood to keep warm. Lacking mountain lungs, I am slow in the steep places, and I start the climb at once, without waiting for the others to come up.

Looking back every little while as I ascend, I see that Karma, arriving at the prayer wall, sets out a sheepskin and lies down, while Tende, Dawa, and Tukten perch on rocks. No doubt Karma will build a fire here and delay everyone with a lengthy meal, thus assuring himself and his wife and child the miserable task, at the end of a long day, of setting up camp in cold and dark, for he is as lightheaded as he is lighthearted, and gives the day's end no more thought than anything else. Every piece of information that this smiling man has offered has been wrong: the climb to this pass, it is plain to see, is not only steeper but longer than the last one.

In the cold wind, the track is icy even at midday, yet one cannot wander to the side without plunging through the crust. The regular slow step that works best on steep mountainside is difficult; I slip and clamber. Far above, a train of yaks makes dark curves on the shining ice; soon a second herd overtakes me, the twine-soled herders strolling up the icy incline with hands clasped behind their backs, grunting and whistling at the heaving animals. Then black goats come clicking up the ice glaze, straight, straight up to the noon sky; the goat horns turn silver on the blue as, in the vertigo and brilliance of high sun, the white peak spins. The goatherd, clad from head to boots in blood-red wool, throws balls of snow to keep his beasts in line; crossing the sun, the balls dissolve in a pale fire.

Eventually the track arrives at the snowfields beneath the summit rim; I am exhausted. Across the whiteness sails a lammergeier, trailing its shadow on the snow, and the wing shadow draws me taut and sends me on. For two more hours I trudge and pant and climb and slip and climb and gasp, dull as any brute, while high above, the prayer flags fly on the westering sun, which turns the cold rocks igneous and the hard sky to white light. Flag shadows dance upon the white walls of the drifts as I enter the shadow of the peak, in an ice tunnel, toiling and heaving, eyes fixed stupidly upon the snow. Then I am in the sun once more, on the last of the high passes, removing my woolen cap to let the wind clear my head; I sink to my knees, exhilarated, spent, on a narrow spine between two worlds.

To the south and west, glowing in snow light and late sun, the great white Kanjirobas rise in haze, like mystical peaks that might vanish at each moment. The caravans are gone into the underworld. Far behind me and below, in the wastes where I have come from, my companions are black specks upon the snow. Still breathing hard, I listen to the wind in my own breath, the ringing silence, the snow fire and soaring rocks, the relentless tappeting of prayer flags, worn diaphanous, that cast wind pictures to the northern blue.

I have the universe all to myself. The universe has me all to itself.

Time resumes, there comes a change in mood. Under the pack, my back is sweating, and the hard wind chills me. Before I am rested, the cold drives me off the peak into a tortuous descent down sharp rock tumulus, hidden by greasy corn snow and glare ice, and my weak legs slip between the rocks as the pack's weight pitches me forward. A thousand feet down, this rockfall changes to a steep snow-patched trail along an icy stream. Toward dusk, in the painful going, I am overtaken by Tukten in his scanty clothes and sneakers. Tukten's indifference to cold and hardship is neither callous nor ascetic: what it seems to be is calm acceptance of everything that comes, and this is the source of that inner quiet that makes his nondescript presence so impressive. He agrees that Murwa is out of the question, and goes on down, still quick and light, to find fuel and a level place to camp.

The steep ravine descending from the pass comes out at last on sandy mountainside that drops into the upper canyon of the Murwa River. Dusk has fallen, and I keep my distance from two herders' fires for fear of the big dogs. Farther on, as darkness comes, I call out, "Tukten, *Tuk-ten*," but there is no answer. Then, below, I see him making a fire; the inspired man has found a stone shed by a waterfall.

Dawa turns up an hour later, and lies down in the shed without his supper. Every little while we call to Karma and his family, but another hour passes, the stars shine, and no one comes. This morning a yawning Karma had excused his reluctance to get up by saying we would arrive at Murwa in midafternoon. Doubtless it was this feckless minstrel who told Jang-bu, who told me, that "one hard day, one easy one" would take us from Saldang to Murwa: two hard days and one easy one are now behind us, and still we are not there. In his airy way, Jang-bu concluded that we could cross both passes in a single day, since neither one, so he was told, was as high or as arduous as the Shey Pass, not to speak of the Kang La. Being ignorant, I didn't argue, though I had to wonder why, if this were true, the wool traders, coming from Saldang, had chosen the Shey Pass-Kang La route over the other Tonight I know. Because the icy north face of Kang La is too steep for yaks, the traveler must break his own trail in the snow; otherwise that route is much less strenuous than the Shey-Murwa route, in which three passes must be crossed. And the descent from the third pass up there, in snow conditions, is as wearing as the climb. I hate to think of Chiring Lamo in the ice and starlight, swaying along near-precipices on Tende's small and tired shoulders; these ledge trails should not be traveled in the night, without a moon.

However, I am too tired to act, or even think. I am already in my sleeping bag when this innocent family appears out of the darkness; hearing Tukten's voice, I end these notes and go to sleep.

JOHN MILLS

*Born in England in 1930, John Mills came to Montreal as
an odd-jobber in the mid 1950s, worked on the DEW Line
in the North, and ended up an English professor at Simon
Fraser University in Vancouver. He has published three novels,* The Land of Is, The October Men, *and* Skevington's
Daughter, *and a collection of memoirs and reviews,* Lizard
in the Grass. *He was nineteen when he had the following
journey in Scandinavia.*

....

THE NIGHT OF LUCIA

Östersund, Sweden—about the middle of December, 1949. Our first
day out was bleak but relatively mild. The landscape lay under a frigid,
grey mist through which the outlines of the thin pines showed blurred
and dark grey. The sky was dark, for thick clouds had grown slowly
during the night and fused with the mist on the low hills. I never knew
whether the road itself was paved or not. Perhaps by now it has become
a concrete superhighway—Sundsval to Trondheim with exits for Ham-
merstrand, Brecke, Östersund and Åre—but then it was covered with
a layer of snow and gravel which had frozen together to produce a dense
substance, the surface of which seemed hard as diamond. I could feel
every ice-embedded pebble in it through the thin soles of my rubber
boots—Wellington boots: the kind a man wears in England for a quiet
day's weeding in the garden. The warmer weather rendered the ice
slippery—a boot would skate on the heavier gravel and I'd totter wildly,
trying to regain balance, plunging the other boot around for a foothold,
but it would slip, in its turn, and I'd land with a bone-shaking crash

342

on the steel-hard road. So from time to time, I'd give up and walk on the heaps of packed, brownish snow on the road's shoulder, but this had become almost as treacherous, to my useless boots, as the gravel itself and it was like slithering over glass-coated screes. Beyond the shoulder was a drainage ditch filled with light, powdery snow under a brittle crust—a boot whacked into the ditch would sink straight down with a crunching sound and fill itself with this finer snow which would melt, then gel into thick, transparent icicles in the tops of my socks. My rucksack was too heavy and too cumbersome, for strapped to the top of it, was a small valise. The arrangement did its best to pull me out of the vertical and would swing heavily to complete the job of throwing me to the ground whenever I started to topple off balance. I improved its stability when we stopped to eat by jettisoning some of the rucksack's contents and stuffing the valise inside.

We had seen no building of any sort, so at noon we stumbled through the unstained, shallow snow of a disused loop road—a resting place for maintenance vehicles. We found some logs and, placing them side by side, built a twig fire in the space between and started the long job of melting snow for coffee. Sam poked at the fire singing under his breath a song popular in those dark, post-war days. "Evening shadows make me blue," he muttered, but without much conviction. He'd not had too bad a time of it, for his boots were of the solid, Vibram-soled type and, what's more, they fitted him. He'd fallen a couple of times but he was by no means the bruised, numbed, and useless object he was trying to encourage. Apart from this, however, he had the invaluable knack of accurate focus. For example I was a man trying to get to Norway against time and under the pressure of future hunger; he, on the other hand, was a man walking along the road, who had stopped for lunch, and who, dressed in warm clothing, was also solving the problem of keeping on his feet. I wished to act in such a way that my movements were planned, meaningful and patterned. . . . Sam knew, without even thinking about it, that coherence lies only in the present moment, and that he would do, in the future, whatever needed to be done. I wanted something to come of whatever I did; Sam did things for their own sake and could not have cared less about the result. He was even, I think, beginning to enjoy himself at that stage.

The two cups of coffee took over an hour to make. We thawed out the sardines, whose oil had become thick and opaque, and I bared my feet, wrapped a towel around them, picked icicles from my socks, then dried the latter near the fire.

It was dark when we started off again.

We had seen no traffic at all, once or twice, we walked past a farm. These had been invisible in daylight, for they were well off the road, but now we could see their lights, a long way off the road, flickering through the trees. We should look, I said, for paths leading toward this river on our left and find a barn to flop in for the night. Let's push it a bit, Sam answered, and see what turns up. This was the last we said to each other for several miles.

Just after dark it began to snow. It was light, small-flaked stuff that seemed, in the darkness, to spurt gently against the skin like drops of ether. It fell into my hair, melted, and began to drip down my face in long uncontrollable and infuriating streaks which disappeared into the neck of my shirt. But two hours after dark the snow stopped, the sky cleared, and suddenly it grew intensely cold. We could see the moon through huge, expanding gaps in the clouds. The strands of my hair began to freeze together and I shoved on a balaclava helmet preferring the constant dripping of water down my face to a frostbitten ear. Except for the echoing crunching of our boots on the fresh snow there was a deep silence into which each sound seemed swallowed, like water in quicklime. We could see the pines as black, feathery silhouettes against the blue-black sky punctured with stars. I became almost hypnotized by the silvery patches of light thrown by the soles of my boots against the snow as I trudged along and it was too cold, now, for my boots to skid easily.

It must have been just before nine o'clock when we heard the car coming.

It began as a tiny, vaguely sensed disturbance in the matrix of silence around us, growing, slowly, until we heard and recognized it, quite suddenly, as a car's engine. I turned, and a mile or so back on the chord across the valley where the road curved, I saw a horizontal cone of white light, dipping and swinging round toward us.

Quick I said, stand in the road.

Stand in the road be buggered, Sam replied, he'll run us down.

The driver swerved slightly to avoid us and swept past, the air eddies in front of the car whipping up thin gauzes of snow and drawing them across the road like the hems of bridal veils. The headlights silvered the telephone wires around the curve ahead.

Bastard, Sam said.

Wait a minute . . . .

The sound of the engine, almost faded into the distance, stopped.

He's stopped for us, I shouted, let's run.

We hobbled forward as fast as we could. My rucksack began to sway heavily until one of the straps broke and it lurched into the snow. Sam shuffled ahead while I hoisted the rucksack on one shoulder and clenched the broken strap against the other. But Sam had stopped on the brow of the hill. The road, after the curve, climbed, then dropped into a valley. There was a house on the left, then another, then two more. Round another bend and we were in a small village, walking along a main street lined with Christmas trees gay with coloured lights. One or two well-fed fur-hatted Swedes passed us on the sidewalk and looked us up and down. The car had not pulled up for us, of course, but at some house in the village. We never even discovered the name of the place. We walked straight through it—no place for the penniless—as though we knew where we were going, struck off along a side path a mile beyond, and found a barn.

<hr />

After our night in the barn we woke cold, cramped, and ravenously hungry. I spliced my rucksack strap with a piece of rope while Sam crept out of the barn, sneaked toward the road and stole a can of cream that stood amid milk churns on a platform by the entrance to the farm. We stirred the mixture of ice and thick cream until it was drinkable and counted our supplies—two cans of sardines, one of beans, half a loaf of bread and a tin of Nescafé—we had no money at all. We gobbled the sardines this time without bothering to warm up the congealed oil. There was no time—we had to be on the road to catch the early morning traffic.

There wasn't any. Two cars went by, then a milk truck whose

driver merely shook his head at us. To keep warm we began to walk.

As the sky grew lighter I had the curious sensation that we were back twenty miles or so, starting afresh from Östersund. There was the same wide valley cut between low hills, the same mist and dark sky, the same interminable, featureless, gently curving highway. It was colder and easier on the feet, for the fresh powdery snow provided a little friction, but, within an hour I had become hungry again and with hunger there grew in me, for the first time, a willingness to discuss alternatives. We can go on like this, I thought, until we drop from starvation, exhaustion, exposure. We were in a part of the country apparently inhabited by suspicious xenophobes who would like as not turn us in to the police as vagrants if we appealed to them for help. And the police would hand us over to our respective consuls who'd confiscate our passports, label us, and send us home D.B.S.—Distressed British Subjects. So much, then, for my dreams of self-sufficiency. It would be the end of the Norway scheme and probably of my relationship with Joan, its other begetter. What love could survive such humiliation? So Sam and I would have to stay on the road and, if we persevered, we'd undoubtedly stumble into Trondheim, miles ahead, a big town with jobs, money, and shelter to offer.

But something else occurred to me. If we hit the frontier without money, bearded, hungry, and ragged, we stood a very good chance of being thrown back. And it was no use trying to enter Norway illegally if I wished to work there and make it my home. The alternative would be to find some place between here and the frontier to find work for a few days, and enter by train and in comparative style. Jumping freight trains was out—there was a railroad along the valley, but again, we had to stay this side of the law.

I thought again about the Swedes—they had been hospitable enough so far—perhaps I was being a little paranoid about them. Surely no one would turn us into the cops purely for begging at his doorstep. On the other hand, northern Sweden in those days was unused to beggars and suspicious of foreigners, particularly those without visible means of support. But it looked as though we'd have to risk it.

We discussed all this at our midday halt. The safest thing, I said, might be to walk back to that village, phone Robert in the Lutheran

Mission at Östersund and get him to wire us some of his girlfriend's money. Sam shook his head. Never go back, he said. Something'll turn up.

Take a look at that sky, he said later. We're gunna have snow up the arse by nightfall. . . .

The grey-misty sky had grown black and sullen toward the South and East and heavy nimbus clouds spread slowly toward us like a dark stain. The valley toward Östersund had disappeared, completely . . . swallowed in the cloud.

We packed up hastily and buried the can. Its contents had by no means satisfied our hunger . . . merely whetted it. My eyes felt gummy from the night's uneasy sleep and I could not stop myself from yawning. I knew that my body was covered in bruises from the tumbles of the day before. My kneejoints creaked as I got up to go, hoisting my leaden rucksack with difficulty over my shoulders. Sam was in slightly better shape but as an Australian was more used, than I was, to large meals. He began to bitch as we walked slowly down the road, about his empty stomach and his increasing physical weakness . . . My gut's shrunk right up, he complained. When did we eat last? . . . Properly, I mean . . . I don't count that bloody porridge at the mission . . . two days ago , . . that's when it was . . . we can't go on much longer, boy, we're gunna drop in our tracks . . . to think I could be back in Stockholm alonga those French bastards . . . they'll be sitting in the warm, laughin' at us . . . stealin' our women . . . keep yer eyes skinned for a house.

But no sooner had we ratified this decision to risk the cops by begging, then the opportunity, such as it had been, to do so, vanished. We had begun, very slowly, to leave the wide valley with its scattered farms and frozen river behind us. The road twisted slightly and rose higher above the valley floor to work its way into denser forest. Ahead of us, in the dusk, the road seemed to be driving toward the flank of a long, high ridge. It looked as though we were going to cross a watershed into the system of glens and lakes that wound their way toward the Norwegian border. There was unlikely to be a farm for many miles. Behind us the sky was black and within ten minutes it had swallowed the grey twilight and we felt the first, hesitant lash of windborn snow.

As we got into the trees the wind dropped but the snow began to pelt down—huge, dry flakes of it which built up on our shoulders and packs and found every gap and join in our clothing. The snow rapidly became ankle deep and then high enough to spill into our boots. The visibility sank to zero. At one point I left the road altogether in the darkness and plunged up to my waist in the ditch. Sam pulled me out and I lay panting and exhausted on the road with the snow building up mercilessly around me. With great difficulty I got to my feet, took two or three steps, then sank into the ditch again. The makeshift strap on my rucksack broke and with a savage oath I released the other strap and threw the whole bloody thing aside. I rested my arms on the edge of the drift, and gasped for breath. I could see only the snow falling rapidly in front of my face and of the road itself and the trees I could see no sign. I could hear Sam shouting in the darkness. I yelled back and he lit his cigarette lighter while I called directions to him. I could see the flame drop suddenly as he stumbled into a soft drift and the light vanished to reappear again a minute or so later. I heaved myself out of the hole I'd dug and lay on the snow. I no longer knew which was road and which was ditch. Sam found me and shook the snow from his clothes and hair and helped me to my feet. The snow began to settle on us as we stood gingerly in one spot, rolling and lighting a couple of sodden cigarettes.

We're off the road, he said. We must've missed the son-of-a-bitch in the dark and gone up one of those bloody farm tracks by mistake . . . and now we've even lost *that*.

As far as we could tell we'd ended up in a tiny clearing surrounded by an almost impenetrable forest of low pines. The tracks we'd made were now completely obscured and even the holes we'd made in the snow drifts were beginning to fill. With Sam's help I found my rucksack and ripped a dozen pages out of a copy of Gibbon I'd been carrying for sustenance and which, of course, I'd not opened until now. We pulled a dead branch off a neighboring pine, shook the snow off it, and broke its twigs. We snapped the branch into three pieces, laid them together on the snow, and stood over the twigs until, with the aid of Gibbon's noble prose, they began to burn. Snow hissed into the fire as we left it to round up more fuel. The fire flickered badly and its light danced back from the wall of timber which surrounded us. Our hunger had died down and left an increasing feebleness which made each step we took an almost impossible effort.

At one point I found myself gaping and dozing numbly in a foxhole my body had inadvertently prepared for me in a snow bank by the trees. I watched myself gazing vacantly at the hissing flames, and at Sam's dancing, gigantic shadow. I heard the damp, smoking crackle of the logs. Then with a snapping sound, and couple of red sparks, the light went out as though it had been flicked off with a switch. Sam had dozily allowed the three branches to burn through and dunk the flame they bore into the snow. I dragged myself upright and forced my way through the waist-high snow to where he stood tearing up my Gibbon and thumbing his lighter.

It's useless, I said. It'll take all we've got to keep the damn thing going. Let's find that path again and make for the farm.

Both of us knew just how mere a gesture this would be. In such deserted country the farm could be miles off along what would now be an almost impenetrable path. But the highway, if we ever found it, would be just as useless . . . there was nothing back the way we'd come and very little chance of there being a village ahead of us. The fire had shown up that the clearing was shaped like a pear and we knew, roughly, where the narrow end of it was. We pushed our way towards it and almost immediately became entrapped by trees. But the snow did not fall so rapidly here and the going proved a little easier. I felt my feet graze rock and once or twice I tripped on a buried deadfall and slid over the other side of it up to my waist. It seemed as though we were fighting our way round the trunks of trees, penetrating deeper and deeper into the forest. Half an hour of it and we gave up. We were far too exhausted to either go farther or to return the way we came.

I shucked my rucksack onto the snow. Let's hole up, I said. Sam nodded and said nothing. We burrowed under the spreading branches of a tree and, with our last remaining energy, dug out a snow cave.

If it quits snowing, Sam said, we stand a chance . . . but if it goes on for a couple of days, we'll've had it.

It was my turn to nod.

I no longer felt cold, nor hungry. I had begun to doze and my body seemed to be floating, upwards on soft eiderdown. I could hear my own blood pulsing slowly around my body and as a faint background whisper through which I heard, every now and again, the creaking of a branch under its load of snow, the snapping of a twig as Sam shifted his position. This, I remember thinking, is not a bad way to die. There's none of the choking terror of drowning, or the agony of death by fire. Here one's life begins to ebb out of the body slowly and painlessly, flowing gently into the cold, dead forest. We'd disappear, that was the only trouble with it . . . it might be years before we were found in this thick, untravelled bushland. We would vanish like dry ice in warm air . . . there would be enquiries from England . . . a perfunctory search . . . but no one would find us here. The cold and my exhaustion had drained me of any regrets . . . at nineteen I was perhaps too young to die like this but at least I'd be spared the horrors of cancer, or the sudden whiplash of angina . . . life's no joke, I thought, when all's said and done . . . a finite series of hot dinners, as a friend of mine once put it . . . it was nothing, and neither was death.

I began to doze.

Sam Harstein was shaking my shoulder. A light! he was saying, there's a light ahead. I staggered to my feet. Outside our miniature cave it had stopped snowing. Had we continued for a few more minutes, fighting through the bush, we'd've come out of the trees onto a huge field. I could see it now, plainly—a lovely expanse of bare snow sparkling in the moonlight. At the far side of it was a house with lighted windows. With a final effort we ploughed our way toward it and bashed on the door.

················

The man who answered our frenzied knocking did not, as the poet sings, gaze about him with a wild surmize. He was clearly a man of action. He rushed us upstairs into hot showers and warm bathrobes then suggested that when we were ready for it we should join the company in the dining room. We'd struck it rich. In the kitchen were the remains of a lavish smörgåsbord—we made short work of it and inroads upon a bottle of aquavit. Only then, with the numbness beginning to leave our feet, did we feel relaxed enough to join the group of people gathered together in a comfortable, bourgeois room which, in itself, was satisfactory contrast to the life we had been living for many weeks.

They are from England, our host said, introducing us, and ignoring Sam's pained expression. And I think perhaps they have walked the whole way.

We sank into deep, luxurious chairs while an old lady in a multicoloured gown explained what had happened to us. Had we not left the road, she said, we would've found that it bends northwards and passes through a village, the first of a chain of them, for we were now in that part of Sweden called Jämptland, a winter sports area on the Norwegian border and which, compared to what we'd come through, could be described as "populated." We'd stumbled on a cart track in the dark—a path which cuts straight across the bend, over a low hill, and into a village. Now it's stopped snowing, she told us in good, though accented English, you'll see the village lights from our windows. Lucky you'd kept to the left, she said, or you'd've landed in dense forest and you'd've had a hard time finding your way out again.

We forced a chuckle.

As it is, she said, you can certainly stay with us tonight and in the morning apply for work at one of the hotels. . . .

We nodded. We'd had enough of the road.

Then we told her about our journey on foot from Östersund and about the hut in the forest where we had tried to become loggers.

These two are luckier than their friends, the host said. Because tonight they're going to see something genuinely Swedish. Have you ever heard of the Night of Lucia?

We shook our heads and Sam raised an eyebrow in enquiry but, just at that moment, a bowl of tiny, icing-star decorated cakes was placed on the table by one of the women, while another carried around a trayful of what looked like small teapots but which contained hot, spiced wine.

It's called glög, our host said. Every year at this time we celebrate the anniversary of Saint Lucia—the Queen of the Light. We eat these little cakes you see here. . . .

And drink the glög? Sam said.

You will see.

My escape from an anonymous death in the woods was still rather too uppermost in my mind for me to enter fully into this festivity, whatever it was. The warmth of the room, the good food, and the civilized company had done much to soothe me but I had begun, irrationally, to worry about the future. How would I get to Norway? Clearly I would have to take whatever job I could find locally but how much of a delay would be involved? I thought anxiously about Joan locked into her ghastly family and into a nursing job she could not stand. To change one's life in England, in those days, needed more than an act of the will—it needed a remarkable stroke of luck; the operation, if you like, of Grace.

It occurred to me that the Norway scheme would amount to very little. Already this journey had taken too long; there was little work to be had and what there was did not last. It was not probable that things would be any better in Trondheim. I grappled with the idea of failure—failure followed by ignominious return and that unfinished business with the British Army.

I got up and walked over to the window. The farmhouse was set on a little hill so that I could see across the whole village. Each house glowed with lighted windows and small Christmas trees starred with coloured lights which reflected back from the snow in soft patterns. The December sky was black—cold and hard as polished leather. I stood for awhile, restless and uneasy, but thinking of nothing. There was a small commotion in the room. I turned from the blackness of the window. A door opened and a girl came in. She was young and lithe but solemn in manner: "did seem too solemne sad." There were tiny lighted candles arranged in a crown upon her head and she wore a white dress that looked like a bridal gown. There was complete silence.

Softly, with incredible sweetness, she began to sing.

ABOUT THE EDITOR

Keath Fraser has traveled in over thirty countries, including India, Peru, Australia, Cambodia, Iran, Sri Lanka, Thailand, Afghanistan, and Cuba. Born in Vancouver on Christmas Day, 1944, he lived for three years in Europe, earning a doctorate in literature from the University of London. He then lectured for several years before resigning to write full time. His fiction is included in many anthologies and he is the author of *Taking Cover* and *Foreign Affairs*, the latter nominated for the Governor General's Award and winner of the Ethel Wilson Fiction Prize. He is currently completing a novel and a story collection. He lives in Vancouver with his wife and son.

ACKNOWLEDGMENTS

The editor wishes to express deep appreciation for the generosity shown by all of the following authors, publishers and copyright holders who have allowed their work to be used freely in this anthology, in order to benefit Canada India Village Aid.

PART ONE *The Very Idea of a Bad Trip*

JOSEPH BRODSKY "Advice to a Traveller" Copyright © 1989 by Joseph Brodsky. Originally appeared in the *Times Literary Supplement*. Used by permission of Farrar, Straus and Giroux, Inc., and the author.

JAN MORRIS "My Worst Journey" Copyright © 1991 by Jan Morris.

GEORGE WOODCOCK "My Worst Journeys" Copyright © 1991 by George Woodcock.

DAVID MAMET "A Family Vacation" from *Writing in Restaurants* Copyright © 1986 by David Mamet. Used by permission of Viking Penguin, a division of Penguin Books U.S.A. Inc.; Faber and Faber Ltd.; and the author.

WILLIAM TREVOR "The Second Journey" Copyright © 1991 by William Trevor.

MARTHA GELLHORN "What Bores Whom?" from *Travels With Myself and Another* Copyright © 1978 by Martha Gellhorn. Published by Dodd, Mead & Company, and Allen Lane. Reprinted by Eland Books 1983. Used by permission of Eland Books and the author.

EDWARD HOAGLAND "Balancing Act" Copyright © 1991 by Edward Hoagland.

PART TWO *Writers and the Fear of Flying*

PAULETTE JILES "Night Flight to Attiwapiskat" from *Celestial Navigations* Copyright © 1984 by Paulette Jiles. Used by permission of the Canadian publishers, McClelland and Stewart, Toronto, and the author.

TIMOTHY FINDLEY "An Unforgettable Journey to Russia" Copyright © 1991 by Timothy Findley.

STUART STEVENS from *Night Train to Turkistan* Copyright © 1988 by Stuart Stevens. Used by permission of the Atlantic Monthly Press and the author.

Thubron. First published in the United Kingdom as *Among the Russians*. Used by permission of Random House, Inc.; William Heinemann Ltd.; and the author.

PAUL THEROUX from *The Old Patagonian Express* Copyright © 1979 by Cape Cod Scriveners Company. Used by permission of Houghton Mifflin Company; Aitken and Stone Ltd; and the author.

MARY MORRIS from *Nothing To Declare* Copyright © 1988 by Mary Morris. Used by permission of Houghton Mifflin Company and the author.

RONALD WRIGHT from *Cut Stones and Crossroads* Copyright © 1984 by Ronald Wright. Used by permission of Viking Penguin, a division of Penguin Books USA Inc., and the author.

CHARLES NICHOLL from *The Fruit Palace* Copyright © 1985 by Charles Nicholl. Used by permission of St. Martin's Press, Inc., and David Higham Associates Ltd.

JONATHAN RABAN from *Old Glory* Copyright © 1981 by Jonathan Raban. Used by permission of Simon and Schuster Inc.; William Collins Ltd.; Aitken and Stone Ltd; and the author.

TED CONOVER from *Rolling Nowhere* Copyright © 1981, 1984 by Ted Conover. Used by permission of Viking Penguin, a division of Penguin USA Inc.; Sterling Lord Literistic, Inc.; and the author.

PART FIVE *Writers and the Effects of War*

IRVING LAYTON "Postcard" from *The Pole-Vaulter* Copyright © 1974 by Irving Layton. Used by permission of the Canadian publishers, McClelland and Stewart, Toronto, and the author.

DIRK BOGARDE from *Backcloth* Copyright © 1986 by Dirk Bogarde. Published by Viking Penguin Inc. Used by permission of A.D. Peters and Co. Ltd.

JAMES FENTON from *All the Wrong Places* Copyright © 1988 by James Fenton. Used by permission of the Atlantic Monthly Press and A.D. Peters & Co. Ltd.

GAVIN YOUNG "The Murder of Hué" from *Worlds Apart* Copyright © 1987 by The Observer. First published by Hutchinson in 1987. Used by permission of Century Hutchinson Ltd.; Aitken and Stone Ltd.; and the author.

JOHN RYLE from "The Road to Abyei" Copyright © 1989 by John Ryle. First published in *Granta*. Used by permission of the author.

CAROLYN FORCHÉ "Return" from *The Country Between Us* Copyright © 1980 by Carolyn Forché. Used by permission of Harper & Row, Publishers, Inc.; Jonathan Cape Limited; and the author.

PEREGRINE HODSON from *Under A Sickle Moon* Copyright © 1986 by Peregrine Hodson. Used by permission of Century Hutchinson Ltd. and Aitken & Stone Ltd.

PART SIX *Classic Questers in Extremis*

AL PURDY "When I Sat Down to Play the Piano" from *Selected Poems* Copyright © 1972

VINTAGE DEPARTURES

Available at your bookstore or call toll-free to order: 1-800-733-3000.
Credit cards only. Prices subject to change.